Criminal Shadows

by

David Canter

authorlink press
www.authorlink.com

Published by Authorlink Press
An imprint of Authorlink
(http://www.authorlink.com)
3720 Millswood Dr.
Irving, Texas 75062, USA

First published by HarperCollins, UK
First Printing, UK Edition, 1994

Second Printing, USA Edition, Authorlink Press,
December 2000

Printed in the United States of America

ISBN 1 92870421 2

Table of Contents

FOREWORD

In the bloody world of crime fighting, scientists often are unwelcome problem-solvers. Among case-hardened detectives, instinct, hunches and experience frequently overrule scientific theory. But once in a while, along comes someone whose theories are so profound, and the research so convincing we can no longer dare to look the other way.

Dr. David Canter is such a man.

In the late 1980's, when he first began using "psychological profiles" to help catch rapists and murderers, it was a novel idea. Only senior police officers and a few psychologists had heard of deriving clues about an assailant's personality and lifestyle from a careful, behavioral examination of the crime and the scene. Few formal studies had been done until Canter painstakingly picked through crime-scene information, and scrutinized details, not as a criminologist, but from his perspective as a psychologist.

In less than a decade, Canter's well-documented theories —along with some not-so-authentic copycat versions—today are generally accepted by a growing number of police forces throughout the world—theories as profound as reading crime patterns to determine where a criminal actually lives.

Thanks to Canter's laborious studies, investigators now have a set of practical behavioral principles to help precisely predict an unknown criminal's domestic circumstances, employment and character, and to catch culprits who might otherwise allude police for years.

Canter's original work now forms the foundation for a number of systematic studies on criminal profiling underway by psychiatrists and psychologists, worldwide. He has pushed investigators' understanding about violent criminal behavior beyond personal insights and intuition to a new level of scientific comprehension. He rejects traditional "reasons" for criminal acts, such as genetic make-up, birth trauma, lack of self-control, or social pressures. Instead he examines what drives a person beyond the bounds of socially acceptable aggression into the realms of criminal violence.

In this book, Canter takes us on a fascinating journey through his groundbreaking theories, reminding us that criminals live as "normal" people hidden in our midst, not necessarily as monsters we can readily see. He dissects subtle variations in the underlying "themes" that drive vicious offenders, and shows us how to use these "stories" as clues to a criminal's personality and identity.

Canter's double-sided mission is to help solve rapes and murders, and to understand both the root causes of violence and the journeys that lead criminals to the darkest places of human existence. Not only does Canter's work broaden our knowledge of criminal behavior, it provides the framework for an important new field, Investigative Psychology, in which criminology and psychology can, at last, harmonize as a single force against violence.

Criminal Shadows is essential reading for anyone involved in law enforcement. In this quest we view a criminal's acts of violence through the shadows he casts, and by what Canter calls "the criminal's own inner narratives."

By learning to read these criminal shadows, we can become better investigators, and hopefully help make the world a little safer for us all.

—Robert D. Keppel

Robert D. Keppel is President of the Institute for Forensics in Seattle, Washington. He retired after 17 years as the Chief Criminal Investigator with the Washington State Attorney General's Office, and has 25-plus years of homicide experience. He has participated in more than 2000 murder investigations, and was chief investigator in the Ted Bundy murder cases in the Pacific Northwest. He has authored a number of books about serial murder, including his latest, *Serial Murder: Future Implications for Police Investigations.*

Chapter One
A BETTER NET

In July 1980 the body of an eight-year-old girl was found by the roadside in Staffordshire, 164 miles from where she had been abducted. For eleven years a coordinated search by six police forces was unable to find the man who had killed her. During that time two more young girls were murdered by the same man, and at least two others were abducted by him, escaping alive. Investigators were stumped—as they often are, and admitted little hope of ever catching him, until a suspicious neighbor tipped police.

The search for the child's murderer highlights the problem of finding a criminal when there is no known connection between him and his victim. Though modern police forces can fill rooms with details of possible suspects, they are faced with the enormous task of finding the one deadly needle in their haystack of paper.

Is there an alternative to waiting for a criminal to make a mistake? Can huge resources and fast computers avoid the need for the killer to "reveal his hand", as in the 1980 case, when the killer doubled back unaware that he had been noticed? Must investigators hope for "good luck", for an alert neighbour who happens to be in his garden at the right time? Must detectives rely on glimpses caught by witnesses, known modus operandi of convicted villains and house-to-house trawls to snag possible suspects?

Despite the use of a specially-dedicated, vast computer system containing details of thousands of suspects, a solitary, middle-aged man, named Robert Black, who had first been convicted of assaults on children a quarter of a century earlier at the age of sixteen, completely eluded police investigators as the serial murderer. Until his fortuitous capture in September 1991, countrywide searches had failed even to include his name as one of the 185,000 people whose details had been amassed.

Senior police officers leading the investigation privately admitted that they were likely to catch him only if he "showed his hand" again. This euphemism proved accurate. A village shopkeeper, working in his garden on a hot summer's day, saw a six-year-old girl being forced into a van. He called the police who stopped the van when it returned through the village. The girl's father was the police officer who opened the van doors to find his terror-stricken daughter inside, bound in a sleeping bag, almost suffocated.

Subsequent inquiries led to Black's arrest and conviction for the murder of three young girls as well as the abduction of a fourth.

It is now possible to bring all this intensive activity and high technology into sharper focus by studying the way a criminal embraces the crime, and how he chooses to commit it.

A criminal indicates something about himself from the way he acts; something that will help sift the possible suspects or even point to places where a likely suspect may be found

To implement new ways of focusing police investigations, we must find the answer to a fundamental question: specifically what does a criminal reveal about himself by the way he commits a crime?

A criminal may divulge what shoes he wore from his footprints. His blood type can be determined from any body fluids left at the scene. But he leaves more at the crime scene than these material traces. He also leaves psychological traces, telltale patterns of behavior that indicate the sort of person he is. These traces are more ambiguous and subtle than those examined by the biologist or physicist. They cannot be taken into a laboratory and dissected under a microscope. They are more like shadows, undoubtedly connected to the criminal who cast them, but they flicker and change, and their origins may not always be obvious. Yet, if they can be interpreted, criminals' shadows can indicate where investigators should look and what sort of person they should look for.

Changes in the law, and the growing pressures on police forces around the world mean that they are increasingly in need of such help. The lone detective, so popular in fiction, has given way to organized teams that require systematic guidance. Senior police officers are seizing applied scientific psychology as a way out of this impasse.

Enormous strides have been made in analyzing material clues, while the interpretation of psychological shadows has made only a few faltering first steps. This book is an account of my involvement, as a psychologist, in a number of police investigations in which I took some of those steps.

Pioneers in Profiling

In trying to interpret criminals' shadows, I follow many other footsteps. People throughout the ages have expressed views about how to identify a criminal in a crowd. Shakespeare, for example, has Julius Caesar making what later proves to be an accurate prediction.

Sleek-headed men and such as sleep o' nights.
Yond Cassius has a lean and hungry look;
He thinks too much: such men are dangerous.

The idea that thoughtful, lean and hungry-looking men were potential criminals, or that certain physiognomy or physique are typical of murderers or thieves is steeped in generalized, untested notions about characteristics that are typical of many different types of people. Similar stereotypes exist today in racial prejudice that assumes certain actions are typical of people with a particular skin color. The blossoming of biology, medicine and psychology in the last century challenged such superficial views that a person's appearance could be correlated in any way with expected behaviors. In particular, medicine had shown that madness and evil could be seen as illnesses, rather than the result of witchcraft and demon-possession.

After Daniel M'Naghten was acquitted of murder "by reason of insanity" in 1843, physicians became more involved in the legal process, especially in determining whether the accused suffered from "mental illness" produced by brain dysfunction. The growth of medicine also led to their increasing involvement in criminal investigations as pathologists. Their work further encompassed treatment of criminals regarded as mad rather than bad. It is therefore not surprising that, by the 1880's, medical officers thought it appropriate to offer opinions about offenders, based on their clinical and forensic experience.

Dr Thomas Bond, in one of the earliest of such opinions, wrote a letter to London CID Chief Robert Anderson, in November 1888 (a document that survives to this day), about the likely characteristics of "Jack the Ripper".

> The murderer must have been a man of physical strength and great coolness and daring. There is no evidence that he had an accomplice. He must in my opinion be a man subject to periodic attacks of homicidal and erotic mania. The character of the mutilations indicate that the man may be in a condition sexually, that may be called Satyriasis. It is of course possible that the Homicidal impulse may have developed from a revengeful or brooding condition of mind, or that religious mania may have been the original disease but I do not think that either hypothesis is likely. The murderer in external appearance

is quite likely to be a quiet inoffensive looking man probably middle-aged and neatly and respectably dressed. I think he might be in the habit of wearing a cloak or overcoat or he could hardly have escaped notice in the streets if the blood on his hands or clothes were visible.

Assuming the murderer to be such a person as I have just described, he would be solitary and eccentric in his habits, also he is likely to be a man without regular occupation, but with some small income or pension. He is possibly living among respectable persons who have some knowledge of his character and habits and who may have grounds for suspicion that he is not quite right in his mind at times. Such persons would probably be unwilling to communicate suspicions to the Police for fear of trouble or notoriety, whereas if there were prospect of reward it might overcome their scruples.

Donald Rumbelow, *The Complete Jack the Ripper*, 1987, pp. 140-41

Dr Bond was drawing on his professional experience, yet the possibilities he proposed would be considered thoughtful and intelligent by police today. Indeed, when FBI agents acknowledged the "Jack the Ripper" centenary by drawing their own account of the offender they produced a description that essentially matched Bond's.

Bond adds a psychiatric flourish with his reference to "diseases" such as satyriasis or religious mania, but essentially he combines a number of reasonable speculations to form a hypothetical word sketch of the criminal. No one was convicted for the Whitechapel murders so the accuracy of Bond's "profile" cannot be confirmed. Neither are we sure the senior investigators of the day gave it credence. It is unlikely that they ignored it completely. Detectives often form a view of the person they seek, whether or not they write down a description. Drawing together the various strands known about the perpetrator, and using this summary as a template against possible suspects, is a natural way of giving shape to the potentially confusing range of possibilities that emerge in a large investigation.

The idea that idiosyncratic habits would give clues to hidden aspects of a person's identity was recorded as long ago as the Old Testament. Gideon chose his army from those men who did not kneel to drink at the stream, preferring those who lay down. The former were secret idolaters and therefore less likely to fight the infidel with total commitment. Morelli, the outstanding Victorian art historian, maintained that he could distinguish fake Old Master paintings by minor details such as how an ear or nose was portrayed. Predating psychoanalysis, he insisted that the large matters of composition and subject were open to conscious control and therefore readily forged, but that details regarded as trivial by the painter would reveal his true identity.

Twentieth-century psychology promises that even the most trifling aspects of human behavior, for example when a person crosses their legs or forgets a name, can have profound significance. Although many attempts to fulfill this promise have failed, notably in such areas as handwriting analysis, there have been some small successes. One relevant example is the careful observation of Germans suspected of war crimes at the end of World War II.

Lionel Haward, then a young psychologist, worked as an RAF officer, on a team attempting to identify war criminals. He drew a list of factors, such as mode of dress and likely possessions, to help screen people suspected of being high-ranking Nazi officials. The checklist made it easier to decide who bore closer investigation. This was a direct precursor of my own activities. When I first became involved with police investigations, I was in the same department of psychology as Haward, then Britain's leading forensic psychologist. He retired from the department not long afterwards, but not before hc had supported my early attempts to follow in his footsteps.

Not long before Lionel Haward began searching for Nazi officers, the psychiatrist William Langer was commissioned by the US Office of Strategic Services to produce a profile of Adolf Hitler, focusing on how he would react to defeat. A few years later, in the mid 1950s, the New York psychiatrist Dr James A. Brussel gave a detailed account of the man whom the press had dubbed the "Mad Bomber of New York" because of his sporadic use of home-made explosives to terrorize the city. Brussel even went so far as to say that the "bomber" would be wearing a neat double-breasted suit, with the jacket buttoned. Despite his help, the bombing continued for more than ten years. When the criminal, George Metesky, was apprehended, he was attired just as Brussel had described.

By the late 1960s, psychiatrists' now widely involved with criminals in treatment programs often were asked by police for their views on the character of a perpetrator they were trying to find. In September 1974 Dr Patrick Tooley offered an opinion on the characteristics of the murderer of Susan Stevenson, who was attacked on Great Lines Common in Kent, dying from her wounds soon after she staggered to the local police Station. Dr Tooley made the following proposal:

> The man is aged between twenty and thirty-five years, possibly a psychopath with previous convictions. Generally one could expect too from his record that he had made a number of court appearances, was convicted at an early age and had possibly been in a special home; likely to be a manual worker and either unemployed or frequently changing jobs. Previous convictions could include unlawful sexual intercourse, drunkenness, robbery and assaults generally.
>
> Father absent—mother restrictive, sexually prudish and devoted to son and spoils him. He, in turn, resents

this and has a hate complex towards women. Despite that, he wants an affair with a woman but cannot make a normal approach. He does not mix socially and walks alone, in open spaces. He could be a "peeper" but seldom resorts to indecent exposure.

Tom Tullet, *Clues to Murder*, 1987, p. 155

When the murderer, Peter Stout, was arrested, Dr Tooley's comments proved generally accurate.

Peter Stout's background was revealing. He was aged nineteen, single and had one elder sister, two elder brothers and a younger brother. Both his parents were dead. His father had been a drunkard and a bully and was disliked by all the children, but they had all loved their mother. When Stout was fourteen he was convicted of indecently assaulting a woman and he himself had been the victim of attempted buggery when he was ten years old. This fitted exactly into the pattern of the man described by Dr Tooley and there were other things that also matched. He was a loner who went for long walks and he did not mix well with others.

The interrogation of Peter Stout was a long drawn-out process of admissions, half-admissions, then a complete retraction and references to the Devil and "queer turns".

Tullet, op. cit., p. 157

FBI Embraces Profiling

Around the same time that Dr Tooley so accurately described Peter Stout, instructors at the FBI's national training academy in Quantico, West Virginia, consciously set about developing the art of providing similar accounts, called "profiles" of wanted killers. Drawing upon their detailed experience of violent criminals, they incorporated "profiles" into FBI training courses for agents. What originated as class discussions between experienced law enforcement agents became a service offered to police forces throughout the world.

FBI academy instructors wanted to reach beyond issues such as the significance of the murder to the murderer, the killer's personality, his internal conflicts and fantasy life. These aspects are directly relevant to pleas of insanity, and to deciding on treatment for offenders. But the inner, psychological nature of the culprit is not readily open to conventional detection. The FBI agents wanted to get closer to the hunt for the criminal, to point directly to where he could be found.

When FBI agents first began this work they used a usual term to grace their actions: offender profiling. By so doing they created the impression that this procedure was a total package, ready to be employed, rather than the mixture of craft, experience and intellectual energy that they themselves admit forms the core of their activities.

The term "offender profiling" has stuck, creating the impression that it is a distinct process that can be cut and dried and sold by the pound. A term originally used as a vague idea of what a policeman might be looking for in a criminal, is now thought of as an esoteric process:

"Offender profiling" is now given a jargon-laden definition as "a procedure that facilitates interfacing between law enforcement agencies and the FBI, enhancing strategic policing and suspect prioritization".

The first documented use of the "profiling" services of FBI agents at Quantico came in 1974 when the Montana police asked for help in solving a year-old murder case. In June 1973 a seven-year-old girl, Susan Jaeger, on a camping holiday with her parents, had been taken from her tent as her family slept nearby. No sign of her body had been found nor any ransom demand received. In January 1974 the charred body of an eighteen-year-old girl was found in woodlands near the campsite. Convinced that the same killer was responsible for both crimes and that he would be known to them, but unable to identify' anyone definitely, local police approached the FBI.

FBI agents proposed that the murderer was a young white male who kept very much to himself. They suggested that he did not live far from the campsite and was therefore already likely to have come to the attention of local police officers. The possibility that he may have kept mementoes of his victims was also noted.

This description closely matched David Meirhofer, a suspect named by an informant. No strong evidence connected him with the crimes, and he had taken both a "lie-detector" test and a "truth serum" interview without implicating himself in the killings. At the insistence of the FBI, Susan's mother kept a tape-recorder by her telephone. When, as predicted, an anonymous caller telephoned and said that he had abducted Susan, her mother was able to record his voice. It was identified as that of Meirhofer. A search of his home revealed the gruesome body parts, kept as "souvenirs". He later admitted to both murders as well as two others of local boys, before hanging himself in his cell.

The continuing successes of the FBI profilers captured the imagination of journalists and novelists long before most detectives in Britain or America had any idea what was happening at Quantico. Fiction writers readily moved into the richer, psychological pastures opened up by these developments in criminal detection. In Ruth Rendell's thrillers of rural murder, as in Thomas Harris's American massacres, the character and lifestyle of the offenders is often more significant than the detective. Fiction, as ever, was in advance of real life, but it did capture a move in police work towards a desire to understand the nature of the criminal and how his personality may be revealed through his crimes.

The shift from looking for clues to looking for a person has created a new and different approach to detection. A specific clue directly linked to a specific characteristic gives way to looking for patterns in behavior that add up to a certain style of life. Conan Doyle's fictional detective, like Agatha Christie's, often bases his judgments on some very specialist, typically technical knowledge, such as access to rare poisons, impossibilities in the event sequences described by the suspects, rare skills available only to the culprit, or other one-to-one relationships between known aspects of the offence and identifiable quirks of the villain. The examination of the character of the criminal, as revealed by the behavioral traces he leaves at the crime scene, is an attempt to get beyond a mere list of clues in order to recognize a pattern, an identifiable silhouette, a distinct shadow cast by the offender.

In the interests of a good plot, fictional police officers are often more amenable to new ideas and approaches to detection than are their real-life counterparts. Not all police forces have adopted this new style of detection. In my early discussions with police officers about the potential contribution of psychology to detection one detective sergeant, who had been in the force for many years, summarized the views of many of his colleagues when he said, "Why do we need all this new-fangled stuff, Professor? After all, we've got 150 years of police experience to draw upon."

A New Era in Investigation

The process of criminal investigation has changed little over the past 150 years but, as my experiences reveal, many pressures from inside and outside the police forces are now producing rapid changes in the meaning of detective work and how detection is carried out. A systematic, scientific understanding of criminal behavior is increasingly central to those changes.

We can now examine the well-known Victorian serial

murder case of "Jack the Ripper," in a new light, using today's more sophisticated investigative tools to test for accuracy against known facts, as we shall see later. The original investigators in the case, used a step-by-step procedure, and a large team of policemen. House-to-house inquiries were conducted, lists of suspects were compiled and many people were interviewed, forensic material was collected and examined.

A close reading of that investigation shows a basic process of identifying suspects, tracing them and deciding whether to examine them more closely or to cross them off the list. This is still the pattern of a major inquiry today. There are, of course, important differences: evidence is much more carefully collected and examined; physics, chemistry, biology and pathology now contribute to a larger degree to the interpretation of stains and fibers, cause of death, and all the other information that provides evidence. The law has also changed, especially in relation to what is acceptable evidence and the forms of expert testimony that can be drawn upon. However, the stages through which police officers go to apprehend the offender are still much the same. The paper-and-ink record-keeping is done by computer, but otherwise the inquiry leading to the conviction of most killers is very similar to the inquiry that "Jack the Ripper" evaded. The computer often adds little to the success of an inquiry when compared, for instance, with the lucky break that led to the arrest of Robert Black.

A computer had been installed for the enquiry that found Black because it was believed that it would help to overcome the problems that had beset an earlier major investigation, the "Yorkshire Ripper" inquiry.

Completed a few years before the search for Robert Black, the Yorkshire Ripper enquiry had been widely regarded as ineffective. The consequences of its failures still echo around government departments and police headquarters throughout Britain. It was an enormous inquiry in the tradition of leaving no stone unturned and eventually led to the conviction of Peter Sutcliffe for the murder of thirteen women.

By the end of the Yorkshire inquiry in 1980, more than 150,000 people had been interviewed in order to eliminate them from the lists of suspects. The equivalent of a small town had been involved in house-to-house searches: 27,000 residences in all. Unlike the Staffordshire case some years later, Peter Sutcliffe had come into the interrogation net on at least five occasions, but had been released each time without raising any suspicions.

The search for the "Yorkshire Ripper" involved three different police forces and rooms filled with card files. Each police force kept its own separate system. It is reported that when these were eventually housed in one place there was fear that the building would not withstand the weight of all the paper. Peter Sutcliffe's name is reputed to have been in all three sets of files but this was not known until the end of the investigation. In its aftermath, much investment was made in computer systems, the idea being that a computer would have spotted the recurring name.

This search for a mechanical solution to the problem of disentangling all the leads and information generated by a major inquiry has meant that all British police forces now have computers that bury investigating officers under data. Exactly what to do with the data or how to use them is still hotly debated. Centralized indexes for "Crime Pattern Analysis" and for listing the modus operandi of known offenders are maintained, but they still rely enormously on the expertise of the human operators and the sense that they can make of the records they hold. Confidential studies of these systems also show that they make a real contribution to far less than one in ten investigations that use them. It is also salutary to note that many of the existing police computing systems cannot communicate directly with each other, data being sent by motorbike when combinations of records are needed.

The existence of this vast data set leaves open to question, for example, the direct implications of recurring names and their relevance. What direction could an investigation take when it is known that a name has recurred? To have significance, a name must hold some meaning for the investigating officers, and computers are very poor at giving data meaning; they are much better at numbers, frequencies, percentages or straight description.

For a person running the inquiry, key aspects of any suspect are crucial. These include their having the opportunity to commit the offense and how that fits with what is known about their modus operandi: (the distinctive actions of an offender which link his crimes together and link him to his crimes). To locate the suspect, anything that might be publicly available about him can help; where he lives—and how—are the most obviously important characteristics. Therefore any information that may help in locating a suspect will-be seized on. But this can cause its own problems if that information is unreliable. In the "Yorkshire Ripper" investigation a taped message, believed sent by the killer, misled the police.

Taken as genuine, the tape was submitted to phonetic analysis of the accent by experts at Leeds University. This enabled them to pinpoint the village from Wearside where that particular Geordie accent came from. Sutcliffe was excluded from the-inquiry because he had a very different Yorkshire accent. Police later realized that the tape was a hoax; rumor has it that it was sent by disgruntled police officers who did not realize the serious outcome (not unlike the letters supposedly sent by "Jack the Ripper" a century earlier). By the time police considered alternative possibilities, a great deal of time had been wasted, and more victims had been discovered.

The phonetic experts in Leeds were not, initially, aware of the fact that none of the victims who survived attacks by the "Yorkshire Ripper" had said he had a Geordie accent. Once it became apparent that every possible suspect who had a Wearside accent had been eliminated from the inquiries, these broader discussions took place. This led to the conclusion that the tapes were a hoax. Eventually, after the largest investigation ever mounted into crimes that affected people's daily lives throughout Yorkshire, it was old-fashioned police routine and the alert actions of a police sergeant, Bob Ring that led to the arrest of Peter Sutcliffe.

Sergeant Ring had made a routine check of the number plate affixed to a Rover car parked while the driver was "doing business" with a prostitute. This revealed that the plate belonged to a Skoda rather than the Rover. Subsequent questioning in a police station and a follow-up of the driver of the car showed that he had been a suspect on previous occasions but each time had been dropped from the investigation. He may well have been crossed off the list again if Bob Ring had not remembered that Sutcliffe had gone for a private "pee" before being taken in for question-ing. When he searched the spot he found a hammer and knife that were eventually linked to the murders. Presented with this evidence Sutcliffe confessed.

Two years after Sutcliffe was caught, two teenage girls were murdered near the village of Narborough just south of the city of Leicester. The detectives given the task of finding the killer were determined not to make the same mistakes of the Yorkshire case. They had computers, and the possibilities of DNA "fingerprinting" were just emerging. These new tools, however, were used indiscriminately. The investigat-ing officers decided they would take blood samples from every man who could possibly have been near the crime scene at the time of the murders. This included men of all ages and backgrounds residing in villages throughout the entire area. For months, over 3,000 blood samples filled the laboratory, waiting to be tested. Investigations today can still produce the same overload, generating long queues of samples taken from even the most unlikely suspect.

In Narborough, this massive forensic onslaught nearly failed. If the culprit, Cohn Pitchfork, had not had a work-mate whose friend was a relative of a policeman, the fact that Pitchfork had got someone else to take the blood test in his place might never have become known to the police. With the large number of samples being taken, like a routine survey, it was not possible for the investigating officers to make detailed checks on the identities of all those who came to give blood.

Many senior officers now recognize that a behavioral analysis can help to identify the most likely suspects. An order of priority can then be assigned to the testing of each suspect. With a more focused approach it would also be possible to check the identity of everyone giving a blood sample.

All these manhunts took enormous effort, and very nearly failed. They were not searches for arch villains, brilliant minds that outmaneuvered the plodding police and covered their traces with fiendish cunning. Robert Black returned through a village where he might have been seen abducting a young girl; Sutcliffe carried incriminating weapons with him when he visited potential targets the police were known to be watching; Pitchfork left semen that, even before DNA, could be used for blood-typing.

To check an offender's view of police effectiveness, I spent some hours talking to "Andrew", a man convicted of a series of violent crimes. I asked how he managed to evade capture when so many police looked for him. He answered that he constantly expected to be caught, he made no plans to avoid detection and was surprised that they took so long to capture him. As in many other cases they had waited for him to show his hand, spotting him running away from a victim he had left in an alley.

To idea of pouring resources into the investigation in the hope that something will turn up must be replaced with a very different style of investigation, one in which various possibilities are weighed and the most fruitful courses of action are given the emphasis they deserve. This more scientific approach requires that investigators have a rich understanding of criminal behavior and have the information and analytic tools to act on that understanding. Changes must occur throughout police training and management; changes which have implications far beyond the drawing up of "profiles" to help identify suspects.

The Need for a Better Net

Recognizing these demands, Surrey's Chief Superintendent Vince McFadden (who was to prove so significant in bringing me into police investigations) summarized the challenge to present-day police forces: "Sometimes we cast our net so wide that the fish swim through the holes." His plea was for a more studied approach to fishing for criminals, working out carefully who was being sought and where they were most likely to be found, using a smaller, finer net to increase the probability of the fish being caught.

There is another pressing reason to develop a smaller, better net. In the past police in Britain could spend virtually as much time and effort as they considered necessary on a murder investigation. The scale of this effort strikes police in the United States as beyond belief. In some large US cities a murder investigation will be dropped if the couple of detectives assigned to it do not solve it within twenty-four hours. In Britain, often ten officers can be assigned to one murder investigation for six months. Now, though, police forces have budgets for special inquiries determined at the start of the financial year and must make that cover all except the most unusual contingencies throughout the year. Inquiries have to be self-consciously managed as effectively as possible. One experienced officer, in charge of a murder inquiry into a gangland slaying, put it this way: "I've got two hands tied behind my back. That's the way the law's gone down. I'm investigating two dead and five injured and I have to look at my overtime."

Beyond financial constraints, the legal system now demands a change in how detectives work. The 1984 Act of Parliament called the "Police and Criminal Evidence Act", widely known as PACE, grew out of the great disquiet felt by the public during the 1970s and early 1980s when ambiguities and confusions in the law appeared to give the police rights that were too easily abused.

PACE made the ground rules for contact between police and public much clearer and in so doing reduced the areas in which police officers could use their discretion. Previously a suspect could be kept for questioning as long as seemed appropriate, provided various routines were observed. The right to remain silent under questioning also had little legal force. PACE, now regulates the amount of time a suspect can be kept under arrest, the length of an interrogation session, meal breaks, and even the rules of contact during interrogation. In the past a police officer could hint that he would keep a person in the cell until he or she confessed, or lay out objects found at the crime scene and indicate that the suspect's fingerprints were on them. Although the officer had to be very careful not to transgress the bounds of legal propriety, the officer had considerable freedom of action. Now the slightest use of subterfuge or pressure can undermine or even invalidate any criminal charges in court.

Other pressures on detectives also strengthen the need to become more effective. Communities sometimes are less sympathetic to the police and less prepared to help an inquiry than in the past; a more mobile population, makes the search for suspects difficult, and the public is more aware of the prevalence of violent crime, especially where the offender is unknown to the victim.

Whether they like or not, senior police officers are alert to the need to stretch beyond their current methods. They know they must challenge the cherished view that "150 years of experience" are all that is necessary to solve crimes In the past, detectives could treat speculation about a villain's personality and background as something to chat about in the bar. Now they need to pull that discussion out of the realms of instinct and gut feeling and put it on much firmer footing. One important new skill for them to learn is to read more precisely the shadows that we now know criminals cast.

Chapter Two
FIRST PRINCIPLES

In 1985 I was invited for lunch at Scotland Yard. Two Metropolitan Police officers, Detective Chief Superintendent Thelma Wagstaff and Detective Chief inspector John Grieve (now both Commanders), wanted to discuss the feasibility of detectives using the behavioral science of psychology to cope with the challenges and difficulties they faced. They had heard of my earlier research identifying behavior patterns of people caught in burning buildings.

Thelma had done a considerable amount to heighten the awareness of the Metropolitan police of the need to change the way rapes were investigated. She had been successful in establishing programs of training for women police officers involved in rape investigations and setting up clean and comfortable interview suites for use with rape victims. The idea of using behavioral science to help find a rapist appealed to her as a way of increasing the success of investigations, especially of sexual assaults against strangers. We discussed how the approach I had taken to studying traumatic fires could be relevant to police investigations. We explored the possibility that psychological research could contribute directly to detection, complementing experience, intuition and footslogging with scientifically established facts and principles.

At the time I had never heard of "profiling", but the whole idea of reading a criminal's life from the details of how he carries out his crime was enormously appealing. It presented a challenge to the very heart of professional psychology. Was our adolescent science robust enough to give an account of a person when he was not sitting in front of us, when all we knew about him were the shadowy traces he had left at the scene of the crime? Were we now ready for a combination of scientific psychology and criminal detection—a method that could save lives? The detectives and I agreed we would explore the possibilities together.

Some months later, I happened to read about a series of rapes in the London Standard. The newspaper had devoted its front page to a description of a series of twenty-four sexual assaults committed in London over the previous four years. Police believed all involved the same assailant. Sometimes the attacker was alone. At other times he had an accomplice. The list gave only brief, incomplete details, but there were some dates and times. I wanted to see if there were any obvious pattern in the list. I sent a note to Thelma Wagstaff, and began to examine the information. Two general psychological principles struck me.

People Influence Each Other's Actions

First, we know that people influence each other's actions. The difference between attacks involving two men and those involving one might tell us something about both individuals. According to the January 9, 1986 London Standard, all the assaults had been linked by police, so why was there a variation in who had committed the crimes? What might that indicate?

Human Behavior Changes Over Time

Second, most human behavior develops and changes over time, often in direct relation to the consequence one experiences from an action.

What was changing here? Did time and one's relationships with others indicate the character or lifestyle of these
offenders?

How, exactly, did "changes over time" relate to "the
influence of other people on the criminal's actions."

Most of us live through a daily and weekly cycle that
shapes what we do and when. At that stage I had no basis for
thinking that violent criminals were any different.

By checking through details of the rapes reported in the
London Standard I was able to draw up a simple calendar of
events, listing the offenses committed by two people together
in one column and those by a man alone in another. This
work essentially was no different from the research
psychologist's commonplace examination of rows and
columns of numbers to describe human action. I reduced
complex actual events to the simplest possible form, hoping
they would reveal central themes, and tell their violent story.

I wanted this rudimentary table to show any hidden shape
within; a light that would reveal the identity of the criminal
beneath his vicious actions.

The resulting chronological table, with days and times
arranged in a column for either a two-man or a single assault,
turned the newspaper descriptions into a manageable, and
intriguing summary. Some days of the week and times were
missing (it also later became clear that the *London Standard*
has got some details wrong). But I was looking for broad
patterns. These were more likely reliable than precise details
that might later prove unfounded. Any pattern at all could be
a bonus, the cautious basis for additional explorations. I sent
the calendar of assaults with my thoughts about it in a letter
to Thelma Wagstaff, curious to see if it made sense, and
whether my conclusions added anything to what detectives
already knew.

I wondered if anybody had prepared a summary table
like the rough one I had drawn. The table showed that the

individual acting on his own in the series of crimes, did so very recently. The attacks where both had been involved tended to come in runs.

I had no evidence that the "one" individual was responsible for all the single-man crimes. But, if he were, one could see a possible relationship between the two men as a duo committing the whole series. (See Table 1, next page.)

Several months later, as a result of a report I sent to Detective Wagstaff, summarizing the results of my analysis of the *London Standard* report, I was asked to visit Hendon Police College in North London where a new incident center had been established for the rapes and two murders.

The walls were covered with hand-written charts, listing victims of assault, and descriptions they had given of their assailant and of the attack. Features such as the use of a knife, or the binding of the victim, were underlined in different colors. Other charts used these critical features to show similarities between the cases. The listing of every detail seemed more confusing than helpful.

Thelma Wagstaff and three high-ranking police officers met me in the room. They wanted action—from me.

Beside the rape investigation (called the Hart inquiry) two separate murders were being investigated. That morning they had agreed to coordinate different teams of detectives, led by a senior officer. Forensic evidence and some unusual actions in the offenses had led them to conclude that the rapes and murders had been committed by the same man.

The situation would turn out to be one of the largest detective inquiries ever undertaken in Britain, certainly the largest coordinated effort since the "Yorkshire Ripper" inquiry almost ten years earlier. I had been summoned to help catch this man before he killed again.

Chapter Two: First Principles

DATE	TWO ATTACKERS	ONE ATTACKER
1982 June 10	Thurs 00.30	
July		
August		
September 15	Wed 00.05	
September 21	Tues 00.30	
September 24	Fri 04.15	
October		
November		
December		
1983 March	Sat 00.30	
1984 January	21.00	
February, March		
April, May		
June	00.10	
June6		Wed 16.30
June 8	Fri 14.10	
July 15	Sun 01.00	
August		
September		
October		
November 22		Thur 22.00
December 7		Fri 19.25
December 11		Tues
1985 January 26	Sat 00.30	
January 30	Wed 19.45	
February 2 (2.)	Sat	
February 24		Sun 20.45
March 1	Fri 0-2.00	
March 3	Sun	
April		
May 22		Wed
June28		Tues
July 14	Sun	
August		21.25
September 22		Sun 21.00

Table 1 Chronological list of sexual assaults in London adapted from the article in the Standard.

With no experience of police investigations and little knowledge of criminal behavior, the police wanted me to use whatever skills I might have as a psychologist to contribute directly to a major inquiry into rape and murder. The analysis I had in mind would be time-consuming. Commander Vince McFadden assigned two police officers to help me. Thus began my journey to see if a criminal's actions really could systematically reveal his key identifying characteristics.

A mere coincidence had linked the two murders and the rapes. Detective Superintendent Charlie Farquahar was leading an investigation into the murder on 29 December 1985 at Hackney Wick in East London of Alison Day, a nineteen-year-old secretary. He learned from a "Crime-watch" TV program of the murder of a fifteen-year-old girl, Maartje Tamboezer, near a village outside Guildford 40 miles south of London. Maartje Tamboezer's body had been found in a wood in the spring of '86, a few weeks before my visit to Hendon. The wood was covered in bluebells. With a poignancy rare for police officers, they had called their investigation the Bluebell inquiry.

Something about the television account of the Guildford investigation made Charlie Farquahar wonder if it was linked to his inquiry, Hackney Wick lay a good distance away.

He talked to the Surrey police, and a closer examination of forensic evidence revealed gruesome links in the way the murders had been carried out . The killer had used a ligature to strangle the victims. He cut the clothing and used it as a gag The facts were unique to these two murders. The criminal attempted to set fire to one body, especially the pubic region, something never before seen in a British murder inquiry.

Comparisons of the murders and rapes in London also pointed to similarities, especially in the way the victims' hands had been tied and the offender set fire to tissues with which he had wiped the victim after the sexual assault. A relatively rare blood grouping was found both in semen at the rape scenes and on the body of Maartje Tamboezer. The Hart inquiry had nearly shut down for lack of progress when the links to the murders were discovered. Setting up the combined operation was a last-ditch attempt to find the perpetrator.

We knew we were following in the footsteps of the Behavioral Science Unit of the FBI, since made internationally famous by the book and film *The Silence of the Lambs*. However, neither *The Silence of the Lambs* nor the publications and lectures of FBI behavioral science agents indicated how to produce an "offender profile". The published accounts revealed FBI agents' experiences, and some of the theories they have found helpful. But they offered no systematic, applied approach for investigating officers.

The police officers assigned to help me turned up at the University of Surrey, on the dot of nine on the Monday morning. All they knew was that they were to help with "the profiling" Rupert Heritage and Jim Blann were both detectives with many years of direct, hands-on experience in solving serious crimes. We had to teach each other a lot about our respective worlds. Rupert was joined by Detective Constable Lesley Cross, an intense, steely woman. She clearly saw her job as part of the helping professions, improving people's lives by reducing crime. Where Jim and Rupert were prepared to try the research trail I mapped out, Lesley wanted more fundamental answers. She wanted to know why.

The first task was to try and work out which crimes had actually been committed by the same man. I decided that we should begin with the rapes because they provided much more overt behavioral information.

A small research room had already been set up in the Guildford police headquarters by Detective Superintendent

John Hurst, who was in command of the Bluebell inquiry. Behavioral analysis became the focal point of the activity in this unexpected setting. I made frequent visits to this strange laboratory, as much out of curiosity as to supervise the research, watching the painstaking process of analyzing the actions that took place in every offense.

Looking for More Detail

Rupert and Jim began by listing, and then comparing all he actions that had happened in every rape. The charts contained the same information originally pinned to the wall at Hendon, but there were two main differences. First, we aimed for far more detail about the criminal's actions: did the assailant say anything to the victim before he attacked her? Were the victim's clothes pulled off, cut off or torn off? What sort of threats were made to control the victim? Exactly what sort of sexual activity took place? How did he deal with her after the assault? We soon had more than a hundred such categories describing the thirty or so assaults that may have been committed by the same offender.

Using the Computer in a Different Way

The second important difference from the initial wall charts was the way we utilized the computer.

For many years I had used computers to help find patterns in data. This time, the computer's task was to compare every crime with every other, across all the actions, and to indicate, by degree, the similarities and differences between crimes. We were concerned that using the university's powerful and somewhat public computers might breach the confidentiality of the material. Fortunately, some new software I had had custom designed for my laptop computer, provided the privacy and ease of use we needed for the whole investigative team, some of whom were inexperienced with computers. Ironically, the software had been paid for out of profits I had made on market research projects studying people's preferences for biscuits. I had wanted programs that could be used by respondents in group discussions at the back of pubs, so it had to be very easy to use and very portable.

I let Jim and Rupert loose on it.

We improvised at every step. Police officers were seconded to help so that no specific budget was assigned to the work. They borrowed a computer and used software that had been paid for by an advertising manager. I fitted in, for free, whatever time I could sneak from the university. Since then, despite our obvious successes, not much has changed.

We got the computer to compare every crime with every other by taking into account all the actions we had recorded for each crime. The analysis would not have been possible if done by hand. It would have taken too long and would have been open to many more mistakes and distortions.

Discovering a Subset of Crimes

Each pair of crimes was measured for similarity, based on how closely related the patterns of actions in those crimes were. We discovered a subset of crimes that were very similar indeed. The analysis also drew attention to changes occurring in the criminal's behavior from one crime to the next.

The lone offender showed increasing assurance as the crimes continued. He spent more time with his victims, especially after the sexual assault. On some occasions, even after he had bound a victim to rape her, he sat and talked to her. We identified certain consistencies, including: the tying of the victim's thumbs behind her back, which investigating officers had already used as a link between the rapes and the murders; the questioning of the victim about herself and where she lived; the apparent self-disclosure by the assailant about his ignorance of the locality. This subset of crimes convinced us that the behaviors probably could be attributed to one man, not two.

We had moved beyond detailed physical descriptions of the criminal, into a new realm of investigation.

Descriptions given by the victims varied considerably. Sometimes he was described as having short black hair, sometimes it was longer ginger hair. Estimates of his height and build also differed from a short five and a half feet to over six feet.

But strong similarities emerged when we considered how the attacker always approached his victims first before returning to rape them. What he actually did and said before, during and after the sexual assault were key to the investigation.

He typically passed his victims, often speaking to them briefly, then grabbed them from behind threatening them with a knife. In many cases he restrained the women so that he could carry out the rape, fastening their hands behind their backs, using a binding made from their own tights. He also spent time with many of the women after the rape, finding out their name or giving them instructions on how to find the way home.

But these actions were not always the same, and that sent us back to the computer to search for more trends, sometimes simply by a process of elimination—excluding some behaviors and adding others to study the computer results.

The essence of the offender, his character or what some psychologists would call his "personality" lay behind the computer trawls.

Questioning the Commonplace

We all are aware that there is something about ourselves

that makes us distinct. We see that uniqueness reflected in how we think, feel and act. Perhaps with less certainty we also recognize the distinctiveness of other people. It is commonplace to meet a person after an interval of months or years but still to see them as their "old self", still talking and acting in ways that we know are typical of them.

As any psychologist might do, I began questioning the obvious and commonplace.

What is consistent about a person from one situation to another? What remains constant from one time and place to another time and place? There are so many ways in which people can differ from each other, what are the major differences that help us to identify each person? It dawned on me that these general questions bore a sharp edge when applied to criminal investigations. Information in an investigation is usually restricted to what a criminal does and says in the act. In such a situation researchers haven't the luxury of asking the criminal specific questions about himself, or to perform certain tasks that might reveal his identity. We needed different theories and explanations that would accommodate the limited material typically available in an investigation. This is not to say that years of scientific psychology are irrelevant and I had to start from scratch. Instead, I was forced to decide which were the dominant, robust themes of psychology that could be applied even in such a constrained and limited human action as violent crime. I concluded that violent crime is always a transaction between at least two people; therefore it must reveal something about the way in which the offender deals with people. We had to consider not just the fact that he was prepared to commit a violent crime, although that would never be forgotten, but also all the other implications of his actions, the way he related to other people, especially women.

Acts of violence can take many different forms and be

preceded and followed by a great range of behaviors. I believed that, taken together, these variations can tell us a lot about the offender's ways of interacting with other people.

Among the plethora of differences psychologists explore about the way people relate to each other two seemed especially relevant to the varieties of violent crime.

A Need to Relate to the Victim

How prepared was the criminal to try and relate to the victim? This mirrors years of debate around terms like "outgoing", "extrovert", "sociable", or even "warm" and "considerate". Within the context of violent crime the key issue may be the attempt to strike up or imply a relationship or not. Given the distorted nature of the relationship in a violent assault on a stranger this must be seen through the eyes of the offender. Does he demand of the victim any sense of him as a person? Requests that she kiss him, or asking her name or whether she has a boyfriend (as this offender did) may all indicate a man who is trying to convince himself that there is some personal, even intimate, contact involved in the assault. Perhaps this would indicate that he has attempted such relationships in the past with varying degrees of success?

A Desire to Dominate

A second distinct theme, long recognized by social psychologists, is the desire for dominance. All violent men want to control their victims so that they can satisfy their urges, but criminals want to explore and relish the experience of control itself. They want to deliberately frighten, demean and insult their victims. Would that indicate a desire to dominate in other aspects of their life? The particular offender we were studying only exerted enough control to rape his victims, so it raised the possibility that he would not be known as a very powerful, secure individual.

Our investigation had made progress. But the offender would not wait for us to develop our scientific theories.

He killed again.

Another murder bore many hallmarks of the previous two. On May 18, not long after my visit to Hendon, Anne Locke a thirty-year-old secretary working for London Weekend Television disappeared after catching the late evening train to Brookmans Park in North London. This was close to the Hertfordshire border and therefore another police force became involved in the investigation. Her badly decomposed body was not found until 21 July, but the indications from the binding of the fingers and the way it had been set on fire were that she had been killed by the same man who killed Alison Day and Maartje Tamboezer.

Rupert's Maps

To keep some track of all the crimes over the four years from 1981 to 1986 Rupert had carefully marked their locations on a map of London. When I saw this I suggested to Rupert that he produce a separate map for each year. He did a beautiful job. Using a transparent acetate sheet for each year, he carefully colored in the locations of each attack, using red for the attacks committed by two people together and green for the lone rapist. There were only three years, there being no linked crimes for 1984. Small squares marked the location of each of the three murders.

Sitting on a high stool, nursing my cup of coffee, I watched as Rupert showed me first the locations of all the crimes. Then he peeled off the acetate layers, going back in time, lifting off those including the murders of 1986, followed by the removal of the sexual assaults for 1985, leaving the handful of assaults carried out by two people together, or one alone, in 1982.

What the layers told me seemed obvious enough; so much so that I assumed the police investigation team had already worked out the location in which the lone criminal must have lived. Casually I pointed to an area of North London circumscribed by the first three offences and said with a questioning smile, "He lives there doesn't he?"

Map of London with the Location of Duffy's Rapes and Murders marked on and the Area in which he lived at the time of his first offences

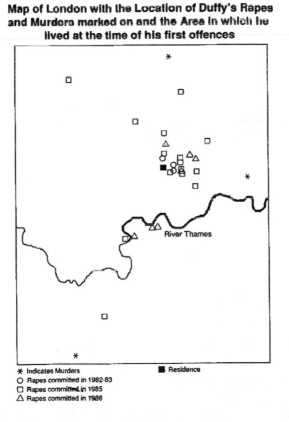

✳ Indicates Murders

○ Rapes committed in 1982-83

□ Rapes committed in 1985

△ Rapes committed in 1986

■ Residence

In retrospect, I cannot say exactly why I suggested that we look at the crimes year by year. My experience examining human behavior has taught me that often patterns can be revealed if the data are broken down into logical subgroups. For example, to study the responses that a large sample of people have to where they work, can make more sense if the information is divided by departments.

The Shape of Change

Psychology often presents individuals as if they are frozen in time and space, describing their score on an intelligence or personality test, how they remember or what their inner conflicts are. All imply that people are fixed and that a description of them at one point in time will inevitably be true of them at another. Yet, while there are profound consistencies in how any person feels or acts, change is also inevitable. The shape of that change may be the most consistent characteristic of a person. So, the variations in the attacks over time I had first noted continued to intrigue me.

A complex mixture of possible explanations can account for even the simple fact that a person chose a weekday to commit a crime. The shadow cast by a criminal's actions does have a recognizable shape.

The shapes I saw in the rapes were changing. Something was happening to the criminal as he committed more and more crimes. The fact that police were convinced he had progressed to murder, after rapes was the clearest possible proof that he was changing.

Here another theme of modern psychology occurred to me as centrally relevant. Everyone changes through life as a result of experiences. However, these changes, as many psychologists throughout this century have shown, are not haphazard or arbitrary. Within any particular sphere of experience changes take place with increasing differentiation and refinement. Furthermore, changes in one aspect of a person are almost invariably reflected in other aspects. A person who tastes many wines, just like a person who uses many computers, or a doctor who treats many patients, not only becomes more able to see (and smell) subtle differences between the subjects of his experience, differences that others are unaware of, he is also more able to distinguish the wines, or computers or patients, or locations for violent crime or ways of controlling victims into more refined categories. This increased discernment makes the person more sensitive to the nuances of the situation or the subject.

An experienced person often can think more abstractly, can see outside the experience itself and look down upon its implications. The most dramatic examples of this personal evolution have been shown from studies of children's thoughts and feelings as they grow up. Psychologists have charted the growth from concrete, self-centered childhood in which a child's own place in the world is totally dominant, through to self-conscious adolescence in which more general principles and alternative perspectives can be perceived and acted upon. There is growing evidence that such developmental processes occur whenever we are faced with new realms of experience. It therefore seemed feasible that this prolific rapist had learned directly from his own experience of the crimes and that this learning process had made him more subtle and sophisticated But it was certainly not clear how that process had led him on to kill.

The constant question that Lesley Cross had asked me was, why had the criminal gone on to murder? He had been successful as a rapist without being caught. He appears, on occasion, to have been almost considerate to his victims after the sexual assault: telling them which train to get home, offering them money for the journey, or a cigarette. Then he murdered three women, one after the other. Why?

Today we have various possible explanations, but in the summer of 1986 the only thing I could say was that the existence of that very question was the most important thing we knew about him. He had changed his actions. That had to be a clue to who he was and where we could find him. But at that moment I did not know how it could help us.

We had the geographical details of many offenses. We knew there was a change over time. Did the geography show any change over time that might be relevant?

Rupert's maps showed an explosion of crimes. The area covered was growing each year. The criminal had not moved on to a new set of locations like some predatory animal that has eaten the game in one region and therefore moves to new pastures. It was more like a marauding brigand whose confidence grows as he continues to evade capture, spreading his dark, influence over an increasing area of the map—the region of each succeeding year encompassing the preceding year. Was the offender exploring ever further from some base? If he was then the most likely location of his base would be in the region of his first known crimes. According to this line of thought, his initial attacks would have been when he was exploring the possibilities close to home; when he was with his accomplice who might have some steady job, for whom rape was an exciting pastime, not a mission; when he was not yet committed to being a "rapist".

Together with these conjectures about where the offender might live we were collecting others in the Guildford police station. Our ideas about the culprit were growing. We were probably slipping into a relaxed academic exploration, but Vince McFadden wanted to know whether his seconded police officers and borrowed computer really were going to get anywhere with the psychologist from the local university before there was another murder. He urged me to hold a briefing for all senior officers assigned to the teams.

In July, 1986, I invited the Metropolitan police, the Surrey police and the Hertfordshire police to meet in my offices at the university—a pleasantly unimposing setting for them to hear my deliberations.

We pulled together some thoughts about the perpetrator,

using what little we could gather from the FBI, our own, simple first principles, and the statistical data-reduction techniques we had developed. The notes I produced for the meeting were a rudimentary set of headings.

PRELIMINARY PROFILE

Residence
Has lived in the area circumscribed by the first 3 cases since 1983.
Possibly arrested some time after 14 October 1983.
Probably lived in that area at the time of arrest.
Probably lives with wife/girl friend, quite possibly without children.
Age etc.
Mid to late 20s.
Light hair.
About 5'9".
Right handed.
"A" secretor.
Occupation
Probably semi-skilled or skilled job, involving weekend work or casual labor from about June 1984 onwards.
Job does not bring him into a lot of contact with public, in all probability.
Character
Keeps to himself but has one or two very close men friends.
Probably very little contact with women, especially in work situation.
Has knowledge of the railway system along which attacks happened.
Sexual Activity
The variety and mixture of his sexual actions suggest considerable sexual experience.
Criminal Record
Was probably under arrest at some time between October 1982 and January 1984.

His arrest may not have been a sex-related crime at all but an aggressive attack, possibly under the influence of alcohol (or drugs?).

I presented the "preliminary profile" using an overhead projector, talking through the points and trying to explain the thinking that had led to them. Copies of the list were handed out, but like most seminars with new students there was little reaction. They thanked me for my efforts, and the policemen and women wandered off across the grass to their cars. I continued to have meetings with Rupert and Lesley but these became rarer and little was added to our ideas.

Another teenage girl was attacked beside a railway line, possibly by the same man. Her mother's timely search for her had frightened the man away. Was he going to kill again before the police got to him? I was given no indication of the directions in which the police inquiry was going and began to think the seminar in the hut had been a waste of time.

Our Profile Proves True

In late November 1986 I saw in the local paper that a man had been arrested for the murder of three girls and a number of rapes. I immediately telephoned Rupert and asked him what was happening. He indicated that a lot was going on but he could not speak to me about it then.

A few days later I got a telephone call from Vince McFadden. I still remember the sensation at the back of my neck when he said: "I don't know how you did it, or if it was all flannel, but that profile you gave us was very accurate and useful to the investigation."

The remarkable accuracy of the profile surprised everyone, especially me.

The huge trawl of possible suspects had led the police to identify nearly 2,000 people who might have committed the rapes and murders, many because they had a blood-group similar to that left at the crime scene which was present in less than 10 per cent of the population. One of these, John Duffy, came into the list of police suspects because he had raped his wife at knife-point after she had left him. Before they were legally separated they had fights in which he bound her to have sex with him against her will.

In the initial stages of the police inquiry Duffy had not been a prominent suspect, reportedly ranking 1,505th on the list. His assault on his wife had been regarded as what police officers often call "a domestic", merely a contretemps between a married couple. Some officers had assumed that a person involved in such domestic violence was not the sort of man who would go on to kill a stranger in a deliberate, planned way. The prospect that such violence within a marriage could be an indication towards later violence against strangers is still not widely understood.

After Duffy had initially been interviewed by the police about the assaults on his wife, the story took another bizarre twist. He staggered into a police station badly injured, saying he had been attacked and had lost his memory. He was admitted to a psychiatric hospital to be treated for "amnesia". He was not under very strict supervision at the hospital, as detectives later discovered, being free to come and go during the day without his absence being noted. It was also curious that the only patient he befriended in the hospital was a man who had strong delusions of having murdered someone. (One day a novelist will explore the relationship between a murderer claiming amnesia, denying any knowledge of a violent criminal past, and a mental patient tormented by his own mistaken belief that he has taken somebody's life.)

Duffy, buried deep in the list of suspects, closely fitted the profile. He was the only one who lived in the Kilburn area, the predicted location, and one of very few who matched the majority of other characteristics. Police launched a large-scale surveillance to watch the suspect. His activities convinced McFadden that Duffy was the man they were looking for. He was arrested.

An acquaintance of Duffy, who practiced martial arts with him, came forward, admitting that he wounded Duffy at his own request. Duffy had told him he wanted to have an excuse to fake amnesia, believing that the wounding would be accepted by police as so traumatic that it could have produced a loss of memory. Forensic evidence of fibers on his clothing were linked to those found on the bodies of his victims and very unusual string, made out of paper, was found at his family home. This string was the same as that used to bind his murder victims. Identification parades linked him to the rapes as did the original blood-typing.

The subsequent court case drew heavily on the ideas behind the profile, giving a story-line to all the disparate facts. John Francis Duffy sat throughout showing little emotion. A small, slim, fair-haired man, bordering on the ginger, with a pock-marked, weasel-like face, he passed notes from time to time to his counsel, but otherwise might have been a casual spectator who would have gone unnoticed in the street. The jury had no difficulty in finding him guilty of two murders and five rapes. He was sentenced to life imprisonment with the recommendation that he serve at least twenty years.

Checking the Duffy Profile Against Reality

Now that Duffy has been prosecuted as the "Railway Rapist" (as the press called him), we can see that only his height was overestimated, from victim statements, and the exact timing and pattern of his previous arrests were wrong. The seemingly uncanny accuracy of everything else encouraged us to believe that it may be possible to develop general psychological principles and procedures to help detect violent crimes against strangers.

Since that first "profile" we have continued refining the processes we used to help catch Duffy. The remarkable positive outcome from the back-room discussions and computer analyses in Guildford police station laid the basis for future developments. Some of the main arguments are memorable, as well as some of the discoveries we made along the way about what could and could not be relied on in a police investigation.

We have learned that physical descriptions may not be as accurate as accounts of the criminal's actions.

We now know that descriptions of a criminal's appearance can be systematically biased. Thus for each victim who overestimates his age there can be one who underestimates it. But, if we can identify a group of offenses that we can be reasonably sure were committed by the same man, then the common elements of the descriptions given by the victims could possibly be taken as a reasonably accurate description of the offender.

Duffy was twenty-nine when he was arrested, so victims' estimates of him, ranging from early to late twenties, were reasonably accurate. The inaccuracy in height estimate, though, was an important mistake. It serves to show that some general bias, among even a number of independent victims, is possible. It suggests that victims can be so traumatized by a man who has violently assaulted them that they consistently remember him as taller than he was.

Rupert's Maps Disclose a Dramatic Discovery

The geographical distribution of Duffy's crimes revealed where he was living at the time of his first known rapes. It is easy to forget that his rapes covered the whole of greater London and the three murders were at three distant points on the very edge of London. Looking at a general map of these crimes we may have thought he lived anywhere in a fifty-mile radius of central London—an area that houses about a third of the population of Great Britain. He might even have been traveling in from further a-field. Yet he was the only one on the list of police suspects who lived in the area we had indicated. His marauding out from the early, less apparently planned sexual assaults to the carefully conducted murders at the furthest distance, strongly suggested an increasing determination and forward planning in his crimes.

Familiarity and convenience were significant factors in shaping the locations Duffy chose for his assaults, at least initially. But when he was convicted we had no idea how generally such a principle might apply. In his particular case we found that even the later rapes happened in areas he already knew. After the trial Rupert discovered that virtually all locations in which Duffy carried out his sexual assaults were close to places that he knew from visiting relatives or close friends, or from his recreational activities. This throws an even more chilling light on his killings. It is difficult to believe that the murders were casually opportunist or accidental. There must have been a plan that took Duffy so far from the central London that he knew.

Here was a man, then, increasingly dedicated to crime, developing into a cold-blooded killer. That was the development process I had glimpsed in the patchy picture of rapes in the London Standard. He had become a lone attacker, increasingly devoted to assaults, raping women whenever he could. Perhaps the early attacks when he had a partner were seen by both men as chance opportunities, but as the partner became more aware of how obsessed Duffy was perhaps he pulled out, wanting no part of activities he could see would lead to arrest?

Throughout his trial, and for many years after, Duffy claimed amnesia for his actions around the time of the rapes and murders. Consequently, no examination of his own count of what went on has been possible. He did have a known accomplice, arrested with him for earlier physical assaults and burglary but there was not enough evidence to bring that man to court for the joint rapes. Recently though, apparently after much soul searching in prison Duffy has admitted his crimes. In doing so he has incriminated his accomplice, claiming that the murders were the result of each egging the other on to more extreme violence.

Duffy's prior criminal history for stealing was another suggestion in the "preliminary profile" that could have been peculiar to this particular man. Perhaps some special circumstances trigger sexual crimes in a man who has previously been a law-abiding citizen, so no record of him would exist in police files. There is a different possibility. Many police officers believe sexually deviant criminals progress from voyeurism and indecent exposure through sexual assaults and on to rape. Searches through previous criminal records are most likely, therefore, to be for sexually-linked crimes. However, clinical studies of sexual deviations do not strongly support this career path. While there are exceptions, many convicted rapists have no obvious antecedents of voyeurism, indecent exposure or less serious sexual assaults. They do, though, often have convictions for theft and violence. So, many possibilities must be considered when delving into previous convictions. Every possibility exists from no previous record to prior sex-related crimes and other criminal activity. Then, there is an added complication. The criminal may never have been caught or convicted for the crimes, and in some trivial offenses, such as "peeping" no records may be available to investigators.

Our proposal that the "Railway Rapist" had previously come to the attention of police officers for non-sexual crimes was therefore only one of a large range of possibilities. The fact that we were correct in this one case, our first, indicates that discernible principles may exist to link what a criminal does in his crimes with the sort of offenses he may have been arrested for in the past.

Police Thoroughness

One assumption which needs further testing is "police thoroughness" A man who had committed as many criminal assaults as the "Railway Rapist" was unlikely to have come to crime all of a sudden. Even if there had been some trigger that set him on a particular spree, the fact that his response was a series of violent criminal activities suggests prior criminal involvement in his life—a life beyond the law. It is the number of crimes that is central to this argument. The same might not be expected to apply to one sudden outburst. We knew the "Railway Rapist" had committed a lot of crimes during a known time period. We therefore had every reason to think that he had also committed other crimes not linked to the identified series.

The principle behind "police thoroughness" is that many men are brought to police attention for a great variety of crimes. In Britain, as many as a third of adult males may have a criminal record. Furthermore, when a major inquiry is launched the net is usually cast widely in the search for possible suspects. It seems likely that someone who commits a series of grievous crimes has his name logged somewhere in police records. The problem lies in finding him. If police are thorough in their search for prior records, perhaps they can improve their chances of success.

Looking for a Central Theme

We assumed that the "Railway Rapist" had been caught up in some police investigation during his long period of crime. The problem for Vince McFadden was choosing among the 1,999 suspects those on whom police resources should be expended. Who should be looked at closely? Our suggestion, presented in the profile, of looking for a non-sexual criminal history was based on the idea there is some central theme, core or objective to a series of crimes, that represents the criminal's way of dealing with other people. A man who rapes many women then starts deliberately to kill his victims shows a central violent nature. In planning some of his sexual crimes he may have had that violence under control to the extent of avoiding immediate detection, but possibly in other situations his aggression would be less under control, more overt: a brawl in a pub, a fight with his girlfriend.

I think of this as the electrician and the ladder principle. In studies of industrial safety I have found that, typically, electricians who have accidents do not do so by electrocuting themselves; dealing with electricity is such an ingrained habit that they automatically take care. If an electrician has an accident it is more likely to be produced by some part of his job that does not require special skill: he falls off a ladder through stretching too far, or bumps into something because his attention wanders. I speculated that a committed criminal, as Duffy became, is skilled at avoiding arrest when he is consciously going out to commit crimes, but drops his guard and reveals his true criminal nature when involved in activities that he does not think of as criminal, like forcing his ex-wife to have sex at knife-point.

Criminal's Own Actions Point to Earlier Crimes

We learned from Duffy's crimes that criminals some-times may betray—by their very actions—that they have been previously investigated. In one case, after he had raped a woman Duffy combed through her pubic hair, presumably so that no traces of his own hair would be found. He also wiped a number of his victims with tissues then set fire to the tissues to get rid of evidence of semen. He was found to have a box of matches with tissues in it, called by the prosecution "a rape kit". Setting fire to the pubic region of his murdered victims was one of the factors that convinced the police that it was the same man who had committed rapes in which he wiped the victims. All these actions revealed a detailed knowledge of forensic investigation. He most likely came by this knowledge through being examined himself after his assault on his ex-wife.

Testing Our Conclusions Against Fact

To test our various conclusions, we added elements together in different ways to see if they would reveal other possible characteristics. In this case we felt these violent crimes had been planned and the offender had taken care to avoid detection. Would this not be more typical of an older man unlikely to be overtaken by the impetuosity of youth? The majority of crimes are committed by young men in their mid- to late teens. Violent, serious crimes such as rape, murder and armed robbery come later in a person's developing criminal career. The studied murders of Duffy were very different from sudden violent outbursts, revealing Duffy's criminal maturity that I rightly assumed was a reflection of his age. He might have been a lot older, in his late thirties or even early forties as many serial murderers are, but that would have been unusual for a rapist who is usually in his early to mid-twenties. The combination of possibilities led us to estimate that this rapist and murderer would be in his mid- to late twenties, an assumption borne out by witness descriptions. As it turned out, we were very close. He was twenty-nine when he was arrested, having started on his crimes in his mid-twenties.

An older man with a history of sexual assault, but probably without any other sort of criminal history, who rapes and eventually murders is most probably unmarried. More of the men who are convicted for rape are unmarried than are married. But in Duffy's contacts with his rape victims he typically approached them first to ask directions, or by a similar subterfuge made contact to give them a false sense of security before assaulting them. After some of his assaults he seemed confident enough with his victims to stay and talk to them, even on some occasions giving them advice on how to get home. Here then was a man who was comfortable being in control of women, who could approach strange women without fear of rebuff. Yet we knew that he raped and violently murdered some victims as well. Women were an obvious vehicle for his control and sexuality. It seemed likely that he would have wished to have a woman available to him, a wife. The profile therefore proposed that he had been married.

Another Clue: Breakdown in Relationships

Here, then, was the birth of another possible principle that we could develop and test on future cases: a consistency principle. The ways in which he deals with his victims tell us something about the way the offender deals with other people who are significant to him.

It would be strange indeed that a man could have a deep, caring relationship with his wife and still go out frequently with a friend or on his own to rape and then murder. Every published case about such men reveals an exploitative relationship between the offender and his partner. On the surface they may seem to be happily married but, more so than in many marriages, it does not take much to find the disruptive chasm between the couple: either an accepting gullibility on the part of the woman, cynically abused by the man, or a woman kept in a subservient role by vicious manipulation. By the time the man is involved in violent crime the relationship may have broken up completely.

The breakdown of this relationship, indeed, may have escalated the criminal's activities. Feelings of anger and frustration, sometimes confused with thoughts of protecting oneself from investigation, or a belief that he is meting out crude justice, are often aggravated by personal traumas. A violent relationship with a woman was therefore a reasonable conclusion in Duffy's case.

When the original profile became public knowledge some authorities commented that it was all very obvious that a man who raped and murdered women was antagonistic towards them. But this anger with women could as easily have resulted in lack of contact with them. It would certainly have been a reasonable assumption, at a superficial level, that the offender had never established any long-term relationship with a woman. How could he rape and kill and still have lived with a woman? This assumption fails on two counts. First, it does not allow for changes in criminal activity. For a younger assailant, lack of close contact with women of his own age would have been a reasonable assumption. For an older attacker prior association with a woman seemed more likely. Secondly, he indicated to his victims through conversation that in some curious way he wanted a relationship. This points to an earlier, perhaps failed, attempt to establish a relationship with a woman.

The third clue to a relatively long relationship with a woman was the variety of sexual activity revealed in the sexual assaults. Scientific study shows that sexual activity is shaped by a learning process. The more opportunity and experience a person has for sex the more varied his or her actions are likely to become. This variety can also be enhanced by access to sex manuals and pornography, but first-hand experience has the most potent effect in all aspects of human behavior. The number of offenses linked by detectives allowed me to see a man who carried out every form of sexual behavior he could with his victims, indicating that he had probably had a long-standing female relationship.

The Criminal's Relationships to Others

But what of this relationship? Would they have had children? The viciousness of Duffy's assault on the fifteen-year-old Maartje Tamboezer was difficult to associate with a man involved in bringing up children himself. His aggression toward this schoolgirl was carefully planned, without any empathy for his victim. I thought, perhaps naively at that stage, this could not be the action of a man who had been a father. (At that stage I did not know of Colin Pitchfork, for example, who killed two adolescent girls while he was married with young children.)

What kind of job, if any, would a potentially violent man have—a man who was antagonistic towards women, but who planned his assaults with confidence, going ever further to carry out his most vicious attacks? He clearly exploited and used people.

He also would be intolerant of those who made demands on him, so any job he had would be unlikely to be a "service" that brought him into direct contact with those he served. His preparation and planning indicated an ability beyond laboring work; the intellectual skills he brought to his murders indicated he even could have learned a trade earlier in life. If he did have some semi-skilled job, how could he commit crimes so often during the working week without any fear of being missed? The simplest assumption was that he worked on the weekend, or had a very casual job. His exploitive, confident style with his victims could easily have been reflected in a poor work record, a man who was often absent from work for no apparent reason. Or he might have had to travel around to carry out his work on his own, so that absences could go unnoticed for some time. The work of a travelling carpenter for British Rail, with hindsight, is a far more obvious and detailed possibility than I would have dared propose in those early days of our work, but the general tone of my suggestions was close enough for police investigators to see the logic.

As we know, Duffy used a unique method to kill: he tied a tourniquet round his victims' necks that he then tightened with a large stick taken from the scene. He used this brutal garrotte to kill all his victims, yet such a method had never been seen before in a British murder. How were we to interpret this dreadful signature?

Carpenters learn about tourniquets, though, most frequently in first aid. First aid manuals point out the dangers of this method of stopping the flow of blood from a wound: "If digital pressure will not stop the flow of blood, it may be necessary to apply a tourniquet but this should be done as a last resort. The tourniquet is a dangerous instrument. The tourniquet should be applied between the wound and the heart (but not around the neck)."

A man intent on murder could easily have read such innocent instructions differently. Other martial arts and survival books found in his possession could have reinforced his awareness of how to dispatch his victims.

The arrest of Duffy and the subsequent details that emerged helped to fill in the picture we had formed in our profile. Other questions we had posted during our discussions at Guildford police station began to be answered during the trial. On one occasion, his former wife told the court: "He said he had raped a girl and said it was my fault." John Duffy had found that he was infertile and some of his most violent assaults took place after he discovered that his ex-wife had become pregnant by another man after she left Duffy. So anger and frustration could be seen as triggers for his actions.

But why did he kill? Why did a man who had avoided

capture for at least three years when raping his victims and letting them live go on to kill? There was some possibility the Hart investigation had so run out of steam that if Duffy had not murdered he would have escaped detection altogether.

It turned out that we may have had the answer to this central question all along, embedded in the ideas inherent in the profile. As the *Daily Telegraph* reported:

> In December 1985, his fifth rape victim was taken to Hendon magistrates court, where Duffy was appearing on an assault charge brought by his wife.
>
> Although she failed to recognize Duffy, he recognized her as she peered at him. He came to a decision that any future women that he raped would be silenced.
>
> He killed Allison Day 27 days after his court appearance.

It all added up to a man increasingly caught up in violence, entangling himself in crime. The more he tried to shake off detection the tighter he pulled the net around himself. Swimming through the murky waters of violent crimes the ill-formed silhouette of the criminal turned out to have an even more interpretable shape than I had hoped for my first involvement in a major crime investigation. The outline provided by the profile became a silhouette that needed very little adjustment to contain the full image of the perpetrator.

Criminals Leave Behavioral Traces Too

Forensic scientists know what the French Criminologist Edmond Locard advocated in the early 1900's: "Every contact leaves a trace." He was thinking of the physical, biological traces that criminals leave from their clothing or where their bodies have touched the scene.

Our work, leading to the arrest of Duffy, suggested that

there was a more subtle meaning to this notion. The contact that an assailant has with his victim leaves a trace of the sort of person he is. There appears to be a behavioral strand to forensic science as well as a biological, chemical and physical one.

When the court proceedings were over, the full significance of our work became apparent. The Surrey police investigation team had a special tie designed to commemorate the case. It had the small image of a bluebell woven into it, a salutary reminder that a schoolgirl had been viciously killed one spring day. If it had not been for the time it takes a complex police investigation to unfold, her killer might have been arrested before he had been able to kill again.

I had tackled the problem posed by police as I would any other research question: I collected all the available, relevant information and attempted to tidy it up to see what central themes it would reveal. The computer had certainly helped in imposing some order on the unruly data. The sequential maps had also been of great value. But neither the computer analysis nor the maps, or any of the other tables and lists we prepared, would have told us anything more than the charts that filled the walls of the Hart inquiry at Hendon, if I had not had some systematic way of interpreting them.

Rupert Heritage, an experienced detective who had never operated a computer or worked with a professor before, nor claimed any knowledge of psychology, was convinced that we had opened a new way forward for criminal investigation. He asked to study with me at the university. Only then did I realize that our team had made a true breakthrough in criminal investigation.

Chapter Three
ENRICHING INTUITION

In the film, *The Silence of the Lambs*, Jodie Foster portrayed Clarice Starling, a new FBI agent, trying to apply what she had learned about "profiling" at the FBI academy in Quantico, VA. The film showed the use of profiling as a tool for detection originating in Quantico's Behavioral Science Unit.

I was invited to the FBI academy at Quantico to exchange ideas and to observe the FBI lectures, as a result of the interest generated by my involvement in successfully detecting the "Railway Rapist."

The Behavioral Science Unit, a relatively small, part of the FBI academy, provides training in most aspects of law enforcement for the FBI and for the Drug Enforcement Agency (DEA) as well as other city, county and state police agencies. Topics as diverse as predicting future patterns of crime and forensic photography are explored and taught in a large complex of interconnected lecture rooms, offices, residences, laboratories and sports facilities. Programs are intensive and all-embracing. They include sending in a team to counsel staff after one of their number has been murdered, and re-acclimatization procedures for people who have been living under cover for long periods of time; there are programs on crimes against the elderly, weapons training, computer literacy and a fitness program that leaves the students more athletic than they will ever be again. Lecture courses are accredited by the local University of Virginia, so each has a syllabus and recommended reading lists and all the paraphernalia of academia that can be presented in digestible chunks to keen students.

But the lifeblood of the Behavioral Science Unit is murder and violent assault, threats and abductions. Those students who come to take the courses become part of a team of active practitioners who are trying to find links between violent crimes across the United States and to give guidance to law enforcement agencies the length and breadth of the land and beyond.

The FBI, controlled by the US Government, contributes to violent crime investigations only by invitation, unless the crime is a federal one (such as kidnapping or a series of related murders) that crosses state boundaries, or involves federal property. They can be brought in as experts separately from the evidence of police investigators. All this puts the special agents at Quantico in a unique position. They are the back-room boffins, the consultants to criminal analysis.

Birth of the FBI Behavioral Science Unit

In the early 1970's, the FBI became aware from classroom discussions about ongoing cases that using experienced agents as lecturers provided trainees not only with a wide range of material, but with access to as many approaches to crime-solving as possible. Agent lecturers offered a perspective unattainable in any other context. In the deep passageways of Quantico, special agents began to realize that if they were directly to assist investigators on the job, they needed a new technology, a process that would be attractive and useful to field officers. It had to be an inviting product, not easily available from the local store. A system, a bundle of skills based on special knowledge, would have to be fashioned then introduced into the real world. Out of these aspirations the Behavioral Science Unit was born.

Most visitors to the Behavioral Science Unit have to master a new and macabre vocabulary: vampirism, cannibalism, satanism, autoerotic fatalities, equivocal death syndrome, threat analysis, sexual sadism (by comparison, well-known terms like "masochism" and "bondage" seem benign). This vocabulary has been created to describe the stock-in-trade of the special agents and their instructors. Here, words like "horrific" and "appalling" quickly lose their meaning to be replaced by a sanitized jargon that allows crimes more brutal and vicious than any fictional conceptions to be discussed with calm enthusiasm by virtuoso investigators. One such was Roy Hazelwood, Supervisory Special Agent Instructor, a small, precisely-featured man who orders his steak very well done and cuts it into many small shreds before he starts to eat it, almost as if he were making sure that it did not contain any hidden forensic material. It is not at all difficult to imagine him imposing hygiene and good order on a red-light district in Vietnam as he did as part of his military service. He was our mentor and guide when Rupert Heritage and I visited the FBI academy in January 1990. By then we had established our credentials well enough, from involvement in a number of cases, to be welcomed to a refresher course (or as they call it "retraining") for graduates of the academy, all of whom had spent a year at some point in the previous decade studying with the master "profilers".

The style and details of each profiler's approach emerged as we observed their discussions of ongoing cases. It seemed the epitome of detection, a Sherlock Holmes-style inquiry. For example, with a set of photographs and little other evidence they tried to establish whether a hanging was, in fact, a suicide; what they call an examination of "equivocal death". Trainees' comments came with confidence and precision: "Drug pushers do not hang their victims, they knife or shoot them; there was no sign of trauma, therefore no support for murder; the complexity of the knotting was best explained by a number of attempts to carry out the suicide; the car found with the keys in the ignition, but locked, explained by the victim wanting the car, rented by his girlfriend, to go back to the rental agency without her getting into trouble; a place near where he worked so he would be familiar with it."

"I like it," Roy shouted, when he was told that the man had previously attempted suicide. Forming a view of the event became a battle to defend an idea.

One evening the FBI agents started talking about the video Roy had shown us that morning of an autoerotic fatality. They had all been shown it at one time or another as part of a training session. It seems that to gain sexual arousal a man had been filming himself in the act of self-strangulation, but he had slipped and accidentally hung himself. The notion that such an activity could be erotically arousing to anyone rather surprised me and that it should be filmed even more bizarre. The material in the training film discussed by students over dinner, like any other lecture demonstration, perhaps captures most directly the mood and character of Quantico. Even scurrilous jokes about the film, obviously often repeated, went round the table. These asides showed that they, like most intelligent students, were critically perceptive of those who taught them—the experienced FBI agents who had put "offender profiling" on the map. They regarded these senior agents as having a "seat of the pants" party line, accepting their approach as broadly intuitive.

The cases they had described earlier in the day were off the scale of my experience and well beyond anything Rupert had come across; murders encompassing vampirism and cannibalism, in which parts of the victim are eaten and their body fluids drunk; sexual sadism with extensive bindings and torturing of victims; a number of autoerotic fatalities. It was a new world, or abyss, of criminal horrors.

The Fellows, as the refresher students are called, seemed much more human than their teachers. Perhaps that is the

real contribution of John Douglas, Bob Ressler, Roy Hazelwood and the other experienced agents who teach what they
now call Criminal Investigative Analysis: the cold look at
mutilations and bodies. They show their students the value of
a controlled emotional response to the crimes they explore,
making sad, ironic comments.

Understandably, students with limited experience are far
more emotional, talking of leaving a room at the horror of
listening to tape-recorded screams, wincing at even the
thought of the teenager who filmed himself hanging himself,
and the mother who was filmed discovering the body.
Fellows showed more distress at these horrors than the grand
old men, and they changed my view of US law enforcement
officers, especially FBI agents. They listen, and have a
curiously liberal attitude containing tough undertones.

None of the people I met looked or sounded like the
media image of agents. The character Jodie Foster portrayed
in *The Silence of the Lambs* has no real counterpart. More
typical was an overweight middle-aged man who admitted
that adrenalin no longer rushes when he hears there has been
an armed robbery.

It was the intelligent amassing of experience that the
students valued in their supervisory special agents. There
was little research. For them, research is collecting interview
material, but little systematic use is made of it. It is another
notch on the belt. For instance, Roy mentioned in passing
that black murderers do not mutilate or go in for necrophilia,
but he did not take this a step further to make a general
statement about white murderers being more bizarre, nor did
he feel the need for any detailed evidence or back-up data.
Bob Ressler said he had a bunch of statistics somewhere but
he clearly did not give it much credence or significance. His
own extensive, direct experience was far more important to
him. Like the gifted practitioners they are, they wish to be
evaluated on the effectiveness of what they do; for their

recommendations to ongoing investigations, not on the richness of their conceptualizing or the statistical significance of their background evidence.

Detailed knowledge of devious criminals is the basis of the special agent's understanding. For example, the obsessive nature of many violent offenders came through again and again. In one case, a shoebox was found in a garage, which contained every bit of paper on which the woman of the house had ever written a note to the murderer, whom she employed. This collection alone revealed how besotted with her he was. There were also a few photographs he had managed to get of his victim. He nursed his fixated passion for the woman—an exaggerated version of a secret desire that unfolded into a series of attacks on many others, including couples. Also in this same box was an ordinary women's magazine advertising clothes as well as a mildly erotic picture of a pair of legs used to advertise tights: one of the most striking illustrations of how turning women into objects, even for other women, feeds the fantasy life of men who turn to murder. That seemingly innocuous photograph in the shoebox said it all.

The importance of considering victims' responses was also a topic of classroom investigations; the strength and will of ordinary folk dealing with violent crime. Students showed warmth toward the victims, admiring how their determination can be fired by the injustice of an assault. One particular victimized couple had trainees cheering when the husband described how, after he had been stabbed, his ire against the assailant increased when "he wiped the blade on my shirt". Severely wounded, but insulted by his attacker the victim was "determined to get him". So although his wife was strapped, spread-eagled by a man who had already killed eight women, the husband struggled successfully to overpower the killer. Roy said laconically: "We call that the will to live."

FBI Lends Credence to Patterns

The central discovery made by the FBI in their development of "profiling" was both more profound and direct than
their writings indicate. They found a pattern, a shape, to the
actions of violent criminals, a shape that was overt enough
for some criminals to be aware of it themselves. They did
cast unique, identifiable shadows, not random markings as
might have been expected. Aware of the essence of their
discovery, I was reminded of what atomic weapons experts
said about the espionage that transferred the weapons secrets
to the Soviet Union: the spies may have speeded up the
process of the Soviets building an atom bomb, but the real,
critical secret was the possibility of building such a bomb.
Once the scientific community knew that a bomb based on
nuclear fission was feasible, then appropriately trained
scientists could work out for themselves how to make such a
weapon. The critical secret was revealed at Hiroshima.

The FBI demonstrated through many highly-publicized
examples that "offender profiling" was possible. Once the
FBI academy confirmed it was possible, I knew that the tools
I had at my disposal could probably do the job too. If you are
told that shadowy ciphers are the letters of a language then
the task of interpreting them is made considerably easier.

Roy Hazelwood corroborated the probability that
continuity and consistency exists in a criminal's behavior—
from non-criminal situations to criminal ones. He pointed out
that if a criminal had been successful in having the victim
feign passion or involvement, it could be due to his ability to
arouse, and thereby control, women—a characteristic that
would also be found in the offender's non-criminal
associations with women.

The same principles apply to the primary distinction that
Bob Ressler drew between organized and disorganized
murderers. It is a simple idea once you spot it. A man who

plans his life and thinks things through, who holds down a job which makes some demands on his manual or intellectual skills, will go about the business of murder rather differently from the casual, confused ne'er-do-well. An organized crime scene may well be produced by an organized criminal. The person who leaves his victim in a hurry with no attempt at concealment may have left many difficult situations in his life in a hurry and be known for his haphazard ways.

The BSU focused on what actually happened in the crimes, not on the introspections of the criminal. That was the FBI breakthrough.

In the subterranean depths of Quantico, the Behavioral Science Unit has a separateness that gives objectivity to its perspective, but its staff needed to turn their insights and experiences into teaching programs. In doing this they faced the problem many practitioners face: a teacher cannot spend the whole time recounting anecdotes of his own successful activities.

Occupational psychologists call the approach to training on the job the "sitting next to Nelly" technique, a time-honored procedure at least as old as indentured apprentices and their crafts guilds. Most detectives around the world learn the practicalities of their trade in this way. But as much as there is to glean from the many valuable insights and experiences of experts such as Hazelwood, Douglas and Ressler, students require a system or a framework in order to feel they are working from established principles rather than trying to emulate the twists and turns of the minds of their teachers.

Here lies an inherent conflict. The expert investigator draws upon his years of experience, particular foibles and ways of seeing the world, his heightened intuition, to think and act as the material he has in front of him demands. As John Douglas says: "You don't learn this stuff in college." Yet on the floors above him, beyond the maze of corridors, arc high-tech lecture theatres, libraries and rooms for study.

Criminals as Fellow Investigators

If intuition does have roots in knowledge and experience then it should be possible to polish and enhance it. But where can that enrichment come from if what you are looking at is rare, hidden from view and difficult to explain? To build up his knowledge and help him to see critical patterns the expert needs another very special expert. FBI agents realized, as many police officers had before them, that the criminals who had committed the crimes were probably in the best position to increase their understanding. Here were people who had a wholly different perspective on the crime, experts of a different ilk.

The agents needed to know the crimes of their interviewees in great detail so that the offenders—perhaps wishing to show themselves in a more heroic light—would not mislead the investigators. This shadow-boxing primarily aims at finding out exactly how violent crimes were committed, what criminals were aware of about police investigations and what they did to avoid detection.

The use of criminals as expert teachers showing agents how to catch other criminals is a much more feasible prospect than might at first seem apparent. Some criminals, once incarcerated, are looking for an easy time in prison and like to break the boredom by talking to interesting visitors. Surprisingly, many offenders were eager to cooperate, though not all gave much useful information.

The people who did contribute to the BSU interviewers, like those who happily take part in social surveys, were fluent, and intelligent. Certainly, the FBI respondents were different from the "typical convict" captured in the pages of learned journals. The latter are below average intelligence, inadequate people who appear to stumble into crime because of circumstances. The existence of intellectually capable people among those who commit a series of murders of strangers is itself illuminating, but it must also be viewed against the reluctance of many violent criminals to talk to anyone about their actions.

So, what can be learned from these helpful, expert criminals? Mainly, they reveal the thought processes associated with their crime: whether there was any planning, if or how they selected their victims, what they did to evade capture and other technicalities on which they have a unique perspective. In the absence of the type of central records available in the UK, access to the criminals allows much more background information to be collected about their lives and what had led them to their crimes. These interviews also become trophies for the agents, scalps showing their valor in battle. Moreover, they assist the interviewer when considering another crime. The agent may remember how one interviewee told him of returning to the grave of his victim on the anniversary of the murder and so recommend surveillance of the graves of victims of other murderers. A convicted killer might delight in describing how he deliberately laid out the bodies of the victims to imply sexual assaults where none had taken place, so the detective would become more alert to the "staging" of a crime scene at other murders he visited.

Particular details may be relevant, but how can the expert go beyond the individual case? How can he go beyond "sitting next to Nelly"? Even when "Nelly" is a hardened criminal who has committed many murders, his experiences will be limited and idiosyncratic. How can this experience be turned into a marketable system or, more importantly, become the structured basis for a training scheme? If you teach you have to impose a system; it cannot be a personal exploration like a novel. Where could such a system come from?

The Role of Intuition and Experience

Paradoxically, the scheme FBI agents developed to summarize their experiences owed more to the similarities between their interviews of incarcerated men and the processes of therapy which many convicted sexual deviants undergo, than to the hard-nosed experiences of fighting violent crime.

A clever detective coaxing details from a man who has killed or raped, may easily slip into the guise of a therapist listening to a client. If the criminal had had any form of therapy, more of a possibility in the USA than in Britain, then he may even have the vocabulary to feed the detectives with motivations recognizable from the clinical textbooks. If the convicts are involved in sexual assaults, then they will talk to their therapist about the anger that impelled them to rape and mutilate, or the feeling of power that so excited them, or how their desire to talk to the girl had got out of control. FBI agents were probably given similar explanations in the interviews they conducted and recognized that the mixture of motivations that clinicians had harvested over the years could be related to characteristics of the individual of use to police investigations.

The BSU set about to create a framework for the different types of rapists, facilitated by Ann Burgess, a psychiatric nurse. By the late 1970s she had already published, with Dr A. Nicholas Groth, a leading forensic psychiatrist, a theory of the role of power and anger in rape. So, when the FBI needed to present their own account of rapists, a wardrobe of types already existed for them to use.

There is a fascinating contradiction here: investigators drew upon their special intuition and experience to identify vicious criminals, yet needed to turn to therapists and their psychological accounts to present their experience as a package. Yet the paradox is more apparent than real. Both explanations come from talking to the criminal and getting his account of the events. The roots are the same, and so come to similar conclusions.

FBI agents accepted psychotherapists' views that variations between crimes are due to differences in the type of psychological disturbance suffered by the criminal. Their accounts of the offender grow out of the psychopathologies revealed within the criminal's actions. It is these different forms of mental disturbance that they use as the touchstone for diagnosing the criminal's "profile".

In examining sexual assaults, the relationship the assailant does or does not attempt to develop with his victims provides significant information. Does he reveal that he is the type of assailant fiercely angry with his victim and women in general, or is he one of those looking for reassurance that what he is doing is not really coercive; who believes that the victim really wants to be raped? The extreme form of anger is revealed when the assailant gains gratification from the victim's response to pain; the inflicting of pain being his sadistic objective.

Sitting between the two extremes of sadism and reassurance are some types of rapists whose desire is to exert influence and power over their victims, to make them experience fear and realize how "significant" their attacker really is. This four-way split between sadism, anger, reassurance and power has become the dominant way of thinking about sexual assaults, assigning each assailant to one of four possible categories or types.

Four Types of Motives

In an investigation each of the four types of motives behind an offense presumably relates to identifiable characteristics of an offender. The sadistic rapist, for example, is expected to be married, whereas the reassurance type is predicted to be single, living with his parents. The anger type is believed to have an action-oriented occupation, and the power type to have a history of property crime. Yet as attractive as this prospect is—using a typology as the basis for deriving profiles of rapists—it does have many problems.

The FBI approach to classifying types of murderer is simpler than their approach to rapists. This framework owes most to Robert Ressler, a confident, hard-talking square-jawed foil to Roy Hazelwood's intense precision. As already mentioned, Ressler suggested that the major distinction between serial murderers is in their "organized" or "disorganized" style of attack. The former plan and restrain their victims before carefully hiding the body; the latter, by contrast, carry out an impulsive attack, fleeing the scene with little attempt to move the body after death. Characteristic criminal behaviors here are thought to reflect aspects of the offender's personality. The organized offender is expected to be intelligent and socially competent with a reasonable work history, whereas the disorganized offender is the opposite.

Hazelwood's rape typology and Ressler's murder dichotomy, like all attempts to assign people to types, do not consider that the boundaries between categories are extremely broad and ambiguous. Many individuals are clearly a mixture of more than one type. Furthermore, even if assailants could be assigned with confidence to a "type", the relationship between such types and offender characteristics is far from precise. Such a classification can therefore act only as a general guide to an investigator, a hook to get him started, but it must be modified quickly by experience with other similar cases and other rather more vague notions of how offenders act. This is often called a hunch or intuition.

The Secret Behind Intuition

FBI instructors happily admit to the power of their own hunches and intuitions. They experience a sudden insight, or awareness, that appears to come from nowhere, yet they know it is based on their earlier experience. There is a Talmudic discussion that illustrates the essence of this experience. The rabbis of old asked each other why, in the opening sentence of the Bible, the word "create" is used to describe God's activities, why not "make" or "shape"? They decided that the profound difference between creating and making the world is that "making" implies putting together existing components whereas creation speaks of invention from nothing. Intuition feels as if it comes out of the blue. It gives a God-like sensation of contact beyond the immediate here and now. Those who are seen to have it appear to have powers beyond the human. It therefore gives them an authority that might be challenged if their abilities were shown to have recognizable, common roots.

I discussed this at some length with Roy Hazelwood, hoping to convince him that such powers are no less impressive if we understand them. He described the sensation he had when he entered the apartment of an FBI employee who had been brutally murdered. Almost immediately, he says, he knew that a black assailant who lived in the vicinity must have done it. It took some probing on my part to extract from Roy what he had been aware of when entering that room. He spoke of the violence of the offense and its somewhat haphazard nature, the type of victim and location.

Sensitivity to Detail

This questioning revealed that, as in all intuition, there are recognizable sources that can be brought to the surface and examined. First there is Roy's particular sensitivity to detail: he noticed that there was soil near the base of a flowerpot by the broken window through which, entry had been gained. This indicated that the assailant had, probably unthinkingly, lifted the pot back up again after he had knocked it over when climbing in. Roy's attention to such details comes from considerable experience of looking at crime scenes and selecting which apparently trivial details will turn out to be important.

Ability to Perceive Patterns

The second component of intuition is the ability to perceive patterns. This applies to all virtuoso performances. Expert musicians see chord sequences in the music where the beginner looks at one note after another. Roy Hazelwood could read the whole scene as violent and disorganized but not frenetic or overtly destructive for the sake of wreaking havoc. Many individual details—where the body was left, the bloodstains showing where it had been dragged, the indications of sexual activity round the time of death—all indicate to an experienced investigator a style of attack.

Background Knowledge

The third constituent of intuition is background knowledge with which patterns can be compared. Here the major differences between science and craft emerge. For the craftsman like Roy, it is particular, personal experiences on which he draws to interpret, assess and develop the patterns that he perceives. Roy's examination of many violent murders had led him to the view that this particular pattern of un-thought-through violence without the indication of really bizarre, ritualistic aggression was typical of black offenders who perpetrated almost casual crimes in the area where they lived.

As a scientist, I would be unhappy espousing the relationship between particular criminal behavior and ethnicity without knowing the supporting data. If I present the ideas as personal intuition based on years of experience it is unlikely that I will be challenged to present the data. Without it, and a clear articulation of principles, it is difficult to evaluate the suggestions made by the expert, or how to calibrate their applicability in different settings. FBI agents have, for example, often said that serial white rapists typically attack women of the same race as themselves, although black rapists will attack black or white victims. But without knowing how they form that judgment its use can come unstuck. From data we have in Britain we know the proposed relationship between the color of the victim's skin and that of her assailant does not hold. This leads to the question of whether it actually holds as a reliable general principle in the United States?

For expert profilers to be successful in helping police investigations it is not necessarily important that the principles they write about or use in lectures are firmly established. The richness of their experiences enables them to deal with actual cases in terms of what occurs to them at the time rather than drawing on any general, published principles. But this does not mean that their approach is casual or fundamentally outside the realms of science. Quite the reverse, they are creating hypotheses, ways of thinking about violent crime. Their experiences provide a rich soil from which systematic tests of scientific research can grow.

Many officers have told me: "When the villain answers the door I will "know" whether I've got the right man or not." They put the word "know" in inverted commas, or use a range of terms like "I have a hunch", "I've got a gut feeling", or the term used by an older generation, "You feel it in your water".

This approach may also be revealed in direct action. The

impact of trust in personal judgment is well illustrated by one case in which I was tangentially involved. The police were looking for an unknown man who had committed a number of rapes at night, breaking into the victims' houses. All these attacks happened within a few hundred yards of each other, the assailant managing to escape quickly each time the alarm was raised.

A special watch of police officers was assigned to the area at night to try and apprehend the man after his expected next attack. Careful instructions were given to all the police officers involved that, the next time a call came in that the man had just attacked, they were to surround the locality and move in slowly and quietly in a coordinated fashion, making a note of everyone they came across. It was thought that the man must know the area well and would therefore be able to slip away if he suspected the police were moving in to arrest him. Hence the need for a cordon around the area that would systematically cut off all his escape routes.

As expected, a subsequent assault took place and the call came through, but the local policemen did not follow their instructions. Those nearest the scene of the offence thought to themselves, "We're very close to this one, let's go and nab him." They rushed to the scene, alerting the offender before they arrived and opening gaps in the cordon. The assailant escaped without being seen by police. All they found was the weapon he dropped in haste as he fled. Later, door-to-door inquiries led to the identification of a strong suspect that was confirmed by DNA, leading to conviction and a sentence of eight years' imprisonment.

Police officers at the scene felt that by acting on their hunch they would get to the offender before he got away. As in all gambles they experienced a feeling of certainty that can be called intuition. They felt they knew the right thing to do despite the instructions they had been given.

Scientists, though, need intuition too. They can be

capricious lovers of any representation of reality, but they can never be free of intuition. The whole basis of the scientific enterprise is faith that patterns will be found, results will be forthcoming from ideas that have never before been tested. This is especially true in psychology where it is believed that ways of thinking about human behavior and experience will reveal shapes and structures that will increase our understanding.

The FBI Behavioral Science Unit strengthened that faith: there were patterns there; the shadows cast by criminals were not arbitrary; they could be read. Even more important was the fact that Roy Hazelwood and his colleagues had indicated the directions in which to look, the sort of patterns that might be expected.

Steeped as I was in psychological research, I came to realize that I offered perhaps a more thoroughgoing scientific approach to criminal investigation, and a desire to develop a psychological way of thinking about "profiling". We needed to look inside the very nature of human intuition in a systematic way, so that the expertise could become more readily accessible to all police investigators.

Chapter Four
CRIMINAL MAPS

The interpretation of the series of maps locating Duffy's crimes seemed obvious at the time, but one clear set of results does not establish a scientific principle. Since then we have investigated the geographical distribution of many crimes. None shows Duffy's distinct pattern. But his maps draw the classic shape that helps us understand more subtle variants of criminal behavior.

To identify which principles are valid, and under what conditions, we must look at the broad landscape.

What principles are available to predict the relationship between where a criminal lives and where he commits his crimes? About the only rule of thumb that FBI special agents offered was that, in some cases, particularly where the criminal appears not to have planned his attacks carefully, he may well live near the location of the first assault. This is the nub of the plot of The Silence of the Lambs: that the serial murderer can be found close to his first abduction and killing. The FBI bases this idea on experience, rather than published evidence, but the direct logic holds true. We can reasonably assume that in the early stages of a person's criminal career they may be rather impulsive and somewhat amateur in their approach, wandering out at night, for example, without a clear idea of what they are going to do, and seizing what they perceive as an opportunity.

Studying the Shadows *Before* the Crime

The key to solving a series of crimes may be found in

working out what happened before the first crime rather than in establishing where the offender went after the most recent incident. A criminal is more vulnerable in his history than in his future. Before he committed the crime he may not have known himself that he would do it, so he may not have been so careful before as afterwards. Duffy left few traces at the crimes far from his home, but carried out his early crimes close to home—a pattern that contributed to his detection. This may be the basis of a generally applicable principle. If we can find the source of the criminal shadow we may be able to pinpoint the culprit.

We had the chance to seriously test our logic when one of my students, Mary Barker, volunteered to do a follow up study on our ideas. Getting details on a number of serial rapes and murders might have been difficult for a student researcher. But details of burglaries were both numerous and available. The general principles we found in studying serious crimes we felt would also apply to lesser offenses. So Mary contacted a local police force involved in crime prevention for access to records of convicted felons.

Mary studied details on thirty-two burglars who had committed from five to seventy burglaries each before being caught. She noted where they had lived at the time and the addresses of their crimes. She wanted to see what geographical patterns emerged for each criminal.

I asked her to get maps for the area and draw out separate sheets for each offender, marking the location of the burglaries and the burglar's home. At that stage it was not at all clear to me how difficult or time-consuming this task would be. The locations, for example, may have been so scattered that it would not be easy to identify them all or find maps to include them all.

A week or two later Mary turned up for a supervisory meeting looking rather despondent: "I've put them on maps like you said. It took ages, but I don't know what to make of it. I don't think it shows anything." She was holding a neat pile of sheets of A4 size paper (210 by 297 mm) on which were drawn dots to represent crimes and a cross to indicate where the offender had lived. Confidentiality had been ensured, by having a code number at the top of each page and no indication of the page from the local street atlas that had been the original underlying map. Only the locations were marked on the white sheets of paper.

"Are these all to the same scale?" I asked, not quite believing what she had discovered.

"Sure. They're all the usual few inches to the mile. That's what you wanted, isn't it?"

"And you got them all on to the same sheet of A4, the crimes and where he lives?"

"Yes, except for the guy who did seventy burglaries, I needed two sheets for him."

I told her that I thought her results were amazing: all the crimes were surprisingly local to where the offender lived.

At the very least, if we could establish general rules relating a criminal's residence to where he commits his crimes it would give the police more of a system for how and where to look for burglars. More important this A4 effect would make further analysis quite feasible. If we could get each set of crimes on one sheet it made sense to start making measurements to find any trends.

The next step, then, was to see if there was a further structure to the patterns on the sheets of A4. One question was whether the crosses usually sat inside the dots. We also wanted to measure distances.

Based on Mary's study of 32 small-town felons, the maps showed that most burglaries can be put on the same sheet of paper as the burglar's residence. There are many conditions under which this relationship might not hold: where a good transport system exists, for example, or if a burglar was looking for special objects and had his own car.

But the run-of-the-mill burglaries Mary researched hinted at something beyond the one-off vicious rapes and murders of Duffy.

The Circle Hypothesis

On further analysis we came up with what we grandly called the "circle hypothesis". This is the idea of mapping all the crimes thought to have been committed by one, possibly unknown, individual and identifying the two crime locations furthest apart from each other. Using these locations as the diameter, a circle can then be drawn that includes all the offenses. The hypothesis is that the criminal will be found to live inside that circle, possibly close to the middle. Just how reliable is this assumption? In some samples of rapists as many as 80 per cent have actually been found to live inside the circle and more than 60 per cent in a central area half the radius of the large circle.

John Duffy had not been so unusual after all.

To explain the "circle hypothesis", let us start from the privileged position of knowing where a criminal lives, or has some sort of base relevant to his crimes. Imagine that location marked in the center of a blank sheet of paper as, say, a small, shaded red square.

An assumption has already been made with this first stage. We propose that the offenders do, indeed, have a fixed abode. In studying perpetrators of serious crimes, such as rape and murder we found them to have a permanent base of some kind; it might be their own home or a girlfriend's place. Fewer than 10 percent are described at the time of their arrest as having "no fixed abode".

Accepting, then, that the criminal does have a base, let us assume that he is determined to carry out a crime, but also wants to reduce the risk of being caught. To keep it simple, let us say that the possibilities for committing the crime, the opportunities, are evenly distributed around his base. Where is he likely to go to perpetrate his first crime?

Maximizing Opportunity, Reducing Risk

In a sense we are trying to learn to think like a criminal, seeing the location of his crimes in terms of maximizing the opportunity while reducing the risk. If we assume that the criminal has a base, then he is likely to have some degree of familiarity with the area around that base, but he is unlikely to carry out a crime very close to home for fear of recognition, or because of the risk of getting drawn into police inquiries. As one police officer succinctly put it: "Oh, you mean dogs don't crap on their own doorsteps!"

The optimum distance from the base to the first crime could be indicated by drawing a small circle, say, at the top right-hand corner of the sheet of paper. Let us label the small circle "first crime". In this simple world the criminal cannot travel very far without getting into unknown territory. Too far and he may not know his way around and easily escape. There may be other risks that he is unaware of as well. The imaginary distance between the "base" and the "first crime" may be regarded as an optimum one, from the criminal's point of view; just far enough to be safe, but not so far that unfamiliarity provides its own risks.

This is a simple, logical argument for how far he would travel to commit his first crime in an area in which there are ample opportunities. But after his first crime the criminal may become aware of new threats to his safety. If he wants to keep the same optimum level of risk, the area in which he attacked is probably no longer safe. People may be more vigilant there. He may be recognized. It is no longer a sterile, unsullied zone. If he is to keep his optimum distance the criminal has to go elsewhere, at the same distance from his base but in a different direction. Assuming the opportunities are the same in every direction, then, for example, up in the top left-hand corner is as good a place as any. We can, therefore, draw a further circle in the top left corner of our sheet of paper, and mark it "second crime".

What is true of the location for the second crime is true for the third, which he must locate at the same sort of distance, although in a different direction, and also for the fourth. The four notional crimes would be arranged on the blank sheet of paper in the four corners like dots on dice cubes. In an actual example we would not expect the dots to be quite so evenly spaced because the actual layout of streets would produce distortions in the pattern.

Once you have committed four crimes, if you want to continue, keeping the same optimum distance from home, then you must return to the vicinity of earlier crimes. A fifth crime, therefore, could be located between the third and fourth, or anywhere else that the criminal felt least vulnerable. Pythagoras would have understood the power of this geometry immediately. To maintain the optimum balance between familiarity and risk you would have to commit your crimes in a circular region around your home: a band of criminal opportunity.

The problem for police is that they would not have the location of where the offender was living marked on their map. All they would have would be the locations of the crimes reported to them. They would have the equivalent of our sheet of paper with the red square for the base removed, leaving just the locations of the five crimes. In my example these form an irregular circle of points with a large blank white space in the middle. So, as you can see, in this simple example, if the police had a map of offences sitting roughly on a circle like this, it would be reasonable to assume for any investigation the possibility that the offender lived near the center of this circle.

The simple, direct logic, derived from a few principles

leads to the "circle hypothesis". To keep the principles basic in this illustration, we have assumed an even distribution of both familiarity and opportunity for crime. We know that such assumptions are unlikely to hold for many people, but even a model as uncomplicated as this can apply to some criminals who have committed a series of crimes.

By assigning the name of a victim to each of the five crime locations, our hypothetical example can be turned into a real map of the murders attributed to the Whitechapel murderer, "Jack the Ripper", over a hundred years ago. In the top left-hand corner for the second crime we can put the name Chapman, and just below it for the fifth, Kelly. In the top right-hand corner, the location of the "first crime", the name Nichols can be written. The bottom two names at the left and right of center are Eddowes the fourth victim and Stride the third. Diagonally across the sheet of paper we can draw the Whitechapel Road, turning the exercise into a specific set of places in Victorian London.

A rudimentary logic may guide the actions even of crimes as strange as those that held London in thrall in the nineteenth century. Whatever the outcome of historical research, or the new evidence that will undoubtedly emerge in the future to keep alive the search for the identity of "Jack the Ripper", the geographical pattern of his attacks does indicate some important points. One is that his killings were circumscribed within a limited area. This suggests both that he was very familiar with that area and that something kept bringing him back to the same limited locality. The most obvious reason is that he lived within the neighborhood circumscribed by the location of the murders, but if he did we will have to discover why he did not spread his crimes further afield, as did Duffy. To answer such a question a lot would need to be known about available victims on the streets of the East End of London in the 1880's, and about available modes of transport. If it was an area where he lived

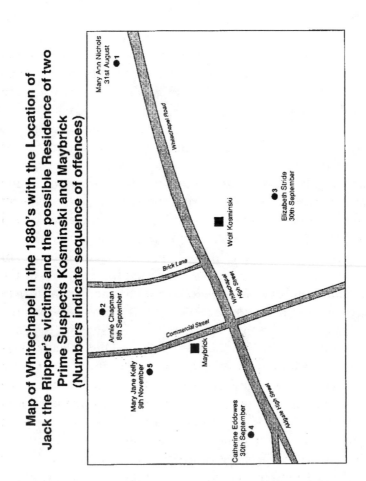

Map of Whitechapel in the 1880's with the Location of Jack the Ripper's victims and the possible Residence of two Prime Suspects Kosminski and Maybrick (Numbers indicate sequence of offences)

it's a reasonable guess that his residence was in the center.

It's interesting to test ideas about the residence of "Jack the Ripper" against the best documented arguments about likely suspects. Historian Paul Begg offers a convincing current-day proposal: that Aaron Kosminski was the "Ripper". Kosminski was an expatriate Polish Jew who worked as a barber in the Whitechapel area. A team of FBI agents and other US experts examined all relevant material and agreed with Paul Begg's view. Some authorities have even suggested that Aaron Kosminski confessed before he died in Colney Hatch asylum in 1919.

Although Paul Begg did not know exactly where Aaron Kosminski had been living at the time of the murders, he did establish where Kosminski's brother was known to reside. This brother had taken responsibility for Kosminski in the mental asylum and probably looked after him before that. It also seems likely, according to Paul Begg, that Kosminski had lived a few doors away from his brother in what was described by the Assistant Chief Constable at the time, Sir Melville Macnaghten, as "the very heart of the district where the murders were committed", at the top end of Mulberry Street. The likely residence of Kosminski could serve as the "base" on our original sheet of paper.

A very different suspect is James Maybrick. Diaries discovered in Liverpool, where Maybrick lived, are claimed to have been written by him as an account of his crimes. The readiness with which many experts accepted these diaries as genuine ignored the important question of why anyone should keep such a potentially incriminating diary, especially someone who had taken care to avoid capture. Maybrick's residence in Liverpool would also challenge the circle hypothesis.

The debate over Kosminski and Maybrick is of more than historic significance. It illustrates a distinction between a person who used a permanent base as a starting point for his crimes, as Kosminski might have done, and the "commuting" proposed by the writer of Maybrick's diaries. These are two very different theories of how the location of a crime relates to the residence of the offender. In our studies of the relationships between the crime location and the offender's residence, commuters have been very rare. Thus more examples are needed to determine if the offender was commuting into an area. However, that Jack the Ripper was a local resident of the Whitechapel area remains a strong hypothesis in the light of the clear sequence and locations of his crimes.

A further point about both Kosminski and Maybrick is both exhibited mental illness. Kosminski ended his days in a lunatic asylum, believing that his movements were controlled by "an instinct that informs his mind". Maybrick is reputed to have indulged in a variety of drugs and was violently jealous of his wife (who was convicted of his murder). Despite the extremes of mental instability typical of both these men, it seems quite feasible that during the commission of the murders the attempt to avoid capture had an identifiable logic. Thus, although there may be many strange qualities to violent acts some aspects reveal overtly logical processes.

These actions probably are not conscious, thus the criminal could not easily hide them. More likely, these patterns are a product of thought habits and behavior rather than conscious choices.

Habits Relate to Spaces

Many habits relate to how we use spaces; though most are not violent. But violent actions have common roots with many other aspects of daily behavior. Actions are unknowingly tied to spatial patterns, a fact that can be seen in public meetings. For example, the next time you attend any sort of talk, make a note of where the people who ask the questions are sitting. People who have systematically studied this will predict that question-askers tend to sit towards the front and towards the middle of the audience. In my own experience, questions are most likely to come from people sitting in the first few rows towards the side of the room that contains the main entrance.

Asking a question involves more than a wish for an answer.

Opportunity

Two processes are at play. One is opportunity, or technical possibility. In some positions it is easier to catch the lecturer's eye, or to judge when an interjection is feasible without being impolite. The second is individual predetermination. A person keenly interested in a topic, or in taking part in discussions, will tend to place themselves where it is easier to catch the lecturer's eye. The person may not even be aware of these actions and what they mean. Typically it is part of implicit habits that we take for granted and notice only when someone mentions them.

Availability

Similarly, a serial killer or rapist will put himself in locations where victims are available and undetected crime is possible, even though he may not realize that that is what he is doing. Like the member of the audience who gets a good seat without intending, necessarily, to ask a question, so the rapist will go to an area where he knows there are vulnerable young women without specifically planning to attack one. But if the opportunity arises to ask a question, or to carry out a crime, the person is well placed to do so.

This may seem a curiously unemotional way of mapping

the logic of a violent criminal. It certainly does not fit the popular notion often portrayed in newspapers, and apparently accepted by some judges, of rapists as sex-crazed beasts who cannot resist the temptation thrust in front of them. Most people can understand a bank robber planning his raid carefully to avoid risk, but surely a sexual assault or a murder is a much more impulsive act? A loss of control?

Most bank robbers plan to avoid risk, as do hired assassins. They may travel a great distance to commit their crimes. Evidence shows that the more emotional the crime, the closer to home it will occur. What the police call "a domestic", the assault of a husband on his wife, or the not uncommon assault of a wife on her husband, typically takes place in their home. They don't usually travel a great distance to thump each other.

Some studies have shown that rapes typically occur nearer to a person's base than many burglaries, especially burglaries requiring real skill, such as theft of antiques, where the burglar must know what he is looking for. So, optimizing one's opportunity may be directly related to the distance over which the search for a target takes place.

The indications are many rapists wander around exploring areas where they hope to see women of interest to them. They put themselves in situations that have particular possibilities, as does the person selecting a seat in a lecture theatre.

The criminal often will go to remarkable length to create opportunities. One man, who was eventually convicted of murdering his wife before she could divorce him; a man with a history of sexual assaults, was found to have kept the most remarkably detailed little red notebook. In it he had recorded, with obsessive precision, a list of women he had seen, where he had seen them and the time to the nearest minute. The notebook records their estimated age, hair color and style, what they were wearing, their car if they were driving, including its registration number.

This seemingly inoffensive little red book, showed that this criminal shadowed many women, perhaps not even knowing himself that he was identifying potential victims. His notes, though, show the extent to which he had systematized his obsession: "29.5.85, blo 30" (presumably, a blonde, thirty years old). A later entry is "Pink/pony. 6.15 pm got on 718 at Bloomsbury St, 6.32 pm got off 718 at Arundel Road." The notebook also contains a strange list with the date of sightings and descriptions of the women summarized with a set of numbers on each line, mainly 8s and 9s. I suppose these are his personal ratings of desirability.

His horrific mind-games gleam through this neat little red book. Here was a man so out of touch with his own emotions that he was compelled to keep a log of potential targets, women he passed in the street, people he had no contact with yet recorded day after day as part of the creation of his private world. The fantasy of having sex with any attractive woman who passes by is not of itself unusual. This type of mental undressing—within the bounds of literary playfulness—generally is accepted as a form of male delusion. What makes the example of the little red book so appalling is the knowledge that it goes beyond the bounds of playfulness and was undoubtedly linked to murder. Rather than revealing what some would call an understandable interest in women, it showed a distorted, obsessive involvement in women as objects. With each note he took he removed himself further from real experience of women as people, feeding the vicious cycle.

Here, impulse and obsession merged with the kind of criminal planning shown in our geographical "circle hypothesis". The circle is just a way of representing the domain, the geographical repertoire over which the criminal operates. Where he lives is often part of that repertoire because it helps to define it.

This cognitive, rational model of the criminal presents him as little different from other men.

The significant difference in his fantasy was in the amount and intensity. Doubtless its intensity increased as it fed on itself. In his day-to-day dealings with other people he may have been regarded as abnormal, although the fact that he was married may have helped him pass unnoticed. Possibly his obsession slowly changed within him. His notebook also shows a frantic preoccupation with the stages of his divorce, the dates and procedures. But in regard to what might be called his geographical activity, he could only be in one place at one time and the places and times were shaped by the normal limits on human activities.

Criminals exist in normal society, limited like everyone else by available jobs, working hours, bus routes or the costs of running a car. The degree of the limitation depends where they are in their criminal development. A young lad who steals from the electricity meter may well do it next door, but the same man ten years later may have graduated to stealing antiques and may travel twenty miles to find good pickings. The early attacks by Duffy and his accomplice were carried out close to home, and the accomplice appeared to be a passive observer. Duffy's later murders that took place many miles away were carefully planned.

This view of a rapist's development suggests that rapists, like most criminals, go through stages of advancement similar to a conventional career. A number of researchers have pointed out the broad similarity that many rapists have to criminals in general. Most convicted rapists have previous convictions for other offences, usually not sex-related crimes. The only general differences between rapists and other criminals is that sexual assault does tend to be committed by older criminals. Where the average age for all crimes is in the mid-teens, sex offenders tend to be in their early twenties.

Diana Scully, an American sociologist, who studies incarcerated sex offenders believes that sexual assault is just an extreme example of men's general reactions to women. But we must remember, criminals are not average individuals; they are violent, often long-standing criminals, still a minority of citizens. There are differences between criminals and the population at large, whether it is the cause or the consequence of their criminality.

While criminals are typically different from the noncriminal population in many ways, their actions often are shaped by the same forces that shape everyone's lives. In terms of their activities, their carrying out of explicit criminal actions, they can be understood as part of the criminal fraternity. But when we consider their actions in time and space, then, unless they are very bizarre indeed, they must be influenced by the same processes and limitations as any other citizen.

Two interrelated psychological processes underlie the "circle" principle. One is the fact well known to criminologists, but sometimes ignored by the police, that many criminals commit their crimes near to where they live. As long ago as the 1930s, sociologists in Chicago pointed out that there were concentrations where most criminals lived and where most crimes occurred.

The second principle comes from studies of how people make sense of and learn to cope with their surroundings, the area of study that has come to be known as environmental psychology.

To illustrate the relevance of environmental psychology, when we were making a television film about my work with the police (called "Helping Police with Their Inquiries", shown in 1991), I asked one of my colleagues, Sean, an easy-going, affable chap, to draw a map of London under the all-remembering gaze of the film camera. He did it without any rehearsal, and I was surprised by how well his drawing showed my point. He started drawing a sketch map, putting a few names to the locations so that it was clearly a map of the area around Covent Garden. I was curious that he had chosen to draw that particular area and asked him why. His imme-diate answer was that he had lived around there and so he always thinks of London with that area at the center. Envi-ronmental psychologists have carried out many studies of this process of sketch mapping and how it reveals the internal representations, or "mental maps", that people have of an area, trying to find out what leads to accurate and to inaccurate mental maps. Their conclusion is as significant as it is obvious: familiarity with an area is the biggest influence.

So, although we don't plan our activities to sit inside a circle, we do operate over an area of familiarity. It is probably quite a complicated patchy shape, this area. The circle is just the simplest shape to take as a starting point.

A personal experience illustrates how surprising the obvious can be. I once startled some overseas visitors who had heard something of my work with the police. They turned up early one summer's evening, when I was not expected back until much later, so my wife took them and the dog to a pleasant country pub a couple of miles away. When, a little later, I turned up at the pub, my friends were convinced it was a piece of subtle detective work, knowing that no message had been left at home. What they had not taken into account was that I knew that there were only one or two pubs that my wife would walk to with the dog.

We are all constrained in the choices of locations we go to by where we know. This may be true of where we look for a place to live, where we go shopping, for entertainment, or to commit a crime. We may read about places or talk to friends, so our familiarity can, in effect, be extended indirectly. We may work out what must exist between two places we know and so extend our knowledge in that way. But the primary knowledge, like that revealed in Sean's sketch map, is determined by where we spend most of our time, typically where we live and work. The criminal who perpetrates a set of crimes in a particular area is telling us something about his familiarity with that area. This familiarity may be entirely a product of his criminal activities, but often it will be influenced by the same limitations that influence us all, where he has his base. Shadows do not float free of their origins.

What of the criminal who deliberately murders strangers at different points in time, the serial murderer? The media image of the travelling loner moving across the freeways of America does not accord with the more structured world I have described. But like many media images it is surreal. In the most thorough examination of serial murderers published so far, Eric Hickey, an American criminologist, studied over 200 such men and women convicted since the end of the eighteenth century. He looked especially closely at sixty-three serial murderers who had been active since 1975. Only about a quarter of these could be classed as travellers. Two-thirds operated in the area close to where they lived. So even for these most threatening and apparently abnormal criminals, some of the general geographical constraints that we have seen in other people may well be relevant.

The geographical mind world that a criminal uses is shaped by subtle processes that might not be immediately available to detectives or obvious even to people who know the offender.

If you ask a Londoner the direct, crow-flight distance from Piccadilly Circus to the Elephant and Castle and then compare how accurate his response is with an estimate of the distance from Soho to Buckingham Palace, you will find that, typically, the first distance, which is across the river Thames in a broadly southerly direction, is overestimated much more than the second distance which is roughly east—west, not crossing the Thames. The river acts as a mental barrier that may be more powerful than its impact as a physical barrier. Even London taxi drivers with, all their detailed knowledge of London's geography are not much better at estimating crow-flight distances than other Londoners. The river, in particular, seems to fill mental space in people's minds, expanding the map that people draw for themselves. Parks and major roads are other typical examples of buffers that lead to distortions in the way people represent the world to themselves.

These distortions are not just mental buffers, They are reflected in how we act. Many London police officers will tell you that villains who live north of the river rarely carry out crimes south of it. "Living on the wrong side of the railway tracks" is a cliché that encapsulates the association between locations and the meaning they have, a meaning usually ungrounded in any direct experience. North Londoners who rarely travel into the unknown territory of South London think of it as distant and unfathomable. Large cities are especially prone to the creation of such distorted images because travel around them can be surprisingly limited as well. Many youngsters in North London have never seen the Thames. I once met an elderly lady in Central Park, New York, who worried because her grandson had just gone off to a summer camp less than a couple of hours drive away on the Atlantic coast. She had never seen "the Ocean" herself and it was linked in her mind to such overwhelming images of huge seas and breaking waves that she felt she had to ask an expert (who could be more expert than an Englishman who must have crossed that ocean?) whether it was really safe for her grandson to be near something as awesome as the Atlantic ocean.

A carousel of influences holds these tendencies together. Where we go depends upon what we know to be available. What we know depends on where we go. Over time in an area we slowly evolve our understanding of what is where from the contacts we have. Someone who moves to London may know the area around tone tube station where they work and around another tube station where a friend lives. One day, accidentally taking a wrong turn, they may discover that the two locations are much nearer than they had realized because, being on different tube lines, their closeness had never been appreciated.

Ask someone who regularly drives through Birmingham, but has never shopped there, how to walk from the station to the Bull Ring roundabout. He will probably have great difficulty telling you. The Birmingham of the regular driver and of the walker are virtually two different cities in the minds of residents. Two quite different sets of navigational skills are necessary to find your way about each of these cities. So, if I asked you the walking route or the driving route and checked the accuracy of your response it would not be difficult to say, from this information alone, whether you were a walker or a driver. Perhaps a not very impressive party trick. But what of its value to a police investigation?

It is possible to walk around the Whitechapel sites related to the "Jack the Ripper" murders in an afternoon (about a quarter of a million tourists do each year). There will never be such tours of Peter Sutcliffe's "Yorkshire Ripper" murders or the scenes associated with the "Railway Rapist" /murderer John Duffy because the scenes are too far apart. Many of Sutcliffe's crimes are over twenty miles from each other and some of Duffy's have over forty miles between them.

The Role of Distance

The very distances over which crimes are committed tell us something about the individual who perpetrated them. In Victorian Whitechapel it is not surprising that "Jack the Ripper" moved around on foot, but if he left the area in a horse-drawn cab why was the farthest distance between any two attacks still within an easy walk? Whitechapel was not the only area of London with narrow streets and many potential victims. We can prudently assume that the scenes of his crimes were within walking distance of each other from where he lived.

Car tire markings were found at some of Peter Sutcliffe's murder scenes. The distance between his killings therefore matches the assumption that these tire markings were produced by a car he drove. But the possession of a car could have suggested to police that the person they sought had some sort of regular income. If you accept that he has a car then you have to ask why all his attacks were in a circumscribed area of Yorkshire. The likely, and correct, answer is that he was familiar with the area and lived within and traveled around it.

Duffy journeyed even further, but the location of some of his rapes and their closeness to railway stations enabled British journalists, without detailed knowledge of the crimes to spot the link to the railway line and dub him the "Railway Rapist". The increasing distances he traveled from a central point certainly fit with a person going to a railway station and then choosing to go off in any number of directions, but this use of the railway system also suggests rather more knowledgeable experience than that of the average traveler. Knowing the main routes north, south, east and west would be unusual for most local railway users. A person employed as a carpenter by British Rail, as Duffy was, would have more specialized knowledge.

**Map of the Locations of Sutcliffe's Murders and his Residence
(Numbers indicate sequence of offences)
(Derived from Kind, S.S. 1987)**

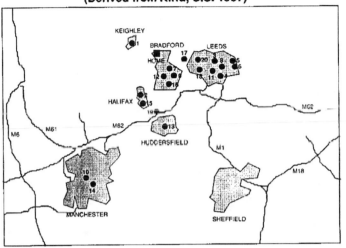

More Successful Profiling Examples

The power of this thinking shows in a couple of additional cases where the principles have been applied with some success. One was the investigation of a series of vicious attacks, robberies and rapes carried out near the southern area of the M15 ring-road that circles London. Apparently under the influence of drugs, a gang set off in a stolen car, ransacking houses. Eventually, as many as ninety-two assaults on houses in the stock-broker belt may have been committed by a gang of at least three men, all in their early twenties. Accomplices are also known to have been involved. During the course of these attacks one man was kicked to death, another stabbed and a woman raped.

The chief investigating officer was Chief Superintendent Vince McFadden, the man who called me to help with the Duffy inquiry. He told me that when he started to lead the investigation he determined to use the "profiling" approach. At an early meeting reviewing the available material, he examined the location of everything associated with the incidents. This included where cars used in robberies had been stolen, where they had been left later and all minor offenses suspected of being linked to the major crimes. This meant that when the $35,000 reward led to a number of tip-offs, it was feasible to identify quickly which potential suspects most closely fitted the geographical and behavioral profile that Vince McFadden had built. Chief Superintendent McFadden told me that the account they developed was so clear they knew when they arrested the first group of suspects that their "leader" was not among them and further investigation was necessary to catch him.

Reading the Trivia

If it is true that all actions are shaped by the same environmental psychology processes, and that therefore criminal and domestic actions overlap, it will be true for trivial aspects of behavior as well as for major deeds. A bank robbery may be planned to take the criminal beyond his normal area of activity, but where he steals a car in order to carry out the robbery may be much closer to home. The "trivia" may therefore turn out to be more indicative to an investigation than the scene of the crime itself. Unfortunately, police records may not store minor offenses so that they are accessible to a major investigation. In the case of the M15 gang, such details helped the police to locate the gang quickly.

The second case was also a series of assaults, this time sexual assaults on elderly victims in an area of the southern Home Counties. The distances between these assaults suggested that the offender had used transport. No obvious rail links existed and the times of the attacks, anyway, ruled out trains. Anyone living in this area of rural Britain will also tell you that buses are not reliable for shopping trips, let alone planned late-night sexual assaults. So, we concluded he had a car. This opened other possibilities. The costs of running a car suggested that he had some sort of job, but the times of day and variety of locations did not indicate a very skilled, reliable form of employment. Any job was therefore not likely to be well paid. So we considered it unlikely that he had a very new car. The required government test on the road worthiness of old cars puts three years as the difference between an "old" and a "new" car, so we could take as a starting point that his car would be at least three years old and probably older. When a suspect who was forensically linked to the offenses was found to have a five-year-old car, no one was more impressed by the power of scientific logic than Rupert Heritage and I.

Where a criminal operates is one of the most distinctive features of the shadow that he casts. It gives a hook of enormous value for any police investigation. It can direct house-to-house inquiries, narrow down suspect lists drawn from criminal records, or provide guidelines for surveillance. This is no secret. The traveling criminal potentially is far more difficult to locate; on the other hand, he can leave a trail that assists his identification, but this requires a readable trail. Through small British towns this might be possible, but across the vast expanses of America it is a different matter. The distances traveled in the United States by some criminals who commit a series of crimes are so large that the FBI reports on profiling rarely consider location material in detail. (They have, however, carried out studies of serial arsonists which show that very simple calculations of the geographical center of a series can, on occasion, indicate the arsonist's place of residence.)

A Geographical Center of Gravity

This idea of a geographical "center of gravity" was also used to good effect in the "Yorkshire Ripper" investigation. Stuart Kind, Director of the Home Office Central Research Establishment, joined an advisory team set up in November 1980 in response to a request by the Home Secretary to assist the Chief Constable of the West Yorkshire Metropolitan Police in finding the "Ripper". It says something of the British valuation of experience over direct, systematic expertise that Dr Kind was the only scientist on this advisory team and that the other four members were senior police officers. Why have four officers? Would four consultant brain surgeons be brought into an especially important piece of surgery? I think not. If a profession has clearly established principles, then any one expert ought to come to the same conclusion as the others.

The value of an alternative perspective can be illustrated, though, because of the involvement of Stuart Kind. Dr. Kind neatly summarizes the idea of a "center of gravity" by referring to a map on which the seventeen "Yorkshire Ripper" crimes had been marked.

> If we mark each of these positions with a map pin and tie a piece of thread to it we are then in a position to consider the following question: "At which single location on the map could be placed an eighteenth pin, such that if we stretched the seventeen threads and tied each loose end to the eighteenth pin, the minimum total amount of thread would be used?"
> Stuart Kind, *The Scientific Investigation of Crime*,
> 1987, p.377

A computer analysis returned the answer: "Near Bradford". This solution was valuable because it refuted the tape-recordings allegedly sent by the killer and found by phonetic experts to indicate a Geordie, not a Yorkshire, accent. Stuart Kind's other considerations offered a similar systematic quality, showing the "Ripper's" base near Bradford. These included a careful examination of the sequence of offenses, leading Kind to conclude that the criminal was at pains to avoid returning to the towns of recent, earlier crimes.

The region Peter Sutcliffe roamed was very unlike the Whitechapel of the original "Ripper". Small towns are dispersed across the countryside between large but not enormous cities. The fact that some of Sutcliffe's victims had the same trade (prostitution) as those of his London counterpart shows both the resilience of that trade and its enormous physical risks. The distances Sutcliffe traveled also illustrate what a number of criminologists have emphasized: that the distribution of possible targets for crime will influence how far criminals travel. Our own studies with burglars graphically confirm the point. Burglars operating in the semi-urban county of Surrey on average travel over seven miles; burglars in the small, readily demarcated town of Cambridge travel on average less than two miles.

Understanding the Criminal's Mental Maps

The mental map a criminal draws is not a fantasy. It is a distillation of his own particular transactions with his surroundings. If we can find out how to interpret the wake left behind by a criminal when he plunges through a community, we can understand those special qualities of his transactions that will lead us to him. The directions and distances he travels are one important indicator of his personal silhouette. This silhouette may change from one set of opportunities to another.

A man was recently arrested in America for attacking a woman in the block of flats where he stayed. During investigations it became apparent that he had sexually assaulted women in South Wales, where he lived. He was on the other side of the Atlantic to visit a friend. In South Wales he had assaulted women in an area close to where his friend lived, often on the way home from visiting him. He would knock on doors of houses where he knew single women lived. Gaining entry by asking directions or for a glass of water, he would then attack them.

Blocks of flats have often been seen as streets in the sky. Each block acts as its' own neighborhood where people are strangers to each other, habitually seen without being noticed. In the large cities of the New World they are direct translations of the urban streets of Britain. The symmetry of the assailant's behavior seems almost inevitable. A comfortable distance from his friend's house he has noticed a potential victim. Eventually he knocks on her door. In Britain this is down the street; across the Atlantic it is a few floors away. In a tower block, though, the population is more clearly defined, so the police could launch a search more speedily and identify their suspect more readily than in Britain. By not taking account of this aspect of the translation of his actions, he was caught.

A man who sets out on a train to look for locations in which to commit a sexual assault, and possibly a murder, is telling us something about himself that is different from a man who wanders down the street to knock on a door behind which he knows there is a lone woman. Both of these men are clearly different from Sutcliffe who set off in his car looking for women on their own walking the streets.

They are all acting within the confines of their own knowledge and awareness. Even when they break out far beyond the bounds of morality they are constrained by their own experience and habits. Like a beggar who makes the same protestations to every passer-by and who always approaches people in the same area, or for that matter like a lecturer who uses the same joke to make his point every time he gives a particular lecture, these habits and constraints grow out of the full panoply of the person's dealings. Through their actions criminals reveal more than just what they are familiar with; they tell us about other aspects of their lives.

We Must Learn to listen.

The consistencies between various studies imply that the offender's venue for a particular crime includes conscious decisions.

Police officers with whom we discussed our findings, initially were surprised, then admitted they had always been vaguely aware of such consistencies. Seeing this as a general principle went further than they were willing to go only on the basis of their own direct experience.

When I first realized the significance of these consistencies, I thought the explanation could be quite simple. "How about this possibility?" I said to any colleague who would listen. "Guys who start off as house-breakers, get used to finding their way around houses. They feel comfortable in that sort of setting. Then if they graduate to rape they carry on with the same habit, attacking indoors. But your street muggers are the outdoor types. Their violence continues in the sorts of venues it started in."

We tested these possibilities against actual examples. Like most elegant ideas in psychology the truth is more subtle and complex.

The premise that our outdoor attackers had no history of burglary, or that our indoor attackers had never committed crimes outdoors did not hold true. We are still trying to tease out exactly what the differences are, but there does appear to be a tendency for the insiders to be the more devout criminals with a longer history and more experience of

crimes like theft and burglary. The outsiders are more likely
to have a history of sexual deviance and relatively little
previous criminal background.

With hindsight this makes sense. Going into a stranger's
house, for whatever reason, is a determined criminal act. A
person would need some experience of what it feels like to
creep through another person's rooms. He would also have
to be prepared to deal with any occupant he came across,
unless he was very careful to make sure the property was
unoccupied. Many convicted burglars when interviewed
about their choice of targets have said that their main
concern was to make sure that there was no one in the house
at the time.

The burglar who cautiously avoids contact with an
occupant is rather different from one who climbs into a
house and sexually assaults the person found there. Such an
assault can never be totally impulsive. Nor can anyone
caught by an occupant convincingly argue that they had no
intention of committing a criminal act. Jumping on someone
in a public place has a different psychological feel. The
perpetrator could see the act as impulsive and opportunistic.
The risks of being caught are higher, and the act demands
less criminal skill or preparation.

The person who asks for a glass of water and, once inside
the house attacks, differs from rapists such as Tony
McClean, who terrorized Notting Hill over a number of
years. He waited indoors for the victim to return home.
Gaining entry by subterfuge implies both a readiness to talk
to the victim and a lack of experience in entering a house by
illegal means. It seems unlikely that such a man would be a
burglar-turned-rapist. Detectives realized that by contrast
McClean showed all the hallmarks of the experienced
burglar he proved to be.

Crime location, distance from home, and mode of transport to the crime scene, are all overt, direct characteristics of

a crime. They can be derived, with some effort, from the available police records. These conspicuous aspects of what offenders do show they differ from each other in important ways. Yet, they are only one aspect of the behavioral styles that distinguish criminals from each other.

How much further can we shine a light down this dark tunnel to help us identify the shadows on the wall?

Chapter Five
CONSISTENT CLUES

Every crime contains a particular meaning to the offender, no matter how twisted it may seem. If we can decipher the significance of a violent act for the criminal, then we can learn to interpret what shapes his actions. We now know there are many similarities in the overt behavior of criminals, elements that can provide us with consistent clues to their identity and whereabouts. The challenge is to know which clues to follow.

We had the opportunity to further search for consistent clues, when UK police officers at Birmingham approached us in the late spring of 1988. They needed our help in investigating a series of sexual assaults by an athletic young man on elderly women living in tower blocks in a limited area of Birmingham.

My associate, Rupert Heritage, and I were gathering more research that would tie offender characteristics to the style of their offenses, and help answer increasing questions from police forces in intractable cases.

Seven attacks had taken place on elderly female victims in tower blocks in the Edgbaston and Druids Heath areas of Birmingham between January 1986 and March 1988. As the police report put it: "Three of the incidents involved genital intercourse or attempts threat concomitant with the definition of Rape in legal terms. The others are serious sexual assaults in which activity is confined to non genital penetration which may have been due to victim resistance, outside interference or cessation of the attack."

Women in their seventies and eighties, often infirm, were

followed into lifts by a stocky young man who overpowered them and took them to the top floor of the tower block, sometimes carrying them up the last two flights of stairs to the landing near the roof. There he raped them and escaped.

In one attack he walked into the flat of a frail, demented lady and sexually assaulted her. The victim was so disturbed that only the medical reports and statements from friends about her distress brought the offense into the inquiry. The victim was unable to give any account of what had happened. Some victims never really recovered emotionally, drifting into depression and senility soon after. One simply gave up the desire to live, and died.

Police determined that one person was responsible for all these crimes. The formal police report stated: "There are strong Modus Operandi links within this series. The consistent use of High Rise buildings, Lifts within, and the removal of the elderly white victim to the upper stairways, all the actions of a black male, have a strength in themselves which would support the treatment of the series as a whole."

Unlike Duffy, whose spreading crimes initially made linking difficult, this offender operated in a small area, in similar settings, and acted in a consistent way.

The local newspaper had quickly elicited a response from a professor of psychology at York University, headlining the story: "Sex Monster Could Kill in the Next Attack." The paper cited Professor Benables (his name is actually Venables, presumably the interview was done over the telephone) as saying: "This man is clearly a psychopath and sensation seeker, the more danger he puts himself into, the more fun he gets." In one assault he had told his victim that his name was Leroy. Professor Benables is quoted as saying: "He may have given this information to increase the risk of getting caught." Without the benefit of access to the full police dossier, apparently, Professor Benables saw this psychopath as getting thrills from sexually assaulting defenseless old women. He also is said to have proposed that the offender "may have sublimated anger against his mother, and is now punishing older women whom he sees as authority figures".

But other, equally feasible hypotheses were possible. The offender may have given a false name to mislead investigators. He may have found older women sexually attractive.

The tower block attacks also had a curious style. The offender was strong and determined, but never overtly vicious. In some cases the victims complained about the cold concrete floor on which he forced them to lie naked. He showed an unexpected, minor consideration for them by putting some of their clothing underneath them. He later remembered, when questioned by the police: "There's been one or two like that, says it's cold. Well I don't want them to be cold do I?"

Police officers expressed special difficulties in understanding these assaults. As one policeman put it, not realizing how much he was assuming about men's attitudes to women: "We could understand it if he were raping young attractive women, but frail old women, I can't see what he gets out of that." The comment reinforced the stereotype of human sexual aggression as having a "normal" form— involving only attractive women, and all else being distorted and bizarre. The conventional view fitted the policeman's own experiences and was therefore understandable, the bizarre was beyond his comprehension.

Separating unfamiliar sexual behavior implicitly leads to the search for some kind of a monster, a person who would be noticeably different from other people and recognized as such by those who knew him. The police felt they needed our help to understand this "monster" who was so far beyond their own comprehension. Precisely because his actions were so bizarre they presented a challenge to our emerging theory of rational, risk-reducing criminals who could be detected by simple logic. Could we wait for a thorough study of sexual attacks on the elderly and do nothing to help reduce the risk that he would kill his next victim before the police got to him? He certainly would not stop until he was caught.

The traumatic nature of the assaults and victims' confusion made the investigation harder. It was difficult to make sense of some accounts. Police thought one victim might have lied about a second assault by the same man. She might have invented the story to try and speed up her move to other housing. Yet the account this woman gave the second time included being forced to fellate the assailant, an act that had not occurred the first time. Other victims had reported similar actions to police.

But the very peculiarities of the case, indeed, also held the distinguishing characteristics that might lead us to the offender.

Reading the Criminal's Constraints

He had a limited repertoire of locations, victims and actions. This man operated in a constrained world. What were the implications of those constraints?

The concentration of the attacks in tower blocks on the edge of Birmingham's city center revealed something curious about the attacker. His familiarity with tower blocks had been recognized by investigators long before they approached me, but why these particular tower blocks? Only when I was involved in making a television documentary about these crimes did I understand how much these particular tower blocks captured the communal anonymity of Britain's second largest city.

The director of the film, Patrick Fleming, had wanted some dramatic shots to capture the abstract notion of the criminal's "mental map" He wanted to show, with visual immediacy, that everyone carries an internal template around

with them for choosing what they will do where. Patrick
came up with the idea of putting me into a small, four-seater
helicopter to fly over the tower blocks where the assaults had
been committed. My task was to be filmed pointing at the
city below, explaining how this bird's-eye view revealed the
likely inner workings of the rapist's personal geography.

From a helicopter Birmingham emerges against the
horizon like something left from a failed attempt to ape
Manhattan on the Warwickshire plane. At 15,000 feet, a
couple of miles away, the tower blocks scattered around the
outskirts of the city center look like the remnants of
children's blocks used to build the office towers that are
crammed together in the middle. They give the impression of
a determined youngster who had started on an ambitious
project systematically enough but eventually lost interest,
shoving the pieces down wherever they would fit. This
creates an incomprehensible bundle of offices and shops that
fade off into the miles of semi-detached suburban residences,
punctuated with asides that are the high-rise towers of
welfare housing.

Air traffic regulations kept us above 1,000 feet, which is
the height from which you can recognize that each back yard
in a housing estate of semi-detached houses is unique, but it
is still not close enough to distinguish what it is that makes
each yard different. Flying at that level I could see quite
clearly the desire for each household to express their uniqueness, but it is equally clear that they can never succeed.

The helicopter pilot navigated closer to the tower blocks.
It was then that I saw how distinctly those clumps of tower
blocks stood between the offices of the city center and the
residential sprawl beyond. In aerial photos I had seen earlier,
the separateness of these particular blocks had been apparent.
But from the air it seemed more plausible that locations for
the majority of attacks had been selected because of their
distinct separateness. Major dual carriageways surrounded

the tower blocks acting as mental buffers. They made the attacker feel that the blocks of flats were a secluded island.

He had moved confidently about this island. There had been no sign of a vehicle; he had even mentioned the use of a bus to one victim. It was possible that he lived in among these buildings, but unlikely. He was not recognized by anyone and had made little attempt to wear any disguise. He was confident and familiar with the scenes of his crimes, but was he alien to them? This was certainly a challenge to the elegant logic of the "circle hypothesis". What of the offender choosing locations to reduce the risk of being known? Was that still a viable possibility in this setting?

The anonymous concrete towers are close enough to the city center to attract many friends and relations, salesmen, casual visitors on their way in or out, but large and anonymous enough for a lone black man to go unnoticed by the victims until he assaulted them. The victims' accepted an unknown man asking for help to gain entry. The distinctness of the island in which the blocks of flats sat would not be so apparent to the casual visitor, only to someone who had day-to-day experience of tower blocks close to the city, probably close to these. He might take for granted the ease with which strangers can come and go in such places. But, would he increase his risk by attacking near his residence?

When police officers brought us maps of the area of the assaults, we asked them to describe the characteristics of the inhabitants of the different areas around the offenses. They produced an account that indicated distinct regions: areas frequented by prostitutes, predominantly black regions with an ethnic mixture. Perhaps the offender was as aware of these different areas, just as were police officers. Perhaps he and they shared a sort of communal mental map. If that were the case, he might think that he reduced risk to himself not by moving a great distance but by moving from one territory to another. In the helicopter I could see how the maps made sense. Against the backdrop of the center city and its complex network of roads, the only distinguishable pattern is made by the busy arteries streaming out from the center, creating physically close, but distinct zones. By crossing a road one could walk into an almost alien location, but still be close to home. I concluded that he lived nearby, and probably in a similar sort of tower block.

Map of Edgbaston with Location of Babb's Rapes and Residence (Numbers indicate sequence of offences)

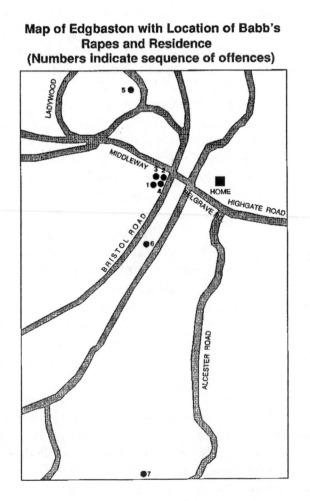

These considerations led Rupert to study the aerial photographs supplied by Birmingham police. One tower block seemed to fit all our discussions. "He must live there," Rupert said, mirroring my earlier confidence in the location of Duffy's home base. But Rupert experienced a conflict I had never had. The detective in him wanted to go to Birmingham and search for the rapist where he lived. Now that he was a university researcher, that wasn't an option. He had to wait for more detailed considerations and an extended police investigation before we found how accurate his suggestion had been.

Discovering the Rapist's Territory

First, we had to know more about how people in the tower blocks lived. The possibility of a man hanging around blocks of flats on many occasions, unnoticed yet living a short distance away, can only be garnered at grass-roots level.

The idea of a "territory" as a distinct, protected area of the city, like an area defended by an animal, was given credence by the films made in the 1950s and '60s about the emerging "concrete jungle". *West Side Story* glamorized the idea with the Sharks and Jets patrolling their protected areas of New York. These strange parallels with animal behavior were convincing. Despite all the evidence showing that animals do not behave in the way humans are said to, high-rise housing in Britain has created a remarkably anti-human environment.

Wandering around the edge of Birmingham city center it is easy to tell that the great boom in building came in the late1960's and early '70s. The architecture is uncompromising. People have to be housed, so what is the simplest way to do it? Not for these designers the flippancies of the 1980s, no post-modern frills. But these tower blocks and slabs were not thrown up in the flush of enthusiasm that destroyed parts of major cities such as Liverpool and Glasgow. These gesture towards play spaces on their roofs and locking systems on entrance doors. The towers built by the corporation for its tenants do not have the maintenance funds to keep the roofs clean or to fix doors that are regularly vandalized. Where a private block of apartments would have a welcoming entrance hall, the high-rise council flats have dark alleys, approached through broken doors, smelling of urine.

Hoping the lift is still working, residents rush through these uninviting entrances, heads averted, to the comfort and comparative safety of their flats. There are no garden fences over which neighbors get to know each other or corner cafés where friendships develop over a slow cup of coffee. This is a planned world where people are placed on the basis of the number of points they have on a form. They will be shuffled into a tower block without fear or favor, concern for color or creed, creating the type of social potpourri that private, unplanned housing never produces. Local authority tenants do slowly manage to swap and change so that clusters of similar people begin to drift together, a black area emerges or one with many old folk.

I remember one local housing authority officer who telephoned me to ask if by painting the walls in his office a different color he could reduce the violence and complaints he received. He thought the problem was external to the system in which he was part. When an old lady complains of being attacked and raped for the second time, police and housing officers think it may be just another ploy to get reallocated. The bureaucrats know that if residents do not have the financial resources then other leverage will be used. A general mood and quality of life unfolds around these insensitive controls on people's lives: violence in the office for allocating accommodation; residents inventing crimes to move on; a network of people treating each other as instruments for personal benefit. That was the world in which the rapist seemed to belong.

The world created by council tower blocks is very different from that created by street-level estates; it has different rules and expectations associated with it. Was the offender a person used to going into other people's private realms, like an experienced burglar? Or was he an impulsive attacker, someone who would grab at a victim in a public place because the opportunity presents itself?

What type of criminal was he? To find out, we needed to examine the details more closely. A composite statement drawn from a number of different victims depicts the harsh reality of these assaults.

> I am seventy-two years old. I have never been married. I have never had sexual intercourse and I was in fact a virgin. I had gone into the block of flats where I live. The external door leading to the block was open, just pushed to. I know that the door at the back of the block was open, just pushed to. I saw no one. I pushed the button for the lift to come. After a while the lift came and the next thing was I was pushed from behind into the lift. I was pushed against the side of the lift. I saw a West Indian male about twenty years old. He was holding me against the side of the lift. I had one of these buzzers in my pocket so I sounded it, but he just took it off me. He told me to be quiet and I wouldn't be hurt.
>
> He held me with one hand and started to press the lift buttons. I kept struggling but he was still holding me. The lift went up and down a few times before it eventually stopped.
>
> He had his sports bag on his left arm.
>
> He pushed me through the doorway leading to the stairs and said we were going up the stairs. I told him I couldn't get up the stairs as I was an old lady.
>
> He then picked me up in his arms as if I was a baby.
>
> He then ran up four flights of stairs with me in his

arms. He then stopped and put me down and told me to walk up the rest of the stairs. I again refused and he grabbed hold of my left hand and started dragging me up. We went up two flights of stairs to the eleventh floor. I knew it was the eleventh floor because I could see the roof area through the glass.

There was a door there that he kicked open and pulled me through, on to the roof.

He pushed me on to the floor on to my back and told me to stop shouting.

I can remember seeing him holding a knife, when he told me to stop shouting. He held the knife to my breasts. I could feel the knife in the middle of my chest. He pulled my skirt and underskirt off.

He pushed me down and sat on my chest, his legs either side of me with his back to my face.

I said, "You're crushing me", but he only said, "I will crush you". Whilst he was sitting on my chest he started to push my woolen tights down. He then pulled my pants down. Then my bottom touched the cold concrete. I told him it was cold and moaned.

He then said, "Lift up, I'll put this under you. It'll keep you warmer" and put my underskirt under my bottom.

I said, "Have you got a mother?"

He said, "Yes."

I said, "How would you like somebody to do this to your mother?"

He said, "I wouldn't."

I said, "Well, what are you doing this to me for?"

He said, "Cos I like women's bodies."

He told me to relax and said, "I'm not a rapist." He tried to get his hand between my legs. I couldn't see what he was doing, but because I kept struggling, trying to breathe, he couldn't get his hand into my privates. I don't know which hand he used.

He pulled my legs open with his hands. I felt his finger go into my privates and it hurt. I was crying. I felt

so helpless. He was so heavy. I could feel his finger
moving about inside. He did this for about ten minutes.
I screamed and he stopped and grabbed his bag and
ran away down the stairs.

Some victims were forced to perform fellatio on him and
complete sexual intercourse, although he never appeared to
have ejaculated.

Some points could be assumed in preparing the report for
the police. The victims had given similar estimates of age
with appropriately younger estimates for the early offenses
than for those eighteen months later. Police agreed that the
offender was black, although his exact racial origins were
not known. His athletic build was described directly by some
victims, but could also be assumed from the ease with which
he apparently carried one of the heavier victims up two
flights of stairs. As in many sexual assaults there was no
indication of alcohol or body odors. Here was a clean-living,
athletic young black man. On some occasions he actually
carried a sports bag in keeping with the athletic persona. He
apparently had no accent that would have distinguished him
locally.

Contrary to some people's expectations the attacker was
not a drug-crazed Rastafarian, but neither was he a violent
assailant demonstrating anger or particular delight in controlling his victims. So where should we begin to make
suggestions about this case? Intensive police inquiries had
revealed nothing, even with a photo-fit picture and extensive
coverage in the city's newspapers. I was sure he must be
local, but how? Why? Where?

Here the matrix of behavior, the patterns that had
emerged from earlier cases, was invoked to help lay this
shadow to rest.

The criminal who sees sex as just something else to take
for himself appears different to the person whose inner

drives lead him to this distorted form of sexuality. The age of the victim does not appear to be an obvious distinguishing characteristic for these two styles of offending. The basically anti-social offender, though, is more likely to be involved in a range of criminal activities, to have committed thefts and possibly burglaries. The clearly deviant offender, however, is more restricted to sexually-related activities.

Was this man a confident indoor attacker, used to taking advantage of domestic privacy, a hardened thief, turned to raping weak victims? Or was his behavior more impulsive, more an attempt to get sexual satisfaction where he could, in hidden but public places? Some shape came into these answers by considering what he did not do. Many attackers of weak victims knock on their doors and talk their way in. Others force an entry into the private realm, then use the privacy as a protection from being disturbed. He did none of this. He followed his victims into lifts then overpowered them. Theft or burglary appeared to be no part of his actions. Here was a man more like those we would attack outside, seeking the opportunity to find a victim. The streets in the sky were just that.

Personal Knowledge

The importance lies not just in his knowledge of tower blocks, but in his confidence in moving around them, his awareness of what to expect where. His later statements indicated he knew very well the lifestyle inside the tower. He knew that he could kick open a door on the roof and get access to a secluded area from which no one would heed screams. He knew that the possibility of a lift opening at a floor with someone waiting was very remote indeed. His pressing of the lift buttons to go to the top floor and then confidently going up the further stairs said as much about him as knowing what music he liked or whether he would prefer to read a book than go to a party. This personal level of knowledge exceeds what could be gained from delivering milk or fixing the heating. It requires at least having lived within places very similar to those in which the attacks took place, probably as a youngster at the age when exploration would reveal their secrets.

After the first offense he made no attempt to disguise himself; so he had no fear that he would be recognized locally. Here was a potentially very helpful paradox: deep familiarity coupled with confidence in anonymity. He operated in a clearly defined area, bounded by main roads, when there were many other potential, similar targets nearby. The marauding pattern, moving out from a base into ever-wider localities where residents may be less alert, is a more common and, indeed, a more understandable pattern.

A Deliberate Choice

What does it mean when a person deliberately chooses not to do that, even though the targets and opportunities are so obviously there?

We concluded that the terrain in which he chose to attack felt safe to him. It provided him with a security that any of the other obvious targets would not. From the aerial photographs and localities given to us by police officers it was apparent that the target tower blocks were all separated from other tower blocks by major roads. A city that has no natural topographical landmarks such as parks or hills must rely on man-made features to give it shape in the minds of its citizens. In such a city the roads take on a special significance. Just as the helicopter pilot used them to navigate because they were the main distinguishing features, so pedestrians are likely to have their mental maps shaped by these dominant features. When the police officers told us about the different areas of the city and the sorts of people who lived in each area, they used the roads as boundaries for defining the different domains. There is no reason to suppose that other people would not do the same.

At least one assault happened some distance away from the main group of attacks, a mile or so away due south in a different tower block. The offense took place after a number of attacks and heavy publicity about them. Here perhaps was the start of the marauding activity, although in later assaults he returned to the area of his initial attacks. If this isolated incident was true to our theory, it indicated the direction away from where he lived. He must therefore live north of the main roads. The distance he traveled was also of interest because it suggested that he felt safe at that length. Perhaps we could also use it to estimate how far north he lived from the primary sites.

There were not many tower blocks similar to those in which he attacked at the appropriate distance, so our hypothesis revealed very few places in which he may have lived, or could still have been living. (Hence Rupert's confident identification of the most likely tower block.)

Selecting His Victims

Beyond these important conclusions on the locality and the security the assailant felt, is the significance of his chosen victims. We could have followed a sort of Freudian interpretation, taking tower blocks as the most obvious of phallic symbols. The forcing of his victims to the top would have metaphorical significance, reflecting his lack of ejaculation during the assaults. (Such an explanation would not have got us any closer to working out where he lived.) So we could also have focused on the frailty of his victims, his curiosity about their genital area and the sexual exploration that characterized many of his attacks. These were important points, suggesting a man who did not have a lot of sexual experience and was unlikely to be married or have had a lasting relationship with a woman.

Here it was clear the victim was a special type of object to him. "I like women's bodies," he said in a distant way, as if these bodies had little contact with the people who inhabited them. This awareness exhibited a remarkable superficiality. He knew he could overpower them, but did not especially want them to be uncomfortable. He was curious about their scars. On one occasion when a victim said an ambulance was coming to take her for a regular hospital appointment he was at pains to say that she would make her appointment.

Again, like the paradox of the locations, was a strange mixture that must hold a clue to his lifestyle. He was showing through his actions with the victims something about his daily life. If only we could read the patterns of his actions we would understand much more about him. The victims were objects to him, but not distant objects, objects he was used to handling. Were these crimes his attempts to explore objects that he had seen only from afar, or had had passing contact with but which he wanted to get closer to? Was this the way he saw them? Did he have some regular contact with women in their seventies? Was that part of his world that he was showing to us in these attacks, possibly even a caring, supportive but distant contact?

From his first attack, though, he knew what he wanted to do. The exploration was determined and extensive. Most of the rapists we have studied had some criminal history. Our matrix showed that the bizarre outdoor attackers were more likely to have previous convictions for sexual crimes than for other sorts of crime. These attacks in deserted streets in the sky indicated a prior sexually deviant, possibly criminal history.

Our report to the police developed these ideas:

> In this series the use of aggression appears to have been no more than necessary to force the victims to comply. Some elderly victims were, within the bounds of their age and ability, quite resistant to the offender. In these instances there was ample opportunity for the offender to retaliate and cause some physical damage and yet he did not. He was probably non-profane in his language and in some cases conversed with the victim in a style which may be seen as indicating a need to relate in some way to her. Overt anger, then, in physical and verbalized form, appears to be absent in these attacks.
>
> The sexual acts performed against the victim were mixed and although resulted in degradation of the victim the question to be answered is whether that was in fact the intent of the offender. Fellatio, vaginal manipulation and penetration are present in the various incidents. It is in the examination of sexual acts together with conversation that enables a hypothesis to be formed. In most cases where fellatio has been required, the conversation had been more reassuring to the victim; in two of the four cases some personal conversation is reported and in all cases conversation of some sexual content was reported. It may be that degradation therefore was not intended and the early anal interests were exploratory acts on the part of the offender. In either case anger is not noticeably present.

Physique

Examination of the offender's activities and physique can be important, too. In the fourth and sixth attacks the offender picked up and carried the victim up flights of stairs to his selected scenes. Not an easy matter, particularly in the case of the victim who is described as of heavy build. Solitary sports interests have been noted in other sexually motivated offenders, bodybuilding, swimming and the like as compensatory activities to re-affirm masculinity. Tattoos were noted in a similar vein but general experience suggests that in the event of a West Indian attacker these are unlikely. Together, the muscular interest, cleanliness, dress and description of hairstyle may be significant. Coupled with the predominant selection of scene and victim the indications are possibly that the offender is obsessive. This would not be uncommon in people with sexual disturbances.

All victims who reported the sight of the offender's exposed penis describe him as being fully erect. The sexual acts committed against the victim would appear to be directed at sexual gratification. However, no seminal discharge seems to have occurred. On one occasion the offender told the victim that he had a handkerchief, which would appear pointless unless it was an indication of his preparedness to ejaculate into it. It cannot be confirmed that this happened. Therefore it is probable that the offender suffers sexual dysfunction in his ability to ejaculate. This is not unusual in sexual offenses.

In related studies we noted that criminals who showed fear of leaving forensic evidence were experienced, and more likely to have a criminal history. Together with the development analyses, the existence of what police call "forensic interference" may reveal that an offender is probably "in the system".

This case did not indicate the attacker had any forensic awareness. No attempts to avoid fingerprint evidence seemed to have been made, and the offender seemed to have only a lay knowledge of forensically important matters, such as fiber transference.

Time Patterns

Time patterns were revealed by a simple table containing

details of day, date and time together with descriptive particulars of the offender. Those descriptions are drawn from the witness statements and show consistencies and patterns over time. The offender was predominantly a weekend attacker at the start of this series changing to weekdays at a time around May/June of 1987. The weekday incidents also occur at a different time of day and in the fifth incident coincide with a change of clothing. On three occasions, each on a Sunday afternoon, the offender has attacked whilst in possession of a sports bag. The consistently later time of day is associated with incidents closer to, and within, the area of the initial attacks.

Development over time was interesting too. Unfolding changes can indicate experience, history and other aspects of an offender's changing situation. Unlike *Modus Operandi* which seeks similar activities over a series, the assessment of development allows inferences to be drawn from a common view that humans learn from experience and mistakes.

In January 1986, in the first incident, the offender was described as disguised by a scarf over his face. This action can possibly be seen as a means to avoid identification which is no more than any inexperienced offender might use. As the series continued the offender abandoned disguise and was more prepared for the victim to see him before as well as during the attack. Seen with the complete disregard for forensic matters, the indications are of an attacker whose level of experience is low at the start of the series, but develops both in confidence and approach.

Control

Further evidence of development can be seen in the type of control exercised on the victim. Physical control of the victim was apparent in the first, second and fourth incidents wherein she was held but not gagged. The fourth incident however, resulted in the victim making considerable noise, screaming and kicking out at the attacker, who fled without pursuing any overt sexual attack.

The fifth incident some weeks later, was the first of a change in control where the victim was gagged by the offender's hand until he could subdue and remove her to the scene of the assault. By the sixth assault a weapon was being displayed and the knife was mentioned again in the seventh attack. The overt possession of a knife, particularly at an incident removed by some four miles from the starting area of the series, may be significant in that the offender felt less secure in that area and required additional means to reinforce his threat. It may also indicate more conscious planning, taking a knife with intent to attack. In the same incident, it appears that the offender fled as the result of the victim screaming despite the presence of the knife. This also may be indicative of the offender's desire not to harm the victim.

Other than the developments already discussed, little evidence suggested this offender had come to the fore as a viable suspect in the inquiry to March 1988. Although his details may be within the police record system, it is possible that he had not been threatened with an interview concerning these attacks.

The series of crimes began with the first four assaults committed in a particularly small area circumscribed by Wellington Road, Charlotte Road and Ryland Road. The main routes of Ladywood Middleway and Bristol Road formed the boundary to the north and east respectively.

This starting area is clearly defined as a group of six high-rise multi-occupancy dwellings. The attacked buildings are in the center of the small group. Within the circle of high-rise dwellings are other multi-occupancy buildings and the area is surrounded by a mixture of housing. The estate probably is recognized by both residents and non-residents.

Following the fourth incident, of October 1986, the first

newspaper report appeared in the *Birmingham Evening Mail*. Later newspaper reports indicate a vigilante presence around the starting area. Had his presence been instigated after this attack, then either the activity of such a group, police presence, or the news story may have influenced the offender to move further away from where he was comfortable.

The development of offender movements through a series of crimes also interlinks with what is happening to him, and around him. Therefore, if he fears being caught he will move offence locations to a place, and at a distance, in which he feels secure to carry out a further attack.

Seven months after the third attack, and following press and police activity, the next assault occurred approximately one mile north of the starting area. Six weeks or so later the fifth incident was committed approximately one mile south of the starting area on a direct north/south axis.

The Criminal Returns

The last known offense was committed in March 1988 and the scene was close to the initial area of the attacks— only a few hundred yards from the first four incidents. The return to that area is significant. The movement in and out of an area has been seen before in other cases, not least the case of the "Yorkshire Ripper".

In the last incident, the offender stripped his victim, reportedly to facilitate escape. This may indicate the offender's insecurity in that location, which is possibly closer to his base, and where losing himself in the anonymity of a larger area is more difficult.

Further consideration of the neighborhood of the attack in the light of information from local police officers makes it apparent that the offender attacked in areas where black youths lived and are not unusual. For example, the fifth assault, although in an area described as being predominantly white, involved a victim who was approached by the offender in a "confidence trick" to gain access to the building. She did not report anything unusual in a black youth seeking entry to that particular block.

No Disguise Needed

The early abandonment of disguise and subsequent attacks indicate that the offender struck where he expected not to be recognized. He was likely therefore to travel into the identifiable areas of the various attacks rather than live in the same neighborhood.

Distances between the fourth and fifth, and the fourth and sixth assaults can be seen as "safe" zones where the offender could continue attacks away from the starting area. In this light, the distance of approximately one mile may be significant. This possible "safety distance" also may be consistent with his move to identifiable areas of similar socio-economic content for future attacks.

It is likely he committed attacks against the elderly before this series. The strong Modus Operandi is present from the first incident.

He is unlikely to have had relationships with a peer age female. He may have had distorted sexual adjustment for his age. Also, he possibly had dealings with elderly people in a non-offense context.

To those who know him he is possibly not seen as capable of such attacks. Cleanliness, and hairstyle with consistent selection of offence venue may indicate obsessive personality, possibly reflected in a controlled individual with a low impulse lifestyle.

He possibly had employment after October 1986. Changes in Temporal patterns between incidents and together with the noticeable change of dress may indicate a move from schooling or institution to employment.

He possibly has lived or has connections in similar high-rise property not within the first attack area but at a distance within approximately one mile from it.

The indications of a local base, together with the race and population factors would indicate the offender possibly lived, or was based in the areas listed below.

Highgate—Probable

Bell Barn Road—Possible

Caithorpe Park—Low probability

Lee Bank area—Very low probability

Police took the report seriously. Intensive investigation had so far been unsuccessful, and senior officers were looking for ways to encourage renewed interest among their colleagues. Investigating officers felt that the report could stimulate further attention to the crimes, not only because of its novelty but because it provided a clear list of factors that could be used to eliminate suspects in the search for the rapist. It was now possible to add to the descriptions from victims of what the rapist looked like, his possible domestic circumstances and lifestyle, an indication of his previous criminal history and the area of the city in which he might live. The profile had revealed a person who was used to being with older women. Perhaps of even more significance to police officers was the realization that the victims were objects of almost conventional sexual desire. Their age was an aspect of their vulnerability and accessibility, not something that was particularly significant in creating sexual arousal.

Particularly important was our suggestion that the offender had a previous conviction for a minor sexual assault. This meant that police officers somewhere in the West Midlands actually knew the culprit and would be able to recognize him from the profile. Yet inquiries in this direction had not produced any suspects who could possibly have committed all the rapes.

A summary of the key points of the profile was published in *Midlands Crime Information*, a localized *Police Gazette*, made available to all police forces in the Midlands area. Officers were asked to consider the profile and suggest the possible identity of the rapist. Many suggestions were submitted, but painstaking inquiries led to all of them being eliminated. A further trawl was carried out. The Intelligence Officer assigned to each West Midlands police station was asked to speak to each serving officer at the station to see if more personal contact could produce suggestions. A number of suggestions were received by the investigating team, but ultimately all were eliminated from the inquiry.

Detective Superintendent Frank Rawlings had not been directly involved in the inquiry, but he was the senior officer on duty with overall responsibility for criminal detection when, one otherwise quiet Saturday morning, he received a report of a sexual assault in a tower block. An elderly woman had been carried to the top of a tower block and sexually assaulted. The assault bore the unmistakable signature of the "Tower Block Rapist". This brought the total to at least eight attacks. Though many of his victims were disturbed and confused, they had given similar descriptions of the offender. Rawlings shared with other police officers the fear that these attacks would continue and that future victims could die whether from the violence of the assault, or after-shock.

Rawlings was at his desk in the CID headquarters of the West Midlands police at Lloyds House in the center of Birmingham, some distance from the scene of the offenses. But he did have on his desk the profile that had been circulated in the *Midland Crime Informations*. So he consulted that, trying to get some further understanding of the offender and possible lines of inquiry.

Rawlings was struck by the possibility that the offender could have had been convicted for a minor sexual offense.

He started to search criminal records held in the Central Information Unit in Lloyds House, for offenders who might fall into the appropriate categories. Early in the alphabet he came to Adrian Babb, who had been convicted for attempting to put his hand between the legs of a woman in the Central Birmingham Library. Although this offense was classified as an attempted indecent assault, it would not be regarded by most police officers as a precursor to violent rape, yet it did fit the sort of offense in the profile, so Rawlings called for the actual case papers. He saw that the offense in the library had been committed against a sixty-year-old woman. Further, the twenty-year-old Babb lived in the Highgate area of Birmingham, that area specified in the profile as being the most probable residential location.

One point noted in the report to police was the lack of "forensic awareness", a term used to capture the difference between a villain who seemed to take account of police investigative procedures, who was aware of what forensic examination could reveal, and one who took no care over these matters. It had been predicted that he was so unaware of forensic possibilities, or paid so little heed to them, that he would eventually leave a trace. The most recent offense had left a fingerprint on the stairs, so it was not a major task to link the new fingerprint to the records of Adrian Babb. The link was incontrovertible and arrest followed shortly.

Babb Fits the Profile

Once aware of the evidence against him, Babb cooperated with his police interviewers and, as became apparent in court, he spent a number of days responding fully to close questioning by police officers. These officers found our profile helpful as a benchmark to help them to test the logic and psychological validity of what Babb told them. His answers also helped us to test further the hypotheses we had formulated about his actions and what had guided them.

He said that he could not recall committing similar offenses in any place other than in a block of flats, admitting quite clearly that he preferred to carry them out in blocks of flats because it was quiet. He was also quite open about the fact that he had never carried out a similar attack. in or near his own tower block because of the large number of people who knew him, and because there were few elderly people in that area.

Seeing these direct answers, so obvious with hindsight, illuminates what a strange scientific quest we are engaged in. The bird's-eye view, as seen from the helicopter, emphasized the focused and particular nature of these crimes, enabling us to formulate a strong hypothesis about what was giving shape to the culprit's actions. Looking on his actions from such a psychological distance we had to form a specific view of what was guiding events. There was no way of knowing if the offender himself was aware of what was shaping his actions, or even if he realized his actions had a shape to them. To find such direct confirmation of hypotheses in the answers a suspect gives a police officer, neither of whom knows of these hypotheses, is perhaps the purest forms of scientific discovery.

The answers Babb gave to his police interviewers also revealed a strange lack of personal involvement in the offenses. He gave an almost trivial explanation against the background of the terror and trauma he caused.

The police asked him on a number of occasions through-out the days of interview what had made him carry out the assaults. He gave two different answers that were never linked by the interviewers or their connections explored. His earliest answer was, "I think it was more of a confusion than anything else after losing the girl that I was with." This referred to a married woman whom he claimed to have been seeing for five or six months, but who had left him for another extra-marital relationship. He also claimed that he had had another girlfriend for about four months before that. In police interviews both these women denied any close relationship or sexual activity with Babb. But whether they perceived a close relationship or not, Babb felt that he had been slighted and saw this as one reason for his attacks on elderly women.

Later in the interviews, when asked why he chose old women to attack he replied, "Their age", saying he didn't know why their age made them targets other than "maybe vulnerability", but he also indicated that it was a sort of retaliation for "getting done for the one in the library, could be sort of like revenge, don't know". He was adamant that he had never assaulted young women and also that he never took much notice of the women he did attack. Indeed he simply described his victims as "elderly", claiming he was "no good with ages at all".

During the detailed examination of the sexual events the police needed to establish if he admitted to rape, defined as vaginal penetration, or to an assault that the law regards as a less serious crime in which no penetration of the vagina takes place. This close examination revealed physiological characteristics that also add to our understanding of Babb's assaults. His response to questions about vaginal penetration elicited the response: "No, can't remember it, but on occasions I've had sex with women before… I haven't really felt like, that it's penetrated. I know like it's there, like 'cos you can tell from the way the girls react but I couldn't feel anything." He had no memory of ever ejaculating.

An only child, he was friendly with a nearby family of four sisters and had systematically stolen their underwear for some time, although his collecting had stopped a little before he started the tower block assaults. The police found this collection neatly labeled with the owners' names, in piles at his house. He had a job as a swimming-pool attendant. The friends he remembered from the pool were young girls, nine-and ten-year-olds, not close adult male or female friends.

The pattern taking shape here fills in the outline we had seen from the crimes themselves. But the reason why our research was necessary became clear when I learned how police officers were trying to make sense of Babb and his crimes.

"You see what puzzles me, Adrian, is that all I've seen of you you're prepared to be a perfectly pleasant intelligent man, that's the impression you've given me and I am quite keen to know what changes a perfectly pleasant, decent man into the sort of man who can do these things that you've done?"

(Pause)

"I honestly don't know."

Of course he didn't know. If he had he would possibly not have continued doing it. By his own admission he stopped in the middle of some assaults and ran away because "I thought no, forget it. Shouldn't be doing this then I just ran off. ...it's sort of like your brain sort of like saying shouldn't have done it, shouldn't have done it, sort of like wipe it from your mind." He found it embarrassing and awkward to talk about these incidents. He said he was very shy and he would not be able to go to a nightclub or talk to women there.

The defense lawyer and the judge, at the close of the trial, debated whether or not Babb was in fact mentally ill. The report to the court from a forensic psychiatrist, Dr Bluglass, was unequivocal. In his interview with Adrian Babb, Dr Bluglass "found no evidence at all of serious mental illness of any kind or disturbance of mental function". The judge was clearly puzzled by this and checked that Dr Bluglass knew that Babb "was stealing women's underclothes and attaching labels to them", which of course the psychiatrist did know. A curious debate then ensued in court in which legal precedents were considered for accepting that a man was sane who had committed such a series of strange, vicious crimes. The purpose of this debate was to establish if Babb should get a determinate, fixed-term sentence or be given an indeterminate sentence conditional on his improving under treatment. In effect, by assigning narrow bounds to the definition of sanity the defense sees it in their client's interest to get a fixed term of imprisonment. Such incarceration has little likelihood of any treatment or help to change whatever is at the root of his offending. An indeterminate sentence would be served in a secure hospital dedicated to attempting to help offenders.

On December 20, 1989 Babb appeared in court, charged with three rapes, taking into account another four, although the police said he had admitted to eleven. The judge in court, sentencing Babb to sixteen years' imprisonment, had said how remarkably accurate had been the profile we had prepared for the police prior to Babb's arrest. In fact, when the police charged Babb because of fingerprint evidence, they called us and said, "Your report was so accurate we thought you had his name and address but were keeping it from us!"

Our report narrowed the area in which Babb lived to one of four tower blocks. It suggested that he was used to being with elderly women and also that he was active in sports. His involvement as a swimming pool attendant, looking after sessions for the elderly, was a remarkable combination of these two predictions. The general description of the offender, his age and cleanliness, also turned out to have been of particular value to the police investigation.

Probably the most significant contribution was to suggest that he had had a previous conviction for a similar offense.

This was our fourth report on an investigation, having been completed eighteen months earlier on 27 June 1988. It was probably more detailed and accurate than the report that led to the arrest of Duffy. Our research confirmed that criminal behavior was, indeed, penetrable. The distorted silhouette produced in a report could be matched, under the right circumstances, to one suspect.

With hindsight, there are some fascinating pointers in this report that we all completely missed. Why carry a sports bag with you when you go off to rape old ladies if you are not en route to, or from, a sporting activity? In either case you are likely to be near familiar territory. The sports bag was seen only on Sunday afternoons, the great British time for amateur sport. It turned out that Babb was on his way back from a football game, probably games that he had lost. (A Dutch serial rapist was a track athlete who attacked near the venue of his meetings, again usually attacking when he lost.) Perhaps the central point was that in the complexity of any investigation it is easy for the police to miss details. The police officers who had arrested Babb for his first assault in the library had never been shown our profile. He was in the records as we had predicted, but they missed him.

The Importance of Variances

Babb commuted a short distance into a particular area to find a very distinct type of victim. His narrow focus of action broadened my understanding of the variations between violent criminals. The tower block investigation in Birmingham taught me to beware of general rules of offender behavior, to look cautiously at any geographical distribution of linked crimes. When Babb was arrested and I learned of his confessions, I was confident that psychological principles and methods could contribute to many different sorts of police investigations, but I also saw the importance of understanding the variations in offenders' actions. It was not enough to recognize their shadows, we also had to make sense of them.

Chapter Six
DISTINGUISHING ACTIONS

John Duffy had taught us that the shadow cast by a violent offender is open to interpretation. Adrian Babb took us deeper into the examination of exactly what rapists and killers do, and where they do it. The crucial part of reading the shadows a criminal casts is to recognize which are his shadows and which are those of another, possibly similar offender.

The task of linking crimes, as the police call it, is enormously important to investigations. In cases where many crimes seem related, police must decide whether to treat the investigation as one major, interconnected inquiry. If so, the inquiry becomes a magnet for resources, and is also scrutinized by senior officers and the news media. Careers are made from effective involvement in a major inquiry.

Hard forensic information is the preferred basis for setting up an investigation of a crime series, such as a shoeprint common to all the crimes, or detailed blood-typing showing the same blood type at different scenes. These days DNA "fingerprinting" is the ideal, but old-fashioned digital fingerprinting will do nicely too.

Specific linking information is often missing. Crimes may have been committed in different police divisions, so that details are not merged, or are distorted by slight differences in the methods of collecting or recording them. The actions of the victims or witnesses may have been so different in each offense that identifying the culprit as the same person can be difficult.

Results of DNA tests can require months to come

through, increasing the risk of more crimes and an escalation of violence before the criminal is captured. He may even escape completely.

In many situations, general aspects of the offenses are reluctantly used as a basis for linking them. These, typically, include descriptions given by victims (for example, a scar or a gold tooth), or very particular aspects of behavior, the *modus operandi* (for instance, entering premises by removing slats from louvered windows).

Deciding whether a number of crimes have been committed by one offender, and therefore that they deserve a special inquiry, is typically done by senior officers after reading statements made by victims and witnesses, together with reports from forensic laboratories and the investigating officers. No statistical or probability analysis is brought to bear, except as it might apply to blood-typing or DNA. The senior officer's considered opinion rules.

The Experiment

Often the actions of a criminal and the descriptions given by victims and witnesses appear so general that the senior officer's decision is a tough one, as we discovered when we carried out an experiment. The experiment was run by Margaret Wilson, a colleague who had worked with me for a number of years on various applied psychology projects. Lynne Martin, a postgraduate research student, (who now works for NASA) assisted her.

Five detectives were given summaries of statements made by twelve rape victims. The statements had been doctored so that any obvious links between offenses, such as descriptions of the rapist or the location, had been removed; all that remained were accounts of what the offender did and said—his behavior. The police officers were asked to decide between them which of the offenses had been committed by the same man. The information they were given was similar to the material available during a typical investigation, drawn directly from existing police records.

The detectives were stressed by their first contact with psychologists, and felt the two women were watching their every move. Despite Margaret and Lynne's protestations, and promises of confidentiality, they suspected a hidden test. They feared their performance then would be judged by senior officers.

We were genuinely interested in how police officers would normally make such decisions. We wanted to use the information to assess how computers could improve their effectiveness. The detectives, however, felt they must demonstrate their psychological sophistication. They were therefore relieved when one of them, "Paul", professed to know all about rape.

"Yes, I read a book on it. There are different types, you see. One lot's sadistic. They don't give a damn about the victim so they'll hang around after and may rape her a second time. All we got to do is find out which are the sadistic ones and that'll be the same villain. Then another lot is sexual rapists. They're perverts. They ask the victim sexual questions. They want her to talk. You often find dirty mags at their house. Another type is the angry rapist who has a grudge against women. They're getting their own back on women by degrading them and taking out their aggression. They often have a domineering mother."

Another detective, lending support to the expert in their midst, said, "Yes, his mother was probably a prostitute."

Paul, encouraged, continued: "One other type is the psychopath criminal. He's just a little toe-rag and so doesn't see rape as a crime. He doesn't really have a motive to rape but some other crime like house-breaking."

Armed with this authoritative review, the detectives closely examined the statements. In one assault the offender had asked his victim if she was enjoying it. This was a clear indication that the offender was trying to seek revenge, and so must be the same criminal who viciously hit his victim when she would not cooperate. In a different attack, money was demanded. This case was seen as involving a psychopathic criminal who must also have done the crime in which the victim was beaten around the face and told not to tell anyone or he'd be back; clearly a criminal worried about being caught.

Through such doubtful analysis the detectives eventually identified four groups of offenses. Margaret and Lynne studied these carefully. They found that every group contained a mixture of actual criminals; if they had been assigned randomly to the groups there could not have been more errors. Paul's ideas had misled the group. They had been less accurate than other officers who just used simple police experience, dealing with direct overt similarities, without attempting to interpret them.

Margaret and Lynne's experiments illustrate only too well the special problems officers faced when they try to determine criminal behavior without the systematic tools of applied psychology, or any other forensic backup.

Unlike the chemist or physicist who works with specially prepared materials and ponders patterns only visible with special equipment, the student of human behavior can access the same material as the nonspecialist. So Paul felt confident in commenting on the actions recorded in a rape as if he were a trained psychologist.

Paul could relate the material directly to the book he had read. He would insist that we all know what violence is, or an act of theft. So when the witness statements recorded actions similar to those mentioned in the book, he felt on firm ground. He was also happy to pontificate because the book used familiar words; ideas such as sadist, pervert and psychopath. Paul did not realize that these words had been refashioned to do a particular job. He took some ideas and absorbed them directly into his own experience without considering that they might have limitations

"If you and me had got together, and ignored Paul here, we could have done quite well," one amused detective said to his colleague.

Paul was not so amused. "It can't be done with the little information you gave us. Have any other police officers been able to sort it out?"

Margaret tried to allay his anger without making matters worse. "We've carried out exactly the same exercise in three other forces so far. In some cases the detectives get most of it right, but," she continued quickly, seeing that he was not satisfied, "there are always some errors. That's why we are trying to develop a computerized system that would support police decision-making."

Paul would not be mollified. How could a young woman really know more about the links between rapes than he did with all his years of detective experience? If he admitted that she did know better without training or background, surely that would undervalue his own hard-won credibility. It is more comfortable to be convinced that some trick-cyclist, sleight-of-hand had been performed to make a fool of him. The expert always poses a threat to local knowledge. Why bother with all this university stuff, when there are experienced officers doing a good job under trying circumstances? Some senior police officers are fond of saying they don't need computers or science to help them find the culprit. They will refer to their criminal intelligence officer and say, "My guy can do it fine by the seat of his pants."

It takes a rather full understanding of scientific psychology to see that it can exceed an individual's experience and even the collective expertise of many police forces.

Contact with forensic scientists has tended to confuse the

issue. Give forensic experts a shoe-print and a shoe and they will be able to say within a known range of certainty whether the shoe is likely to have produced the print. The forensic service has therefore evolved to provide evidence used in court to challenge or support the case against the accused. It is not part of the forensic scientist's remit to say what sort of people buy shoes that leave that sort of print. Even such elementary relationships as that between shoe size and height are rarely offered by forensic scientists. It is the detective's job to find the culprit. The forensic scientist is then looked to by detectives to help prove the case in court.

A curious imbalance exists in this relationship between police and scientists. It is reflected in the difference between an incident room and a forensic laboratory. An incident room is usually an office that has clearly seen better days which has now had extra desks pushed into it. The walls are covered with boards containing names of duty officers, lists of crimes and actions to be carried out. There is paper everywhere and the only books are likely to be a dictionary and the police almanac. Here is an office where men of action, in their brown and gray suits and highly-polished shoes, make contact to get instructions for their next action and write accounts for their superiors of the actions they have already taken.

A forensic laboratory, on the other hand, is filled with equipment. White, Formica-topped tables have low-slung fluorescent lights over them. Microscopes of many sizes and shapes, centrifuges and fume cupboards abound. Here many of the staff are women in white coats studiously looking at the objects brought to them by the police. Most of the scientists will have university degrees, many to postgraduate level. The police officers have mostly left school at the earliest opportunity and have little or no formal training in science.

The detective wants something that will help him

identify the culprit that he can take to court. The scientist is concerned that her credentials as a professional are not sullied. Out of this emerges the language of caution that is so characteristic of reports from forensic laboratories to the police. The favorite of detective stories, "the blunt object", is a product of the forensic scientist being unwilling to go further than the generality that "the wound is consistent with a blunt object being applied with enough force to fracture the skull". Detectives become confident translators of these terms: "It means she was probably hit over the head with the bit of pipe we found in the back yard." In many cases, though, the forensic scientist's caution leaves the police investigation with no direct lines to follow, only the possibility of establishing a link to the culprit once a suspect has been found by other means.

Guidance from behavioral science, then, lends a different feel to an investigation, indicating new ways of thinking about the criminal, or characteristics that may distinguish him from other possible suspects. The nuances relevant to examining criminal actions can strain relationships between police and psychologists, though each has much to learn from the other. The Manchester student rapes investigation proved to be a good example.

Studying the Manchester Rape Case

In the early summer of 1988 police were investigating a number of indecent assaults and full rapes. All had occurred in the same area, south of Manchester city center, not far from the university. It is an area of bed-sits, big Victorian houses divided into one-room apartments, mainly occupied by young men and women, many of them students. Scattered among these houses, which were built a century and a half ago for rich merchants, are multi-story blocks of welfare housing creating an anonymous conglomeration of rented accommodation.

The city had more than 25,000 students, a mobile population with little focus or coherence.

Each rape had been followed up separately but none of the inquiries got anywhere. This was a crime-prone part of the city. Police officers and computers were already over-committed.

Fortunately, the city has an effective sexual assault referral service. It had been set up three years earlier in response to concerns that rape victims were not receiving adequate help. Partly supported by police, this independent unit is committed to the rights of rape survivors. It is "a collaborative service provided by medical personnel, counselors and investigators and a right to choose any or all of these services". Women can approach the center directly even if they do not wish to make a report to the police. Victims are encouraged to report to police and are offered help and support in coping with what that might entail. From investigators' viewpoint, the existence of the assault referral center is a distinct advantage in that most sexual assaults in the area do eventually come to police attention. In the late spring of 1988 some of the staff of the center were already convinced that a serial rapist was at large in the city. By late summer of 1988 the police knew that nine assaults had been committed by black assailants in the same area of the city. All the attacks had been indoors, the victims being young women whom the police described as "living and sleeping alone".

In some areas of the city virtually every house was filled with students, and most young women living alone were students. This density of students caused some confusion in the early days of the investigation because all the victims were found to be students. This led some police officers to assume that the offender was deliberately setting out to attack students. Chance and probability were at work, however. Even a random selection of houses in this neighborhood could produce young women who are all students. Adrian Babb attacked in an area where he would find elderly women. He increased the probability of finding the type of victim he wanted by the area he selected. But he attacked in very restricted areas and the age of his victims was a common characteristic. Being a student is not so obvious, and the area over which the attacks took place was much more widespread. It was therefore more likely that the offender was seeking single women rather than especially looking for known students.

Some officers suspected this series was committed by one man, but there was no solid forensic evidence to link the crimes, only the type of victim, the time period, the car and the general description of the offender given by victims. None of these circumstantial details would stand in court, so detectives do not give them much weight. Furthermore, the resources needed to set up a special incident room were not easily available. With the end of the academic year, many people most able to help the police were dispersing, making an intensive enquiry difficult. Indeed, the criminal might have moved away with the students and taken his awkward problem with him.

In October, with the return of students for the new academic year, one more similar attack took place.

Reading closely through the victims' accounts of the ten assaults, investigators noted the consistency with which the offender asked the victim to take his penis and help him to penetrate her. They found it curiously distinct that he should need this assistance. This characteristic behavior seems to have tipped the balance in convincing senior officers that one man was responsible for all the crimes.

Once police admitted they were treating the crimes as a series committed by one man, students exhibited outrage.

The women students suffered enormous consequences. Special buses were introduced for them, rape alarms were distributed, and patterns of social activity greatly constrained. As the local paper put it: "Students are angered both by the multiple rapist's threat to their security, constricting their lifestyles, and by the slowness of police to admit his presence." Each rape had received media coverage. People reacted by criticizing police for the delay in realizing that one person may have been responsible for so many assaults.

One Individual Responsible?

In their defense, police said it was not until July that they were convinced by scientific tests that one individual was responsible for all ten attacks. In fact, as court proceedings later clarified, DNA results became available only in October, linking the fourth and the ninth offense in the series. The so-called "scientific tests" were based on little more than police experience and intuition, but the pressures on police to make some morale-boosting statements intensified. They therefore announced to the press that they had enlisted my help "to evaluate every detail of the attacks and compile a profile of the wanted man's lifestyle and environment".

At this stage police were confident their offender was a local man who deliberately choose to attack particular students. They therefore interviewed all the victims again, in great detail, trying to establish common connections. Did they have newspapers delivered by the same boy or drink in the same pubs? But no common factors could be found, except the obvious ones, by now buried in the plethora of detail. Indeed, a chart summarizing the offenses had been completed and covered a great length of wall in the incident room.

Detectives were impressed that the victims seemed

unaware of their attacker until he was beside them in bed, having already put his hand over their mouths. Police saw this as an indication that he was an expert burglar, so then they had to decide whether he was "a seasoned criminal or a sex fiend". They trawled all black males who had criminal records, giving priority to those who had been convicted of rape—even men who were now fifty years old, despite the description by victims of a much younger man. They also looked closely at men with convictions for other sexual offenses and aggressive crimes. They eliminated people who were in prison at the time of the attacks or who had a blood group different from that found at the fourth and eighth crimes in the series. None of the DNA tests on 360 suspects examined matched the samples taken from these two offences.

It looked as if a more considered behavioral analysis would help. By analyzing more than sixty solved rapes we had found that the actions of any villain could be broken into discrete components. By examining which behaviors usually occurred in the same crime, such as using a knife as well as blindfolding, had also given us some idea of the shape, or what I call the "structure", of the actions. This added weight to some obvious points. In our sample of solved rapes, no one who insulted or verbally abused his victim would also have complimented them on something, such as good looks. Such, curiously inappropriate, admiration was typical of less physically vicious assaults. To sort out distinctive behavior we have to inspect the finer details of the criminal's actions.

Most of what happens in a sexual assault does not involve vaginal penetration, although police interviews focus on this aspect to legally establish whether it can be classified as a rape, or as a sexual assault. Legal considerations also involve anything that would indicate consent or lack of it. But much, much more happens in an assault to help us understand the offense and the offender. The sexual activity itself may vary. Premature or delayed ejaculation, and a variety of other forms of sexual dysfunction are common, as are acts of fellatio, cunnilingus, or buggery. Any or all of these can be perpetrated on the victim in a variety of sequences and a number of times. Like the police in Manchester, I had assumed early in our research that some aspects of the criminal's sexual actions could be a trademark that would not only indicate links between crimes, but could also point us to characteristics of the criminal.

I supposed that central aspects of the offender's sexual actions would help indicate whether the crimes had been committed by the same man, or different offenders. Consider the following critical points taken from the statements of the victims of the ten offenses committed in the same general area of the Manchester. The victims had all given similar descriptions of the offenders. Had all the acts been committed by the same offender?

If not, how would you distinguish between offenses?

He said to the first victim: "I'm not going to fuck you."

To the second victim: "Get hold of me, hold it, put it in."

Third: "Put this in your mouth."

Fourth: "You do it, you'll have to put it in."

Fifth: "Put it inside you"... "Put it back."

Sixth: "I just want to feel you."

Seventh: "Put it in."

Eighth: "Put this in."

Ninth: "You put it in."

Tenth: "...it fell out. He said, "You put it in. Put it in."

Here the assistance required by the offender distinguishes the second, third, fourth, fifth, seventh, ninth and tenth crimes from those other crimes in which no penetration occurred. In the sixth offense the criminal was disturbed and left in a hurry. We can reasonably assume that the first offense was an exploration and therefore no penetration was intended. This would lead to the conclusion that this offender's sexual style required the victim to assist him with vaginal penetration. If that was so, then what might this say about the characteristics of a persistent rapist who consistently sought such help?

Before developing an intensive psychoanalysis of this intriguing behavior, we need to know how common such a request is among rapists. Curious as it may seem, this may not be a distinguishing characteristic at all. Indeed, without surveying a large number of rapes for the frequency of different actions we do not know if this seemingly curious act is typical of a whole class of rapists. Neither clinical publications nor FBI agents help us to know how common this is.

Detailed examination of the victims' accounts reveals some subtleties in even this most specific of requests.

In the second, fifth and tenth attacks the assailant's demand for assistance reportedly occurred as a consequence of his insufficient erection, making penetration difficult. In the third the demand is to put his penis into the victim's mouth; an action that is common in the sexual assaults on which we have details. Did these differences in the exact context of the rapist's request carry any significance?

The request for assistance dealt with only one of the very many actions that constituted the offence. Consideration of another set of aspects, such as the mode of early control of the victim, could lead to different ways of thinking about the offences. After all, first contact with the victim, before she has a chance to react, could be taken as the offender revealing his own "pure" behavior unmodified by the reactions of the other party to the transactions and so be seen as most essentially characteristic of him. These are the victims' reports of those very first moments of frightening contact.

First Victim: "I don't know what woke me, I think it

was the man's presence and thinking someone was touching me. I wasn't sure what. I was so frightened. He put his hand over my eyes and mouth."

Second: I saw the figure of a man dressed all in black which filled the crack in the door. I realized at that point that he'd also seen me and then he flung the bedroom door open. He walked into the bedroom holding a knife at his shoulder level."

Third: "I turned towards the door and saw a male coming towards me."

Fourth: "I remember waking up and realizing that there was something cold on my neck. Then I heard a man's voice say 'Don't scream. I've got a knife and I'll use it'."

Fifth: "I turned over on to my back from my stomach and saw the man by my bed. He began to climb on to my bed. I started to scream and noticed he was holding a knife in his right hand."

Sixth: "I felt something touch my shoulder and I woke up. I then saw a man crouched down on my right side. I heard him say 'I'm a burglar, I've got a knife'."

Seventh: "I felt a hand being placed over my mouth. Initially I thought it was somebody playing a joke, but when the person said 'Shut up' in a menacing manner I realized it wasn't a joke."

Eighth: "I rolled over and saw a man with a knife coming close to my bed."

Ninth: "As I was half way to standing up I suddenly saw a man standing on the stairs. I was so shocked at seeing the man and immediately started to scream. The man began to come towards me. He said, 'Shut up'."

Tenth: "I became aware of something over my face, surrounding it all over. It was rough on my face and of a voice muttering. I must have said what's up or something. The voice said, 'Shut up'."

Apparently, in every case the victim was asleep when the assailant entered her house. Is there any significance in the fact that on some occasions he was close by her side before she woke up, ready to control her, whereas in others she was already awake before he came near? What about the knife and the readiness or otherwise with which he revealed it? What about his instruction to her to "shut up"?

Beware of Simplified Pictures

This detailed scrutiny of the criminal's action serves to illustrate two central points. The first is that there is a great deal of potentially very important detail here. It is unlikely that any detective can recall all the details of exactly what happened in every case without confusion. Most police officers are therefore likely to remember details that are salient to them and build up simplified pictures in their mind of each incident for discussion and comparison.

Different Details Lead to Different Views

The second point is that attention to different details will lead to different views of whether the offenses are the work of one man or more than one. If we rely on details of the sexual act we may conclude that it is one person. Yet if we take account of whether he wakes the victim or waits for her to awaken we may come to the conclusion that more than one assailant is involved in the series of different offences.

Deciding, purely on behavioral information, whether there is more than one offender can be a complex task. Many factors can lead to changes in the offender's actions, perhaps due to a victim's response. If she immediately fights back or someone comes to her assistance, or if she has taken sleeping pills, then the assailant may react differently. Police officers often look for consistency in a criminal's actions, without considering the interaction between both the victim and the offender.

Crime Settings

The setting carries broader implications too. An attacker in a large house where no one is present except the victim may feel no need to keep the victim quiet or to move her to a more secluded location where he can assault her. If he attacks outdoors, though, these considerations might be uppermost in his mind because of fear of being disturbed. One fascinating question is whether criminals ever deliberately choose to attack in one location or the other, possibly because of what those locations imply for control of the victim, and the risk of being caught. If so, then the choice of location itself may reveal something about the offender and his background, as it did for the "Tower Block Rapist", Adrian Babb.

Consistent Venues

Our studies have shown that the great majority of sex offenders were surprisingly consistent in the venue they chose to carry out their assault. Only a small minority would attack indoors as well as outdoors; they tended to stick to one sort of venue or the other. Early explorations also suggested that outdoor attackers were much less experienced as criminals, more impulsive and bizarre. The reasons appear related to the planning and forethought involved in breaking into a house, compared with the more overtly impulsive quality of an outdoor assault.

Criminals Learn Lessons

Natural variations in the offender's actions may occur as the result of learning or development, as in John Duffy's case. Many other examples abound. For example, one man attacked a woman who screamed and fought him off. The next time, his first action was to control the woman with a knife, then gag her. Here he showed a direct change based on what he had learned from his previous crime. In another example, a burglar was surprised by a woman who shouted "Don't rape me". He broke into the next house with rape as his chief objective. Violent criminals have also learned other, more subtle lessons from their victims. One was told by his first victim that she would swear on her mother's life not to report him. In a later assault he demanded that the victim should "swear on her mother's life" not to call the police.

Internal Developments

Changes may also take place because of internal developments in the man himself, such as his sex drive, or ability to run away quickly. Less obvious lessons may be the break-up of a relationship, or loss of a job. All these possibilities need to be considered while still trying to find the essence of what the man is doing when he commits the crime. A variety of aspects all must be combined. Somehow we have to map out the criminal's actions and see where the map points us.

When we were approached about the student rapes in mid-March 1989, a major inquiry was in full swing. They had eleven people in the incident room, twenty-five outside and twenty more on night patrols. As in so many large police inquiries, even with the advantage of large computer systems, there was a risk of being swamped by the detailed information.

The victim statements were worrying in a number of ways. The criminal's behavior varied in the details of the violence and the amount of time he spent with the victim. Simply looking at the offences as a sequence over time suggested that he was becoming more confident and violent. Rupert and I spoke about Duffy who went on from rapes that were not especially violent to kill later victims. We felt obliged to produce a quick interim report for the investigators, voicing our concerns.

To simplify the material so that some sense could be made of it, we carried out a preliminary computer analysis of the patterns of behavior. This was the same analysis we had carried out on the "Railway" rapes to see if there were some central common theme. Essentially the computer draws a square plot and represents each crime as a dot in that square. The closer together the dots, the more similar is the pattern of behavior of the crimes that those dots represent.

The Computer Analysis of 9 Bed-sit Rapes and 3 Notting-Hill Rapes showing similarity in Patterns of Behaviour (Actions typical of each offence are indicated. The Numbers give the chronological sequence of the offences)

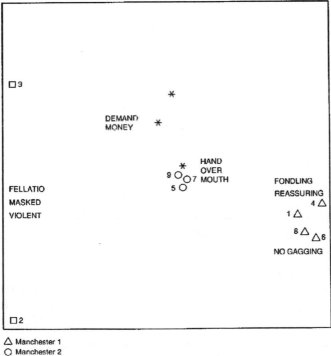

△ Manchester 1
○ Manchester 2
□ Manchester 3
✳ Notting-Hill

Researchers in Israel, less precise than British academics in their use of English, who helped to develop these analysis techniques, call the pictures generated by the computer "maps". They are indeed secret, behavioral maps of the criminal world of the offender created from consideration of his actions. They plot a violent geometry showing how alike are the actions in each crime.

The computer works only with what it is given. If no mention is made to it of the description of the offenders or where the attacks take place, but just their actions, then the computer will plot the crimes in its own neutral box as best it can. In effect, it is performing a very similar task to the one the detectives were carrying out for Margaret and Lynne. But the difference is that it is giving its best estimate, using without fear or favor all the behavioral information that it is given.

The key here is the information that the computer is given. We continued to explore the implications of feeding it details of one set of actions or another, but by the middle of 1989 we were working with ten aspects of behavior, such as the means the offender used to control his victim, his conversation with her and his sexual activity. Our earlier studies had shown that these actions really did capture the full profile of the criminal's activities. The actions selected were critical to the results produced. With different behaviors the pattern produced by the computer could have been very different.

Here, more than anywhere else, the difference between behavioral science and Sherlock Holmes and beyond is most clear. The comparison of behavioral profiles is a comparison of patterns, not the linking of one clue to one inference. The term "offender profiling" does appropriately draw attention to the configuration of the many points that a profile must have. One point, or clue, no matter how dramatic, does not make a profile.

The preliminary maps that the computer generated were very worrying. Trying this analysis in a number of different ways we always found that the second and third crimes in the Manchester series formed an island on their own on the left-hand side of the square plot with all the other crimes over to the right, typically spread from top to bottom. The crimes to the left were clearly more violent than those on the right. Punching the victims and threatening them with a knife were typical of those on the left, whereas in the offences on the right the assailant was more likely to reassure the victims that they would not get hurt.

This could mean at least two things: that the offender had a very varied style of behavior, or that there was more than one offender involved. Whichever of these possibilities we selected we felt that the police needed as rapid a response as we could give them. We decided to draw up a quick preliminary report based on the bulk of offences that held together on the right of the plot, ignoring for the moment those offences that seemed to indicate very different types of behavior. We planned to return to those after we had explored further various other sets of behaviors.

The Manchester Report

On 1 April 1989, within a couple of weeks of getting the details on the ten Manchester offences, a quick report was sent to the police, containing suggestions on directions for police investigations, emphasizing our fears of how these violent crimes could escalate to murder. The report drew attention to the number of strange components in this series of rapes and their relationships to other crimes we had examined. Duffy had gone on to murder from relatively non-vicious rapes. That was a constant refrain to our discussions. In just one case in Manchester the victim had been washed —the ninth. The assailant's intention had obviously been to remove any forensic evidence. But why had he not done that in other cases? Ironically, the ninth case had been linked to the fourth one by DNA, despite the washing, but why had he not been as careful in the tenth case? A sample from that had already gone for testing.

The report we sent to the police was our eighth contribution to an ongoing investigation and only the second to focus entirely on a series of sexual assaults. It pointed out that the offender often appeared calm and in control during the attacks. He did not usually appear to be unduly frightened by shouts and struggles, nor did he retaliate with violence beyond that necessary to control the victims. He appeared to be at ease moving around the various premises, even when others were present, and showed no surprise at finding a young woman alone in a room. The general impression that emerged was of a person who planned his assaults, drawing upon considerable experience of breaking into houses in the area. Our initial analysis suggested that he was targeting particular types of premises in certain areas, rather than particular individuals.

Implied Relationship

His implied relationship with women appeared to be confident, yet distant. From the conversation reported he did not appear ever to try and talk them into submission, implying a typical, rather cold, relationship with women, who were seen as objects for his gratification. The examination of the sexual activities indicated a development from early exploration to going prepared to rape.

Experienced Burglar

The crimes showed the style of an experienced burglar. Previous burglaries could have been committed by the same offender. Earlier cases indicated the possibility of such offenders carrying out relatively opportunistic burglaries and discovering that the flats they had broken into were occupied by a single woman. This then supported their fantasy life, leading to an eventual desire to make contact with such women.

Time Patterns

The times of the crimes were noteworthy for consistency and unusual relation to other series we had considered. They suggested he might be returning from a night shift or be on his way to some form of work.

Variations Over Time

Our report also tried to unravel the variations in the crimes as some form of development over time. The first crime appeared exploratory and our analysis showed that he developed in both the range of sexually related activities and the preparation for those activities. In some of the later attacks he also appeared to increase his use of violent control to force compliance from his victims.

Our computer analysis showed a marked change in activities between incidents three and four and a lesser change from incidents five to six. As these changes in pattern both coincided with a longer time interval between attacks, they could well indicate some change in the offender's lifestyle. The first interval in particular, from December 9, 1987 to June 9, 1988, was especially noteworthy. It was long enough to be consistent with a prison sentence.

Locations

In considering the actual crime locations we concluded

that they were carried out broadly along a North-west—South-east axis, within reasonable walking distance of each other. There is a movement up and down this axis, earlier crimes at the bottom, then up to the top, then back down again. We had observed this pattern in a few other criminals, all of who lived in the area of their crimes. These considerations suggested a base central to the crimes within a particular area.

A Criminal History

A number of factors indicated the offender had a criminal history and possibly was very aware of police investigative procedures. His disguises, socks and gloves, not only showed that he feared later recognition, but also that he chose devices (such as socks) that he could explain to a police officer if stopped. It suggested the possibility he might have been charged in the past with "going equipped" to commit a crime.

Of particular significance was the washing of the victim in incident nine because we had no indication of him even wiping the victim in earlier or later assaults. It seemed possible the offender had had a blood sample taken sometime before incident nine, but that this had not led to any follow-on inquiry, thus he may have thought it no longer important. Given that he had raped on December 8,1988 and washed his next victim on December 19, it was probable that the sample had been taken from him between these dates. The possibility that a sample had been taken before the attack, however, could not be discounted.

In late May, the lab reported DNA results from the last assault, number ten, spurring police to contact us. "The DNA from number ten is not the same man as four and nine," they said, clearly rather annoyed with us. With all our clever computer tricks, why had we not told them there were two offenders? Did this mean that the "profile" we had written for them was useless?

Two Offenders?

The existence of two offenders helped us answer a lot of questions we had been asking ourselves. For example, why had the victim been washed in offense nine but not offense ten? The DNA showed these were two different offenders. Offense nine, therefore, was the last we had for one of the offenders. The offender who committed offense ten had probably never washed his victims. Furthermore, surrounding publicity could have made the criminal aware of the risk he had taken in offense four by leaving body fluids. So the next time he attacked did he try to clean up after himself? But where does that put the man who perpetrated four and nine in relation to offenses five, six, seven and eight? In offense six he was disturbed before he could ejaculate so it was difficult to form a view on his "forensic awareness". But five, seven and eight were complete rapes. Were they his offenses or not?

We now looked at our computer plot with new eyes, attempting to see if that pattern of ten dots could be cajoled into giving up its secrets. To extend our base of information, we fed the computer analyses of crimes by known offenders. These solved offenses acted like beacons in an anonymous landscape, providing identifiable markers for our unsolved crimes. These markers drew stronger distinctions between the crimes, putting two, three and eight into one group on the left of the plot; five, seven and ten in the middle, and one, four, six and nine clearly to the right. The known rapist's crimes were in the middle, closest to the second group. He was a long-standing burglar who had graduated to rape, a married man with young children. We concluded that these were broad characteristics of the one offender, but probably not of the other.

The distinct DNA for case ten was the crucial jigsaw piece. It unlocked the relationships between all the other offenses. We were now able to consider other known features of the cases. In two offenses, one and four, victims noted the assailant wore spectacles during the assault. But four was definitely linked to nine by DNA. Therefore three offenses, one, four and nine, appeared to be produced by one offender, let us call him X.

In three cases—one four and six—the mode of entry was rather clumsy, and unexpectedly distinct, one of climbing in through a back window. The first two here were already linked by the spectacles, so it seems reasonable to tie in six to the crimes perpetrated by X, assigning to him the four cases of one, four, six and nine. They were in a distinct region on the computer map of behavior, especially when the "marker" cases were included. In these the offender was less vicious and further away from the known criminal. Curiously, that fitted with the disturbance during offense six frightening him away. Being less determined or experienced in criminal ways, such a man would be more likely to put himself in a situation where his presence would be noted.

Seeing the computer plot with this new perspective, the results made much more sense. The points to the right of the plot were cases one, four, six and nine. The computer knew nothing about DNA, or spectacles, or the washing of the victim. All it had were the similarities in the action profiles of the offenses derived from the ten actions we had given it. But it was also telling us that one, four, six and nine could readily be the work of one man. In this pattern, offense nine had indeed been the subsequent crime, after four, at which X had left seminal evidence.

The fifth, seventh and tenth offenses also fell in a distinct region of the computer plot. The DNA evidence therefore linked whoever produced a sample similar to that left at offense ten to five and seven, offender Y.

We could say a lot more about these groups of offenses once we recognized them. The offenses of the known rapist, when put into the analysis, happily stood next to the groupings of rapist Y. Was he then the same type of burglar rapist, with X a rather different character?

One further dramatic piece of evidence now emerged once we had assigned the offenses to two different people. The fifth, seventh and tenth crimes, which our analysis had linked to offender Y, were in the Northwestern part of the area of Manchester covered by the ten rapes. Offender X was operating in another, distinct, equally limited area. The first, fourth, sixth and ninth attacks were in the Southeastern part of the original area of the city. Here was corroboration indeed: two distinct areas, each about one-mile square with apparently different people committing their crimes in each area. This certainly paralleled everything else we knew about offense locations in British cities. The scale of territory over which each attacker roamed was well within what we had found for others.

The second, third and eighth attacks were behaviorally very different and also sat, geographically, at the extremes of the two groupings. Offenses two and eight were on the northern edge of the Northwestern grouping and offense three was on the eastern edge of the Southeastern grouping. These offenses therefore remained (and remain) problematic. Do these represent a third or even third and fourth offender?

Our quick preliminary report had undoubtedly confused two offenders as one, although the weight of our inferences to the offenses clustered on the right of the computer plot had meant that it was biased more to offender X than to anyone else. Our suggestions, though, as to the likely base of the offenders now needed further tuning to take account of the two different regions in which the offenders were operating.

Taking the geographical ideas together with the different patterns of behavior revealed by computer analysis, we were confident we could disentangle our original account and generate two distinct "profiles". This required going back to the behavioral material with our newfound understanding.

The distinctiveness of the offenders gathered momentum as we studied the behavior in more detail and closely examined the various computer printouts. The person whose crimes stood distinctly on the right of our plot sometimes wore spectacles during an offense and climbed in through the back windows of houses (apparently unaware that obtaining entry by forcing the front door was less risky at that time of night). He was very ready to tell his victim that he was not going to hurt her, indicating throughout the conversation his own concern about the victim's reaction to him. In one assault the victim had an asthma attack as he was starting to touch her. He left her without continuing the sexual assault, after saying, "I don't want anything, I just want to feel you." This was the man who was beside his victims before they woke up, often with a knife already pressed against them. He was never viciously aggressive, although he hit the victim who had the asthma attack, clearly confused about what was happening, thinking she was playing a trick on him.

The Wimp

As this picture of offender X became clear, Rupert, in the way of police officers, gave him a label to distinguish him, calling him "The Wimp". This was not a wholly accurate soubriquet because the man was climbing into occupied houses at night and using the threat of a knife to force women to let him rape them. What the term did emphasize, though, was that this man was confused about his relationship to his victims. He did not appear to be a seasoned burglar, although he told some victims that he was a burglar.

He was a man seeking sexual contact with women, apparently because there was no other way available to him. Many of his sexual actions were apparently exploratory.

To the fourth victim, X said, "You do it, you'll have to put it in." To the sixth, he said, "I just want to feel you," and to the ninth he said, "You put it in". In two cases he emphasized the victim's actions. This contrasted with the fifth, seventh and tenth in which the three different victims all quote him as saying, "Put it in." Here the instruction was far less personal; it was a vicious demand to facilitate the rape. Rupert labeled this assailant "Macho Man". The slight differences in how the instructions are written in the statements have a strange consistency to them. If this is combined with the more aggressive style of the second offender, then it is possible to hear a difference between the aggressive instruction ("Put it in") and the request for help ("You put it in").

The Wimp, then, had all the hallmarks of a man who had no regular contact with women, who quite probably wandered the streets peeping into windows—probably a lonely man and in the older range for rapists, (typically in their mid-twenties), having attacked through the mounting frustrations of his life. He would have little previous criminal history, if any, and live in the vicinity of the Southeastern part of the city.

Macho Man

We suspected that offender Y, "Macho Man" lived in the area of the Northwest. He revealed many of the habits of experienced criminals, entering by an insecure front door, sometimes disconnecting the telephone, taking chequebooks or other property that could be sold only through the underworld. Significantly, he was a violent man who woke his victims as he entered their room, immediately threatening them with a knife and telling them to shut up. To keep his victims quiet he forced his hand into their mouths with such violence that in one case he scratched the back of the victim's throat. He would tell them to move up and down as he was raping them, saying things like, "You're not doing much for me." This was a man who was used to controlling women. Just considering his approach to the victims showed his confidence in being able to bend them to his will. In the fifth, seventh and tenth crimes the victim's first awareness of the offender was when she felt him close, touching her, either with his hand over her mouth or clearly holding a knife. Indeed, in the fifth offence the victim screamed, but for both the subsequent victims of the same offender, their first experience was of a hand over their mouth. Most of the other victims in the series awoke before the man was close enough to put his hand over their faces. In one case she saw him standing on the stairs before he entered her room.

This "Macho" rapist showed his history of contact with women and exerting control over them. Our computer analysis showed that his behavioral pattern was similar to another known rapist who had a previous conviction for burglary, as well as being married.

At the end of March, before we had disentangled the two (or more) offenders, the police had already identified a man who we will call George as a possible suspect for the ten offenses. A police officer on night patrol had seen him "acting suspiciously" in the area of the rapes. The tenth offense was uppermost in the minds of the police. Suspects at this stage were asked only about that March attack. With the knowledge that they had a good sample for DNA comparison from that attack, George was asked to provide blood. He was more than ready to do so. He had a good alibi for the attack and was clearly confident that he could not be linked to the crime. Indeed, with hindsight we can see that even as a suspect for the ninth attack in December he would have felt safe, having made the victim wash herself. Eventually the

DNA evidence cleared George from offense ten. But evidence for the other two offenses in which body fluid was recovered was still unclear by mid-May 1989.

This lack of clear evidence is difficult to comprehend for people versed in the study of probabilities. The lab could only say that George's DNA possibly matched that found in crimes four and nine, with the odds at three million to one against it being merely a chance association.

In the legal view, there are about thirty million men in Britain, so such odds did not specifically identify George. The police needed to support their already astronomic odds with more information on the suspect.

An expensive surveillance team was assigned to George, revealing that he continued to prowl and peep in some of the areas of the offenses. Although he had no previous convictions police found that he had been cautioned in 1986 for "behavior likely to cause a breach of the peace" when he was found masturbating outside the flat of two girls. By late June 1989 this was added to the identification material from the spectacles observed at offences four and nine. The strengthening of the DNA analysis to one in ten million gave the police the confidence that he had committed the first nine rapes in the series, for which he was duly charged.

Challenging the "One Man" Theory

In Surrey we had not been party to any of these investigative considerations, although two police officers had spent a week with us helping to re-analyze the behavioral information. (Their colleagues had been so impressed that they had survived a week in the exotic realms of a university that when they returned they were awarded a parchment and card mortarboard in honor of their new status.) However, this did not initially add any weight to our growing conclusions about two offenders and the crimes they had committed. Our initial reluctance to challenge the strongly held view of very experienced officers, that one man was responsible for all the offenses, appeared to have led to general doubt about the utility of our conclusions.

At the end of June 1989, George was charged with the first nine of the rapes in the series, but the DNA made clear that the tenth offense was committed by somebody else. It was only when a second suspect, who we will call Martin, had been identified for the last rape that the distinctions we had drawn, with the help of our computer plot, began to be taken seriously.

Martin had come to police notice in the winter of 1988 because a checkbook had disappeared from the house in which the fifth rape had been committed. This checkbook turned up in police inquiries associated with Martin. Linking Martin to the checkbook had been a product of painstaking police research. Fingerprints on the checkbook had been identified and led to a long chain of contacts being un-raveled, Martin being about ten links removed from the person whose fingerprints had been identified. By very careful elimination they were able to focus on Martin as a possible suspect.

Detectives had always considered the possibility that the rapist had taken the checkbook and sold it, so they were not surprised that Martin was happy to help their inquiries by giving a blood sample to compare against semen from the fourth and ninth offenses. They were also not surprised to find that he had good alibis for at least four of the nine assaults. His association with the checkbook had given him an indirect connection with the rape, but at that stage there was no especially strong reason to suspect a seasoned burglar in contact with prostitutes and known to have girlfriends.

Martin, of course, was comfortable in the knowledge that he had not committed the assaults for which his blood samples were taken. He probably also thought that police were so convinced that there was one man for all nine rapes that he attacked again in March. By now, though, he was very concerned that the victim should not see his face, telling her not to look and covering her head with a pillow so that he could escape without being seen. He knew he was in the police records but thought he had already been eliminated through the blood tests that attempted to link him to the wrong cases.

In late June 1989 the laboratory established that Martin's DNA was the same as that found in the last crime of the series. Not only had the checkbook that implicated Martin as a suspect come from offence five, but our analyses had put offenses five and seven into the same group as offense ten. In the process of sorting out who should be charged with what, there were a few days when both Martin and George were being charged with the same crime. The problem was how to explain to a court the behavioral links that tied the fifth, seventh and tenth crimes to Martin. Close examination of statements from the offenses showed that Martin had viciously controlled all three victims by forcing his hand down their throats. Medical officers and forensic scientists were prepared to say that they had never come across that form of control before. It was so unusual that they were prepared to say it linked the three cases without any doubt, tying all three to Martin because of the DNA link to offense nine.

Martin was sentenced to seventeen years. Twenty-three years old, with an extensive criminal record, he was regarded by the police as very much part of the criminal underworld, with suspicions that he was involved in drug dealing and in pimping. His photograph shows a handsome young man looking with open-mouthed confidence at the camera, a person who believed he could steal sex by force in the way he got so many other things he wanted.

**Map of Manchester with Location and Residence
of the Bed-Sit rapes and rapists
(Numbers indicate sequence of offences)**

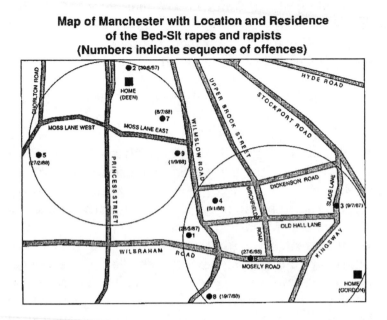

George was described in newspapers, after he was sentenced to fourteen years' imprisonment, as a college failure, a twenty-seven-year-old loner living "in the midst of bright, attractive young people living in flats and houses near his home". He was described as never having had a girlfriend and as being a "mother's boy", but the photograph of a puzzled, bespectacled man with a faint moustache reveals someone who never really understood the extent of the fear and anger his actions threw over a large community. He was trapped by police because they were investigating him for a crime he knew he had not committed. He had not considered they would eventually realize their mistake and connect him with the same blood test to earlier crimes. Even the care with which he had washed his last victim, an indication of the attention to forensic detail that might be expected of an ex-college student as much as an ex-con, was not enough to hide the critical evidence for his crimes.

The victims played different roles in the actions of the offenders. For George the victim was a confused substitute for the genuine relationships he desired. For Martin the victims were just other women to use.

Subtleties are Critical

These cases demonstrate both the difficulty and the importance of distinguishing between crimes that may be linked to the same offender. When only the actions of the offender are available, as Lynne and Margaret's experiments showed, it may be very difficult to decide which elements should be focused upon. Quite subtle aspects of what is said and done may be critical in disentangling the series, and can hold the key to understanding the make-up of each offender. The computer analysis certainly helped us see the wood for the trees and gave guidance on the distinctions between the cases. Once recognized these could easily be defended in court without any need to refer to my complex arithmetic.

The initial concern that encouraged us to give such a hasty response to local police—that the observed variations in behavior could indicate escalating violence—was partly proved in ways we had not expected. Martin, who was confident that the DNA would not implicate him, violently gagged some of his victims with his hand. He may have been prepared to kill if he thought it would guarantee his liberty. He certainly treated his victims as objects significant only to his sexual desires. Perhaps this is where murder and rape overlap closely: in the meaning the victim has for the assailant.

Chapter Seven
OBJECTS OF MURDER

In most, if not all, rapes and rape/murder cases the criminal sees the woman only as some sort of object. The particular type of object he thinks the victim is may hold vital clues to his identity.

Murder in the family, where two people know each other well and have fed on each other's emotions for many years, usually happens as a passionate outburst that explodes into a violent killing. Here one person feels so strongly about another that, as awful as the crime might be, most of us can imagine similar break points in our own relationships.

The murder of a total stranger involves a different kind of aggression. In this sort of crime, the victim plays a role in the life of her assailant, though she may never have seen him before.

Our studies of a number of violent killings helped us establish some important connections between the detection of rape and of murder, rules that might be applied to rape/murder cases in general. We wanted to know how people treat each other as instruments of their own gratification. One particularly helpful case for our research team involved the murder of a young woman in Cardiff

The Cardiff Murder Case

The murdered woman had been well known to the police as a prostitute, working in what used to be called the Tiger Bay area before the docklands development got under way. The scene of her death was described to me over the telephone as "a brothel near the docks".

Like many people, my idea of a brothel had been drawn from fiction and the movies. Then I saw the police photographs of the viciously knifed body of Lynette White, lying on the floor of the room where she used to take her clients, her "brothel". The small, buff-colored room had a dirty, torn carpet and smudged curtains. The bed, a bare mattress with no covers, essentially filled the room.

By the time I reached the room it had been neutralized in the detailed way that only police scientists and scene of crime officers can do. Every drop of blood, every foreign fiber and hand-dab had been examined. All that remained were the faint brown stains on the worn carpet where once the pool of blood had seeped through.

The police photographs of the victim provided a brutal contrast to the artful arrangement of even the most gruesome cinematographic horror pictures. Police photographers never compose their shots for anything other than to clearly record the scene and the body. This usually means emphasizing the wounds and blood splashes, the bindings and the general disarray surrounding most murders. The photographs of the murdered prostitute in Cardiff were the grisliest pictures I had ever seen; more than fifty stab wounds punctured the body, the neck had been hacked, the wrists gouged.

Before the police asked Rupert and me for an opinion, they had talked to every woman who worked on the street in Cardiff and knew a great deal about the victim and her family. She was a young girl born in Cardiff, with little talent and few job prospects. Her mother died when she was young and her father took up with another woman. As such women have done for centuries, she found her way into selling her body to men before she left school, only to be thrown out of her home by her father who felt his honor among friends would suffer. That action condemned her to her only means of survival, prostitution.

Police questioned Stephen Miller, Lynette's boyfriend and pimp. His only source of the money for drugs had been Lynette. Miller was convicted of the murder, but later freed on appeal. Police had also located a number of her punters, regular and less regular, discovering in a matter of weeks facts about prostitution that would take a university research team years to unravel. Officers interviewed known clients of the area prostitutes not as criminals, but as lawyers and bank managers, garage owners and councilors.

The detectives introduced me to the working women in the local pub, near the scene of Lynette White's murder. Most of the half-dozen women were drinking on a break between "Johns." They were indeterminately middle aged, overweight, lacking any overt sensuality, except for the tight jumpers and short skirts that advertised their availability. Anyone who ever doubted the feminist argument that women are treated as objects for the sexual satisfaction of men, need only spend a short time with the few-dollars-a-go, street prostitutes of Cardiff to be convinced how many men can use a woman's body as a source to satisfy their appetite, without any need for or attempt at contact between two human beings, except that which is necessary for the exchange of money.

There is a strange rhetoric that keeps alive the idea that the punters really care. Kevin Toolis, a journalist who specializes in writing stories about the seamy and bizarre, wrote at length about the life of Lynette White. He quotes, without comment, the words of her friends: "She was really a good worker there. She had a lot of nice gentlemen friends, a lot of regulars. A lot of them tried to get her away from Miller." Toolis describes Lynette White as "younger and prettier than most of the other street girls. She had brown curly shoulder-length hair, blue eyes and clear complexion. Her height of 5' 3" accentuated her figure."

The other street girls liked Lynette, and the murder had

shocked them. They therefore cooperated fully with the police. This meant that by the time I visited what was left of the brothel the police could give me a very full account of Lynette White's story, highlighting its unexplained components.

The wounds were ghastly, but their very intensity and variety had to tell us something. There were far more knife wounds than were needed to kill the small woman. They also varied in depth and location of the deepest wounds on the body. Some were powerful, vicious stabs, others almost exploratory incisions. Some wounds did not indicate the violent, almost random onslaught that might be associated with a wild frenzy: yet the hands were almost severed at the wrists and the killer apparently attempted to cut off the head.

As in other actions, such as sexual assaults or even burglary, the details of what the offender actually does in a murder offer us an account of that offender. It is as much a communication about the sort of person committing the crime as posture and facial expression might be in indicating how well a student understands a lecturer. How could this attack be interpreted? The most obvious matter to explore was the attempt to sever the hands and head. Here were very specific actions that should reveal a distinct message. I discussed them with a fellow psychologist well versed in the meanings of actions in patients. His response was immediate: "Wow! What a wonderfully symbolic act—a real attempt to turn the victim into a non-person, to remove her personality. But I wonder why he gave up before he'd completed the task? Perhaps he was overcome with the horror of what he was doing?"

Curiously, the conclusions we drew from this information were similar to those Rupert and I discussed earlier. The clinical view implies that the victim has some personal and emotional significance for the offender and the attack is an attempt to destroy that significance by destroying those aspects of the body that make it a particular person. Therefore, the victim is not just any person as far as the offender is concerned, but special. This implies an established contact with the victim, a familiarity, or relationship. But it is none-the-less a relationship built upon a victim as a body, a person who can be nullified by the removal of head and hands.

The perspective endorsed by Rupert, as a police investigator, was more down to earth. Police identification of the body would be very difficult without the head or the fingerprints. This would reduce the risk to the assailant. If police cannot identify the victim, they are less likely to establish who her contacts were.

This implies that the victim and assailant had an established relationship that could be discovered by the police. No interpretation contradicts another. They all point to Lynette being seen by her murderer as a person whose body posed a threat if it could be identified. The most obvious suspect, then, would be a close associate of the victim, the man she gave her earnings to, for example, her pimp. Such a person would be a prime suspect anyway, and had already been questioned by the police before I arrived on the scene.

The Cardiff Report

Our report to the Cardiff police explored the possibility that the murderer was a client angered, say, by some remark Lynette had made. On all murders of prostitutes, detectives are daunted by the possibility that one of her many anonymous clients could have committed the crime, providing a vast field of suspects, many of whom are untraceable. We kept this option open in our report, but with hindsight it is difficult to imagine the circumstances under which a casual, anonymous client would inflict the number and variety of wounds found here. If a punter murdered a prostitute in a fit of rage, he would be expected to leave as quickly as possible and not linger about trying to cut off her hands. The exception to this would be those cases in which the body is systematically, and possibly ritually, mutilated as when the breasts, for example, are carefully sliced off. Lynette's wounds had none of that surgical quality. Nor were they focused on the breasts or genital areas as "ritual" mutilations often are.

Prostitutes are far more likely to experience violence within close personal relationships than from their clients. The majority of murders happen within an established relationship, not between strangers. Paying for sex is already a form of power and control, a use of the woman as a body. It would seem that such domination would reduce the need or desire to further violate the woman. If the criminal were only motivated to silence a potential witness, say as part of a theft, we would not expected to see such a variety of stab wounds. In this case, anyway, money was found at the scene, suggesting that theft was not a significant motive.

A prostitute's male relationships of a more permanent kind are often based on physical control and acts of violence. How often this violence spills over into murder is just not known. The world in which male and female prostitutes live is extremely difficult for police to penetrate. Many unsolved murders are of people who sell their bodies. In the depth of this ignorance we can only assume that the usual human emotions of rage and jealousy, despair and even indignation can lead the death of a prostitute at the hands of someone they know, perhaps very well.

In our early considerations of Lynette White, we were still open to the possibility of a client having committed the murder. But investigators saw a greater possibility in my argument that the victim and her killer had a relationship.

Our report, while emphasizing the relationship between killer and victim, also focused on the severity and number of stabbings. Any act against another person is carried on a wave of emotion. Different kinds and degrees of emotion are reflected in actions. The number of stabs and their differences, the mixture of tentative cuts and vicious thrusts, the start at severing the head and hands but failure to complete, provide a variety of messages.

The wild frenzy of the murder, but the lack of any fingerprints or similar evidence, also revealed a mixture of approaches to the act of murder. Was this then an attacker with wild mood swings during his attack, frenzy quickly followed by remorse? Or were these different "styles", an indication that more than one person was involved in the murder?

The frenzy of an attack, whether leading to death or not, is also typical of crimes involving drugs or alcohol. As psychologists know, drugs remove inhibitions even in murderers. The wounds may speak of at least two assailants, perhaps more. They also suggest that at least one of these people was under the influence of drugs or drink.

The FBI Behavioral Science Unit might also point out that many elements of the case were "disorganized". The violence and mutilation as well as the thoughtless frenzy and abandonment of the body at the scene are all hallmarks of this type of murderer. In terms of the central behavioral traits of the crime, its distinguishing facets, its labeling as "disorganized" suggests a particular "style" of killing that can tell us something about the life of the killer. This is not the style of killing that a regularly employed professional or skilled worker is likely to carry out. Furthermore, a hardened thief intent on murdering as part of the course of a burglary would choose a victim where there was more likelihood of monetary gain.

This is the type of murder carried out by an impulsive person who easily loses control, who drifts from one way of surviving to another.

Peter Sutcliffe and Dennis Nilsen, who abducted their victims and hid the bodies, presented an organized face to society and dealt with many aspects of their crimes in a similarly organized way. A man who chops at the wrists of a dead prostitute in the room where he has murdered her, then leaves her body in a pool of blood, is no arch villain who plans his life or has a "mission" to kill. He is much more likely to be a small-time criminal with some previous criminal record for acts of violence or petty theft.

More important, the criminal who reveals confusion in his assault is less likely to go searching for his victim. Here is the sort of criminal who rarely travels far from home when he commits a crime. Paradoxically, his lack of intelligence in committing the act makes his patterns easier to interpret. His crimes are shaped by simple, recognizable forces, and by familiarity and convenience.

Our report closely matched investigators own ideas about the murder or murderers. The information pointing back to Miller and his associates, though no evidence had yet linked these prime suspects to the murder. Police even had one of Lynette's close friends undergo hypnosis to see if she could provide any more clues to the actions of Lynette around the time of the murder, it yielded no useful information. As a consequence the investigation was running out of steam, and there were plans to reassign officers to other duties and wind up the inquiry.

Our descriptions of the people who murdered her were taken by the police to point to her boyfriend. Lynette's close associates were re-interviewed, including the friend who had been interviewed under hypnosis. This led them back through a maze of lies and counter-accusations, unraveling an incredible story. During the last few days of her Lynette allegedly was hiding from Miller, possibly trying to forge some new existence away from the sleazy brothel. Lynette's friends reported that Miller and others caught up with her in her first-floor room, attempting to force her to give up any money she might have made. In the ensuing fight she was killed. In court five people allegedly were present during her murder, some as horrified spectators urged to make token stabs so that they would be party to the crime to ensure their silence.

Three of these, including Stephen Miller, were convicted and sentenced to life imprisonment, a conviction against which they appealed, and won partly because they charged police with coercive interrogation procedures.

The murder of Lynette White illustrates how much more work should be done to develop the simplistic typology of "disorganized" or "organized" types of murder. The aspects of an offense, the many shadows it casts, can be examined for what it might reveal about the killer. In this case there was a close familiarity between the murderer and his victim, yet the murder scene itself appeared haphazard, disorganized. Familiarity and contact with the victim surely provided the killer with opportunities for a more careful murder, with less risk of being caught. But the disorganization needed to be examined within the context of a shadowy world of street prostitutes, where people use each other for their own gratification.

People like Lynette who long for relationships beyond unthinking abuse are often destined to become victims. When we examine the context in which she lived her life, we can see how violent crime grows out of the perception of other people as instruments.

A Human Instrument

The investigation of the crime must therefore attempt to understand what sort of instrument the victim presents for the assailant, whether or not the crime is overtly sexual. A direct interpretation of the significance of the victim to the offender is probably the best starting point. The actual setting may help us understand the people who are to be found there and their relationships to each other.

Lynette White was a source of money. Everyone used her as an object. She must have wanted a personal relationship that went beyond all this, love, to keep going, but it was too late for her. Other people did not see her that way. Prostitutes are vulnerable people living on the fringes of legality and therefore at great risk from the other criminals with whom they mix. They are treated more as animate objects than as people who feel and think. The step from being a sexual object to being the subject of violence is a small one. A woman who earns her living from selling her body can be treated without empathy; as a thing to supply money; to be beaten into submission; and as expendable.

The Victim as an Object

But what of other women who become the targets of men's violence? Are there any similarities or differences that can help us catch the perpetrators? Can this evolving theory of the victim as an object be developed to help catch those who kill women they do not know, especially women who do not live a high-risk lifestyle?

The Bhatti Case: A Different Kind of Victim

Mrs Bhatti was fifty-three when she was murdered on Sunday 11 June 1988. She was accustomed to take early walks in the park. Police assumed she got up, dressed and walked along the High Street to the small London park in Southall near her home. This walk would not have taken more than five minutes. She was seen approaching the park at around 5.55 a.m. Mrs. Bhatti was apparently wearing a personal stereo found at the murder scene.

My work on this case illustrates how widely different one case can be to another, depending on the type of victim and her lifestyle.

Witness statements, and the general patterns observed in other settings, drew police to surmise that people walking in the park tend to turn to the left on entering and walk a circuit that brings them round along the path at the far side near Green Drive and then back along the central path towards Boyd Avenue.

A number of people appear to have been in the park around 6:00 a.m., although the majority of them seem to have been at the Green Drive end. None of those identified mentioned anything untoward.

The attack took place under bushes in a little used area of the park. Two separate respondents indicated they often used the bushes as a urinal, indicating the area was reasonably secluded and free for direct surveillance. One witness saw the body and called a passing police officer. She did not see it in the bushes until she was very close, also supporting the view that this was a surprisingly secluded location in a busy, small, urban park.

Photographs taken at the scene showed Mrs Bhatti was beaten about the face, probably with a hand or fist, sexually assaulted orally and beaten a number of times over the head, probably with a cider bottle. She was jabbed in the face, probably with a broken bottle, and received other cuts and abrasions, especially on her wrist. We were informed by police officers that the cuts to the face and wrist were probably post-mortem. The actual cause of death was strangulation. The blows to the head probably first rendered Mrs Bhatti unconscious. Blood splashed on the underside of nearby leaves, showing that the blows took place in the bushes.

This all suggests that Mrs Bhatti was approached and punched into submission. The location of the head wounds low on the back of the head and to the right would suggest that these were inflicted when the victim was down, from the right-hand side. The location of the clothing and other objects indicated she had been pulled into the bushes.

Mrs Bhatti's handbag was found over the fence in the grounds adjacent to the Red Lion Hotel at a distance consistent with it being thrown there. It contained part of a broken bottle. Further back in the park, beyond a fenced-off area accessible over a broken fence, Mrs Bhatti's pay slip was found at about 7.45. This could be called another disorganized murder, but the victim lived far from the high-risk lifestyle of Lynette White. Mrs. Pushpa Bhatti was a gentle teacher and devout Christian, a lay preacher well respected in her community and adored by her husband and three children. Unlike the Lynette White case, in which police had considered many suspicious relationships, in the Bhatti case, they could only suspect those closest to her. Even distant contacts were very unlikely to harbor any grudge against this widely admired person. Two weeks after the killing the newspapers reported that police were "baffled".

The Relationship Between Victim and Setting

Using our emerging principles for relating behavior to characteristics of each offense, we proposed a profile of the offender. Here, we were looking not for relationships between victim and offender, but between victim and the setting of the crime.

The barren room in Tiger Bay defined some lifestyle characteristics of the killer. Such a person, at the very least, had contact with prostitution, which was the only reason the room was ever entered. But, in the Bhatti case, a wide range of nearby residents frequented Southall Park. It was not an unusual place for a female lay preacher to be on an early

Sunday morning in the summer.

Knowledge and familiarity with an area is a prerequisite for many violent crimes, as our early studies showed. Like a person going shopping, a criminal will also go to locations that are convenient. In our report to police we pointed that the killer likely was familiar with the park, based on the particular bush he used, the fact that he threw the handbag over the fence, and that he disposed of the pay slip at the back of the park, in a semi-private location. He would certainly have been wandering around the park before the attack and may well have been a frequent visitor there. The location where the killer had dumped the bag, and the location of the pay slip indicated someone had escaped to Green Drive, possibly in a southerly direction in an attempt to get over the railway line.

As in most murders we have examined, the FBI catchall description of "disorganized" would seem appropriate. The chaotic nature of the crime was indicated by the killer's use of a public location, violence beyond the need to control the victim, the limited attempt to conceal the body, the disposal of bag and pay slip in places where they were soon found, the bottle remains and general disarray around the body.

All these aspects made it likely the assailant lived locally. In fact, our research would place his residence quite near the crime, within walking distance.

His impulsivity, coupled with clues that he lived nearby, indicated this was not his first crime. His other crimes were just as likely to have taken place in familiar, convenient locations, in the same general area. It was probable we would find some form of mugging, indecent assault or rape by the offender less than a mile from this crime in the past five years. Our report urged police to look for these related crimes to help solve the case.

From our study of a number of assaults, attacks outdoors seem to involve pre-selection of a familiar area by the offender, rather than pre-selection or targeting of particular victims. These offenders attack where they are comfortable, in surroundings known to them, surroundings that also provide an easy escape. The victim is then selected by the circumstances in which she becomes available and vulnerable to attack.

Typically the offender would have approached the victim, perhaps conversationally, before beginning the full assault. If that was so, the crime was not a sudden overpowering attack. The escalation of the attack most probably resulted in the victim's reaction, perhaps triggering the offender's "rage". This intensification based on the victim's response occurs frequently in cases we have seen.

Our Profile

Our report elaborated further:

> The offender would be an unintelligent person, working in an unskilled job, if at all. The crime would in part be a product of the offender's sexual problems, linked to a hostile over-disciplined upbringing. Contact with a father would have been intermittent. Instability in the father's occupation was also likely. General statistics would put the offender in late teens to late 20s. The degree of violence might well indicate the middle of this range. The type of impulsive, socially disturbed individual indicated by these characteristics would be less likely to be in a permanent relationship with a woman and may well live alone.

The Question of Ethnicity

FBI agents at Quantico had suggested that people of the same ethnic origins as the victim usually commit sexual homicides. There were some difficulties applying this principle to the murder of Mrs Bhatti, both because photographs did not enable us to determine if an assailant would have judged her to be Indian or Caucasian, and because we did not know if these proposals from the United States would translate to Southall, an ethnically mixed area. We therefore made only the most tentative suggestion that the killer would be white.

We now know there is no simple relationship between the ethnicity of the victim and of the assailant. Local police in Southall reported that people of Afro-Caribbean origin made a number of attacks on Asian women. These points taken together made us lean much more to a member of the local black community.

The criminal background of the offender could be indicated with much more confidence, because our own studies had shown that there were characteristics typical of these sorts of impulsive, violent, outdoor sex offenders. We therefore considered it very likely indeed that the offender had some form of criminal record, possibly for a sex-related crime or for criminal violence or for crimes linked to mugging. Such a criminal history meant that it would not be surprising if the offender had already been considered as part of the ongoing inquiry.

Two weeks before we submitted our report to police in Southall, a rape took place in a cemetery less than a mile from Southall Park. The victim was a twenty-two-year-old pregnant woman who was so shocked by the assault that she aborted. The offender put a jacket over her head so that she could not identify him later. The police traced that assailant through description and sale of objects stolen during the assault. Police knew the attacker, Michael Ogiste, from earlier crimes, but some senior officers did not think that he was the sort of man who could have murdered his victim. When they spoke to me about this suspect they also expressed concern that he closely matched the description in our report except for one feature they thought must be crucial: he was black. We had suggested a white assailant and the officers involved were clearly not able to take account of the cautiousness with which we had made proposals on ethnic origins.

Bhatti's Murder Matches Profile

DNA tests indicated the suspect had been responsible for the murder of Mrs Bhatti, so he went to trial. In later discussions the Southall police quickly pointed out that he was already under arrest before they received our report. Perhaps worthy of note, though, is that working from reasonably overt, systematic principles, we could generate a description so accurate that when our report arrived it was immediately recognized as being a description of a man already in custody. If we had been able to report earlier, might we have been able to save a young, pregnant woman from the trauma of violent assault and consequent miscarriage?

Michael Ogiste was just turning twenty when he was arrested. He lived alone with his mother less than a mile from Southall Park, south of the railway line. He was unemployed at the time of the offense, having previously had unskilled work. When he was eighteen he had been convicted for crimes of theft and violence, and imprisoned. In later informal conversations, local officers pointed out that when Ogiste was arrested the number of sexual assaults reported in the area noticeably dropped. The court declared Michael Ogiste a psychopath and he was therefore considered insane and sentenced "for a period without limit of time".

One strange coincidence was that Ogiste's mother was a strictly religious person, like his victim, active in church life. It may have been that the victim was practicing hymns as she walked around Southall Park on a sunny Sunday morning. A pleasant-looking woman in her early fifties, Mrs Bhatti was hardly a conventional object of sexual desire as Lynette White was, but she represented something to Ogiste. He denies the murder so presently there is no way of establishing what went through his mind when he attacked her. The violence of his attack, none-the-less, reveals he was determined to overpower her; he did not want only to subdue her or make her submit. He stole things from her as well as sexually assaulting her. The victim meant something to the offender. As impulsive as the offense was, it still involved the choice of a location and a victim. The action and its target had significance to Ogiste.

In different ways Lynette White and Pushpa Bhatti were treated as objects by their killers. They were of little significance as people. They were targets the assailant wanted to control and use. Criminals who have virtually no contact with their victims, apart from the attack, exhibit the most extreme form of this behavior.

Steps to Larger Crimes

In one case, we were asked to comment on an attack on a woman walking down a shopping street in the middle of the day. A man she had never seen before suddenly knifed her. The same man similarly attacked another complete stranger a few days later. In another case, a large number of attractive young women each became aware that acid had been squirted at them while they were travelling on the London Underground. Again there had been no contact between the assailant and his victims other than the covert attack with the acid. Perhaps the most revealing aspect of these acid attacks was that it was squirted on their buttocks. In addition, the acid formed a squiggle similar to graffiti. It was as if the assailant was "making his mark" on these victims, like the numbers put on victims in German concentration camps. The pain and distress his actions caused to his victims were not as important to him as his attempt to have some impact on them. Such men appear to have very little contact with women generally, to see them as distant objects. This may well reflect a general disturbance in their relationships with all people.

Knife or acid attacks on strangers are a step away from more directly murderous sprees that catch the world headlines from time to time. The consideration of one of these will serve to illustrate this frightening phenomenon.

Mass Murders, a Different Breed

Around midday on Wednesday August 19, 1987 Mrs Myra Rose found four-year-old Hannah Godfrey and her two-year-old brother walking hand in hand along a road in the Savernake Forest, a thick mixture of trees that spreads out over a few square miles in north Wessex about forty miles north of Stonehenge in southern England. The children had been having a picnic in the forest with their mother, Susan, on the way to visit their grandmother for her birthday. Hannah said to Mrs. Rose: "A man in black shot my mummy." Susan Godfrey's body was found not very far away in the forest with thirteen bullet wounds, having been shot in the back at close range and left for dead where she fell.

This was the first of a number of unprovoked murders that Michael Ryan committed that day. Following his killing of Susan Godfrey, which probably happened as he attempted to rape her, Ryan returned from the forest to his home less than ten miles away. On the way he called in to a service station to fill his car and a gas can. The cashier, who knew him from many previous visits, urged him to pay quickly because she was hurrying off. He responded by shooting at her with an Underwood M1 carbine. Fortunately she was able to hide behind the counter until, the gun eventually failing to fire, he drove away.

At his home in Southview, Ryan loaded his car with weapons and survival apparatus, such as maps and water bottles and a bulletproof waistcoat. He then set fire to the house. He attempted to shoot his dog but, as he later reported, he could not bring himself to do this with his eyes open. Consequently he just wounded it. When he got into his car he could not get it to start. His reaction was to shoot at it a number of times with his Kalashnikov AK47.

He now moved along Southview, shooting with his AK47 and Beretta 9mm pistol at anyone in his path. This included his mother returning from a shopping trip. He shot her twice as she confronted him and twice again in the back where she fell. Walking from Southview to his old school about half a mile away he killed another eight people and wounded a further eight. By the time he ran out of ammunition for the AK47 and was down to the last magazine for his pistol, waiting on the top floor of the school for the police to find him, he had killed seventeen people and injured a further fifteen. His final violent act at the end of the day that led to the newspaper headlines throughout the world associating the name of the small town of Hungerford with "massacre", was to shoot himself.

Later inquiries revealed Michael Ryan was twenty-seven years old when he shot himself, his mother, and a number of neighbors who had known him for many years. He was a quiet, introverted person whose only friend and confidante appears to have been his mother. His father had died, at the age of eighty, three years before Ryan's murdering spree. This death appears to have lifted a load off Michael's shoulders. His father had always been a big, athletically built man, an ex-army captain who dominated Michael and his mother. His mother was twenty years his father's junior and appears to have protected Michael from his father's criticisms as, increasingly, his father revealed his deep dissatisfaction with his son's lack of achievement or success.

Michael Ryan escaped from this ambience of conflict in his many lone walks, which appear to have been increasingly fraught with disturbed fantasies, and a fascination with firearms. From about the age of fourteen he had air weapons and before he obtained the Kalashnikov and other assault rifles he had a collection of military memorabilia. His contacts with others grew more distant as he became involved in his lonely military games, and he had only intermittent casual work. His game-playing spilled over into the far-fetched stories he told acquaintances of being befriended by a reclusive colonel, of learning to fly and so on. By his late twenties it seems likely that most people had ceased to have any real meaning for him. He saw them as creatures who could be controlled by his superior fire-power.

The "massacre" in Hungerford has some spine-chilling similarities to many other tragedies in which a lone individual kills a number of people in one connected spree of mayhem. These events are sometimes labeled by behavioral scientists as mass killings, to distinguish them from serial murders in which the killings happen over an extended period of time and often in a number of different locations. There are many distinct differences between these two types of multiple killings.

The mass murder is typically a tragedy in the classical, literary sense. In a predetermined, almost inevitable, unfolding process, a person acts out an inner rage that most often ends in his own death. It is a form of suicide. Even when the man is caught alive he usually has been narrowly prevented from killing himself. For example Julian Knight, who killed seven people and wounded nineteen others in Melbourne in 1987, during what became known as the Hoddle Street massacre, admitted after his capture: "I was going to shoot myself but I'd lost the bullet I'd put in my jeans pocket."

Shakespeare realized this close association of murder with suicide in his portrayal of Hamlet, whose own death is implicit from the beginning of the play which ends with three bodies on the stage besides Hamlet's. The almost casual killing of Polonius starts the sequence of murders that makes all the others unavoidable. Macbeth, by comparison, is more obviously a serial murderer who, if he is not stopped, will go on killing until force of arms prevents him.

Dramatists, whether of the stature of Shakespeare or lesser mortals, build these individuals into powerful symbols for human experience. They expand the character to capture feelings and emotions that will move their audience to new levels of personal insight. In doing that they move away from the very limited and blinkered view that real criminals have of the world.

Considering only the initial murder of Susan Godfrey by Ryan, the body at the crime scene presents some superficial similarities to the way Lynette White's was found and that of Pushpa Bhatti, but there were important differences too.

The use of an assault rifle to kill a person as she ran away, prior to any sexual assault, shows the extent to which the killer saws Susan Godfrey as an entity to be controlled or destroyed. Lynette White's significance to her killers was revealed by the location in which she was killed as much as by the nature of the stab wounds. She was a resource to her killers. Pushpa Bhatti was murdered in the course of a sexual assault. She represented an opportunity for Ogiste but also a threat. All three very different women in very different settings were dealt with by their murderers as less than fully human, as mechanisms that were to be bent to their assailants' will. They fought against the role imposed on them; in dying they maintained their own humanity.

The majority of murders in Britain are quickly solved, usually because the killer is well known to the victim and often because, filled with remorse, the murderer virtually gives himself up. Those cases where detection is more difficult stretch police capabilities. These are the ones for which detailed behavioral analysis is most relevant.

Another World

Detailed records of murders are now often made available to me on police videos. Their unblinking look at the aftermath of murder shows with clinical precision the difficulty investigators face in solving crimes.

One of the most memorable police videos began with a voice over the bright stripes of the usual color card, matter-of-factly intoning the place, time and date of the crime. The color card jerked out of view and a pleasant terraced house in warm, gray sandstone appeared on the screen with a red-and-white striped plastic tape draped in front. Police officers huddled beside the door, and the background filled with noises of their official conversations over radios.

The camera moved towards the house and the neutral eye took us into the small entrance hail, the cameraman pausing at the door to get his bearings. The police radios were now distant to the breathing of the cameraman and the shuffle of his feet in the debris. Someone asked if the sound was on and got a grunted "Yep".

The stairs at the end of the small hallway showed signs that someone had started a fire there: burnt paper and smoke marked the wall. The camera turned left into the small front room and slowly filmed the charred skeletons of an armchair and sofa. Smoke and the remains of the fire-fighting turned the room into a derelict shell. The memory of the solitary inhabitant lingered in the overturned wastebasket, and shattered lamp over a burnt-out television.

The camera turned full circle and proceeded carefully up narrow, twisted stairs. A small bathroom and kitchen were glimpsed off the stairs with a panning shot that drew most attention to the smoke-darkened walls and overturned waste-baskets. Then, at the top of the twisting stairs, the camera revealed a pile of burnt paper and even more blackened walls. Attempting to get a good shot of these decrepit remains the cameraman stopped at a voice saying, "Don't go back any further." The camera then moved round to the right, passing the doorway to a bedroom, moving across the untidy bed and down to the floor. A chalk-white figure lay there, like an undressed dummy from a shop window. But this was not a model. Its intestines burst through the stomach wall. It was the body of a murder victim.

The shock of this image still echoes within me, although since that first distressing sight I have been called to study far more gruesome pictures of mutilated bodies. That was the moment when I realized how far I had strayed outside the cozy realms of university research to confront the challenge of violent crime.

The attempt to set the house on fire had brought out the fire brigade, and led to the discovery of the body. The fire seemed unnecessary, and increased the culprit's risk of being caught. There had even been more than one attempt to start a fire, in the living room and under the body itself. The attempts had not been effective, although this was an old building with wooden floors. The fire had slowly smoldered for some time. Oddly, the victim's nightdress was found, inside out, behind the front door, but no sexual activity was indicated. The house was in general disarray Boxes of fruit pastilles were scattered everywhere and drawers were full of unused tights.

Police realized that the abnormal features of the case reflected the victim's lifestyle, and could be either irrelevant or the key to understanding the murderer's actions. But which was which?

The case grew more complicated when we all considered

how the body was left. The killer not only mutilated the body but also attempted to burn it. The location and direction of bloodstains and exactly how the victim died can speak volumes about what actually happened. Experts can tell from the angle and direction of a splash whether the blood came from a vein or artery and therefore where the body was when any particular wound was inflicted, thus building up a detailed account of the struggle. The haunting phrase comes back: "Dead bodies don't splash." The grimness of the principle that underlies all forensic investigations throws a shadow over the scene: "All contacts leave a trace". The run of blood next to the body, then, suggests it was moved after death. Why? To set a fire underneath? But if you are going to burn the house down, why stop to try and burn the body?

Careful forensic investigations would answer such questions as what the victim had to eat and when, how long she had been lying there before the fire was started, what accelerant was used, who made the nightdress, where the tights were bought and many, many other minutiae. But the underlying question remained: what was the victim's relationship to the killer that caused such bizarre actions? The key to his identity lay here.

Neighbors and local shopkeepers described the victim, herself, as strange. The police uncovered a history of intense psychiatric disturbance, an estranged husband and little close contact between the victim and anyone else. The thickening plot began to make police officers feel that they were getting out of their depth. They didn't know how such mentally disturbed people behave: how would they react to a casual intruder? Would they have close friends? The detectives felt that they were dealing with people who lived by other rules, unknown to them. This eventually led them to seek help from me.

The two things that cause many police investigators particular difficulties are sex crimes and stranger assaults.

They cannot draw upon their own experience to understand these crimes. A victim who has an unfamiliar lifestyle magnifies their difficulties in understanding what has happened and therefore how to proceed.

Their questions posed a major challenge. Were these violent acts, which may be overtly or covertly sexual, beyond the pale of ordinary experience and comprehension? Was this a search for a distorted human being? If so, what maps and guideposts could help ordinary folk understand this other world?

Police believed there also might have been some sexual motivation. Although the forensic and medical evidence did not indicate any sexual activity during the assault, the naked female body was enough to suggest that possibility. The likelihood that the attacker and victim were strangers was a further reason for police to seek my assistance. Initial investigations had ruled out the husband, who was nowhere near at the time and could have committed a much simpler crime, less open to detection. The victim had so few other close contacts, appearing to live the life of a recluse. Virtually anybody who could have got into the house would have been a stranger to her.

If the investigation of crimes involving prostitutes and promiscuous homosexuals is so inherently difficult, how have violent criminals who have attacked a number of strangers been caught, then?

Part of the need for a psychologist's help in this kind of investigation lies in the fact that there is considerable room for confusion, and a tendency to follow false trails. The woman found dead by the fire brigade may have been killed by any passing burglar, by an acquaintance or relative. It might have been intentional or accidental, part of another crime or the determined objective of the assailant

When the police video came to an end, the images that remained were of the smallness of the house, the winding stairs, the remains of the smoke from the fire and that chalk-white body. It was only after I turned off the TV monitor that I realized we had never seen the camera operator's feet. So, we had never been shown what was happening at key points on the ground as he moved through the building. The latest technological assistance to criminal investigation turned out to be little more than a useful set of images that captured the atmosphere of the scene. We were all reminded to "look at people's feet." Detailed analysis, in this case at least, came from careful study of the photographs and written materials.

Our considerations of the strange mixture of fire and wounds pointed to someone confused about what he had done and why. He possibly did not even know himself why he had attacked a naked woman. He knew it was wrong and wanted to hide all traces. The police had witness reports of a man walking to the murder scene with a gas can. He could have returned to try and wipe out even the memory of what he had done.

The bizarre lifestyle of the victim in the small town where violent crime is so rare provided a context different again from Cardiff, Southall or Hungerford. There was no underworld of vice, no passing criminals, known loner seething with violence. The killer had to be a person who knew the victim, a person this lonely woman would open the door to in her nightdress. This pointed to a local man whom the police interviewed. He knew the victim before the night of the attack and, himself, had a history of mental disturbance.

Unfortunately, evidence was insufficient to arrest and convict him. Until a court gives a verdict, we will never know for sure if our interpretations are correct.

Chapter Eight
STORIES WE LIVE BY

Psychologists and psychiatrists generally say crime has one of three very different causes—biological, social, or psychological. But we will see why these views often are not helpful in everyday detective work. Perhaps there is a more effective answer.

Explanations

The Biological Approach

The conventional approach to explaining the actions of criminals looks for causes within their biological or psychological make-up. The actions themselves are seen as clues to a deeper disturbance. This perspective focuses on the inner sickness of the man, and holds that the criminal will tend to be triggered to crime if conditions are right.

Biological theories of criminality lead to a search for an understanding of violence in the physical make-up of the criminal, whether in properties of the brain or damage to it, hormone imbalance or faulty chromosomes. These explanations can be traced to the discoveries in chemistry and biology that built up momentum at the end of the eighteenth century. They gave rise to a fond belief, still endorsed by many today, that all aspects of human action and experience can be reduced to biochemical formulae. The view that a person was little more than a combination of physics and chemistry enthused Mary Shelley to invent that most enduring image of the evil monster in her book *Frankenstein*.

The idea that human actions can be explained solely in biological and physical terms is still dominant in many explanations of criminal, and other, behavior. People are still often thought of as a conglomeration of mechanisms. Variations in the way their components are built are thought to lead to the differences between people. This is the "monstrous creation" vision. Those who do not fit the norms of society are either badly built or their original programming has got out of control.

Spiritual theories as late as the last century espoused that evil men were put together with missing bits. They did not have "the fear of God before their eyes." Innate depravity made the criminal susceptible to "the seductions of the evil one".

Instead of a clear physical defect, psychiatrists who wished to support the biological basis of criminality talked of a disease that could not be seen under the microscope, but was "mental". Insanity was deemed to have many forms, including "moral insanity". People argued about whether or not a person's soul could be diseased although his mind was not. A pathology, or illness, of the psyche was thought to be the cause of anti-social behavior. The term "psychopath" was born to cover those people who, though not mad or stupid did not embrace the acceptable codes of social behavior. These people formed a catch-all group who fell outside the definitions of psychopathological illness, such as schizophrenia or mental sub normality.

While it is now rare for psychiatrists to discuss diseases of the soul, some terminology hangs on. Many still regard criminal actions as evidence of a hidden mental disease. Just as a person with jaundice can exist normally, though occasionally must take to his bed, so the festering disease within a criminal will sometimes lead him to crime. From this view criminals appear normal but carry about an unseen hole, or badly decayed area, in their persona where guilt or remorse should be. The non-threatening appearance of the criminal is the human machinery working normally, but from time to time the defects in the machinery of the psyche will throw the person out of kilter, producing violent crimes.

The idea that criminals are born that way—made of some sort of criminal material that surfaces when given the opportunity—does not stand up to close scrutiny. If there are biological determinants they must peak in young men from deprived sections of society, because they are the people who commit most crimes. But if they are, why do they afflict only some young men in these sub-groups and leave others unscathed? More importantly, what biological mechanisms would create the unfolding changes characteristic of the development of individual criminals? Why do imbalanced hormones, or minimal brain damage, cause youngsters to steal fruit and older criminals to carry out bank robberies? How do these processes give rise to the limited repertoires that are typical of individual criminals, such as Jack the Ripper's targeting of prostitutes or Babb's selection of elderly women?

Psychotics Not Necessarily More Violent: Professionals who work with that sub-group of violent offenders diagnosed as mentally ill tend to see crime from a medical perspective. These views are clearly expressed, for example, by Dr. Gary L. Malone, well-known US psychiatrist, psychoanalyst, hospital administrator and teacher. He specializes in patients who have been diagnosed schizophrenic or having huge mood swings known as "bipolar disorder". Dr. Malone reflects the predominant view among the American psychiatric professions that "bipolar disorders and schizophrenia are genetically inherited, neuro-chemical illnesses". They have shown that an excess of dopamine in the brain is typical of people diagnosed schizophrenic and that bipolar disorders are related to increased electrical activity throughout the entire limbic system—the part of the brain where emotion resides.

This does not show that the biochemical and electrical activity actually causes the illness, but it does make clear that it is an important part of the illness. This is especially valuable for therapy because it leads to the proposal that medicines that change the neuro chemical imbalances, such as Haladol or Thorazine, will be beneficial. Dr Malone points out that 90% of patients being seen by psychiatrists in the US are on some kind of medication. "In a recent poll of members of The American Psychoanalytic Association, 60% of patients specifically under psychoanalysis were taking, and reportedly responding to, medication". He sees this as "supporting the argument that such illnesses are, indeed, neuro chemically based."

Dr. Malone adds that a great deal of research, however, has shown psychotic patients are not any more prone to violence than the general population, except in cases where drugs and alcohol are also involved.

Typical results indicate that marginally less than one in twenty people in the general population are likely to commit a violent act. For psychiatric patients the figure is slightly above one in twenty. But among psychiatric patients dependent on drugs and alcohol, the chance for violence rose to almost one in two. In contrast, purely drug and-alcohol-related acts of violence in the general population rose from one in twenty to about one in eight.

So although drugs and alcohol increase the risk of violence the risk is increased much more for the mentally ill.

However, Dr Malone, agrees with many other experts that "mental illness has no common thread tying it to serial killers". He says for example "The Son of Sam probably was a bipolar psychotic, able to stay secretive for a long time.

Ted Kozinsky, on the other hand, moves in and out of psychotic, magical thinking. He is likely a bipolar variant with psychotic features." There is no single form of mental illness that creates serial killers. As Dr Malone puts it, "a combination of factors account for violent acts".

Biological elements may account for certain psychological differences between people. This could contribute to their general characteristics so that under certain circumstances they might be more prone to commit a crime than a person with a different biological make-up. But this chain of influences is so long and marginal that for practical purposes it is not useful to investigators. The important, yet subtle, differences between Martin and George in their student rapes in the Midlands did not seem related to their genetic make-up. The idea that Duffy may have had minor brain damage could not help determine where he lived, so that he could be caught. In a section of Chicago's homosexual community neighbors knew that Jeffrey Dahmer had unusual sexual proclivities, but any biological explanations would not have made local police take the potential for serial murder in that community any more or less seriously.

The Psychological Approach

A second explanation, in contrast with the biological model, focuses on psychological mechanisms in the mind of the violent criminal. For millennia the fall from grace has been seen as the product of the conflict of desires, eating of the forbidden fruit. Psychologists no longer talk of "sin" but the ideas they draw upon do relate.

Beyond the Biblical account of human frailty, the tragedy of Oedipus is probably one of the earliest visions of this inner human conflict. In this Greek tragedy the central character attempts to act honorably but his fundamental human weaknesses and lack of full knowledge inadvertently lead him to kill his father and marry his mother. Try as he will to live a virtuous life, the original sin, present within him at birth, ultimately leads him to his doom, destroyed in the battle between different desires.

More recent psychological theorizing has seen this battle between inner forces as a precarious balancing act. If the balance swings one way or the other, mental disturbance results. Many psychological theories focus on the mechanisms people use to keep their experience of the world in balance. For example, if people do something logically at odds with views they have expressed—such as eating meat when they are declared vegetarians—then they will reinterpret their experiences in order to maintain a coherent view of the world. The lapsed vegetarians will say they did not want to insult their host, or that it is only red meat they will not eat. In other words, people change their beliefs to fit their actions.

Faulty Valves

Another view of the internal psychological struggle is that people have to control their emotions in order to stay within socially acceptable bounds, but the process can be faulty. So, it is argued, they may be "over-controlled", their feelings eventually bursting out when they can no longer be suppressed. Or they may be "under-controlled", reacting emotionally to many minor incidents. The balance is there-fore seen as similar to the pressure valve on a water boiler. If the valve is faulty then violent behavior may be the result.

Compensation

Still reflecting the idea of a balance of desires, some psychologists believe that crime compensates for deficien-cies in a person's experience. He may feel weak in non-criminal life, but committing crimes makes him feel strong. The inner conflict here is a self-imposed mismatch between achievement and potential. The criminal feels put upon by others and seeks power through his crimes. Like Oedipus, the criminal walks a tightrope between what he knows is acceptable and what he feels is honorable. In many situations he acts acceptably; he is a good father-and husband. But his fall is ordained. Eventually his actions will reflect his true desires.

These notions of inner conflict may get closer to distinguishing between criminals when we have them before us in court or in therapy, but the theory presents a fundamental problem when used to help investigations. If everyone has the propensity for many conflicting motivations, how do we know which is being represented in a crime? A person who is fundamentally good may allow his inner badness to burst out into violence. So a violent act will lead us to look for, say, a controlled person who normally shows no signs of violence. In Freudian terms the "compensation" resolves problematic personal relationships. It is the young man put upon by a domineering mother who goes out to attack other women in retaliation against the mother he is afraid to challenge. But the opposite of this argument is also tenable. If someone who is without a conscience commits a violent act then we must look for a person who is known to be violent. The hostility is not "displaced" so it may be displayed in many non-criminal situations.

The inner conflict, compensation/displacement approach therefore always leaves a major question for any criminal investigation, if there are always opposite possibilities, which is relevant to any criminal situation? In a violent crime are we looking for a man known to be violent or one known not to be? The answer may lie in the details of the violence, but this implies there is a certain sort of violence typical of a man known generally to be violent and another sort for the person who is not. Perhaps, then, we should discriminate between types of violence, rather than types of inner conflict. Explorations of the psychological processes may provide some understanding of violence, but it cannot help reveal the repertoires that characterize criminals, or why the changes and developments in a criminal's activities should occur.

Knowing that Babb might have hated himself for what he was doing, or that Ogiste was trying to compensate for some perceived sexual inadequacy, might help us a little in any subsequent interviews with suspects. It is not really the stuff that police officers can ask about in house-to-house inquiries. How could the knowledge of Nilsen's psychopathology have speeded up his apprehension? The writer Brian Masters argued that Dennis Nilsen killed his homosexual lovers as a form of compensation for his inability to relate closely to other people. By keeping their bodies with him, it was claimed, he was finding some form of company to fill his loneliness. Whether this explanation has any validity, we should not base any investigative strategy upon it.

The Social Approach

The third general approach to understanding violent crime is the social perspective, contrasting with the biological and psychological views. Here the causes of crime are seen as a network of personal contacts that show people the criminal path. This idea was the foundation of our modern penal system. The reforming Quakers believed that if a man were separated from the villains who had led him astray, put into solitary confinement with the Bible to study, then this would correct his errant ways and reform him. The power of this social perspective was encapsulated in the term "reformatory". In the USA many prisons are still called "correctional" establishments. If you believe the cause of criminality is based in fundamental biological or psychological deficiencies, then you will not believe that you can "correct" a person by locking him up. The determination of the courts to keep young offenders out of prisons, away from the company of older criminals, serves to illustrate the irony of the failure of prisons to achieve the Quakers' goals.

The social explanation of crime is very different in emphasis from the other two perspectives. Oedipus, like *Frankenstein's* monster, is a solitary figure. Neither of them is part of a criminal sub-culture, tutored in the ways of crime by their close associates. Those around them are mere artifacts, there to create the means whereby they can be led to self-destruction. The solitariness of these fictional characters reveals that similar conflicts are expected to erupt in other times and other places. Those conflicts are thought of as the essence of humanity. In these stories there is no emphasis on the possibility that they may emerge out of social transactions.

Although *Frankenstein's* monster was the precursor of many modern fictional automata, these later translations lost a theme central to Mary Shelley's book. She presents the ugly creation of Viktor Frankenstein as developing into an evil fiend only when he is ousted by society. This has a number of consequences in the evolution of the monster. One is that he is never able to develop productive, warm relationships with other people, thereby becoming increasingly callous. The second is that the only illustrations he is given of how to behave are those of other people reacting viciously to him. One other most important consequence, central to *Frankenstein's* tragedy, is the monster's desire to have a female of his kind made with whom he can form a mutually supportive relationship. As we all know, Viktor refuses this request, realizing that there are some fatal flaws in the make-up of the fiend that would only be magnified if he had a sexual partner with whom to produce offspring.

Mary Shelley's novel leaves us questioning whether the evil nature of the monster was really created by a lack of emotional shape and support, as would be expected of any child abandoned by its family at birth, made worse by the vicious way he is treated. The novel then, rather than the monster himself, provides a perceptive example of the third general class of explanations for criminal behavior. It emphasizes a criminal's social group and the way he learns to act, being taught by those around him. Many current assessments of criminality are sympathetic to this social perspective, seeing crime as endemic within particular families and sub-sections of society.

The social explanation—that criminals are generally drawn from a limited range of social backgrounds—clearly holds validity, but it cannot be the whole story. John Cannan killed at least one woman and violently assaulted a number of others, yet he came from a comfortable, middle-class background and the other members of his family had had no contact with the law. The same could be said of many notorious serial killers and men who rape a number of women. The society these men keep does not obviously provide them with violent criminal models to copy. The same society, whatever its illustrations of violence, does not appear to have led many of the brothers and sisters of vicious men into similar patterns of behavior.

The inner, secret nature of violent crime, the very "alternativeness" of the criminal stories they live, is possibly one of the strongest challenges to the social learning perspective. If the violence is a secret part of the hidden thoughts of a criminal, how can it be shaped by contact with other people? The criminal fraternity itself condemns rape and child abuse, describing such offenders as "nonces" because what they do is of no instrumental value—a nonsense. So how does a sub-culture support it? There is also the related problem of how people learn hidden, secret patterns of behavior. Social processes are open to view. Yet the brutal actions of Duffy, Dahmer, and thousands of other violent men, are secret creations of their own.

Social explanations emphasize what makes people similar to each other rather than highlighting the crucial differences that lead to the identification of a suspect. For instance, an awareness that the killers of Lynette White mixed in the same milieu as she did is a useful starting point for the inquiry, but hardly goes beyond what many detectives would have immediately assumed.

The biological, psychological and sociological explanations all take steps towards understanding and investigating violent crimes. Although each has major flaws, in combination they provide foundations for further study.

But, to take these ideas a step forward the system of explanations needs to be set in motion. All the approaches we've discussed here are essentially static. A criminal is seen as being assigned his behavioral pattern either at birth or when he joins a criminal group. The inner conflicts have been viewed as part of a person's psychological make-up that emerges in a particular way under given circumstances. All these fixed views of violent actions belie the very obviously dynamic qualities they embrace. They continue, and usually change, over time. We therefore must consider further aspects. This brings us to themes regarded as fundamental by the founders of modern scientific psychology.

Development and Change

James Sully, heralding the dawn of modern psychology, wrote one of the first major British textbooks in the field in 1891. He started the book by emphasizing that mind is a process of growth or development:

"The ultimate problem of psychology is, indeed, to explain all the higher and more complex mental states as products of development. Hence the most important class of laws for the psychologist are the laws of mental development."

> James Sully, *Outlines of Psychology,*
> 1892, p.7.

On the other side of the Atlantic, around the same time, William James, arguably the father of modern psychology, wrote: "Every smallest stroke of virtue or vice leaves its never so little scar".

> William James, *The Principles of Psychology,*
> 1890, pp. 30-31.

Both Sully and James illustrate a stream of psychological thought that has seen the human state as being in a continuous process of change. The mind is always in action.

This view of human nature contrasts with that held by psychologists who focus on the fixed structures of the human condition, hard-wired into all aspects of experience. From the static view, a person's intelligence, ability to detect differences in musical tones, discriminate subtle differences between colors, their right-handedness or even how impulsive or sociable they are, are all considered as a particular aspect which, if not fixed at birth, is certainly fixed by adulthood. Many of the explorations of these psychologists are of the state and structure of an individual, often focusing on the particular human capabilities that are common to all individuals. Even when such psychologists look at the differences between people they are concerned to describe the traits that people exhibit, the characteristics which are typical of them in all circumstances.

The academic debate between those who search for common, static structures within the human psyche and those who look for dynamic processes of development was reflected in the less abstract discussions I had with Rupert Heritage and Lesley Cross about the "Railway Rapist". We needed to identify those aspects of the rapist's actions that were consistent, typical of him. These helped us to recognize the crimes that he had committed and link together his rape series. But we also knew that he was changing his actions as the crimes progressed. The physical description of an almost diffident, apologetic offender in the early assaults also fitted the description of a much more determined and aggressive offender in subsequent rapes. We need to know how offenders develop and change as well as their stable, consistent characteristics.

Sigmund Freud, born in Austria in 1856, has had the most widespread influence. Although there is much to be said for Hans Eysenck's glib aphorism, that what was true in Freud's theories was not new and what was new was not true, this has not stopped generation after generation of students, in many different disciplines, utilizing the rich metaphors of Freud and his followers to comment on everything from advertising to xenophobia.

Of particular interest to the debate between static and dynamic qualities of human processes is the fact that although Freud and his very many followers were concerned with the basic structures of the mind that were common to everybody, they none the less elaborated a developmental process through which everybody went. They argued that it was distortions in this process of development that gave rise to the variations between people, and especially to the variations in their mental states.

Freud primarily focused on the early stages in a person's development, the first few years of life. Later followers started to put the critical episodes in human development into a life-long sequence. One of his most broad-ranging followers was Erik Erikson who sketched out eight major stages in life in which particular interpersonal crises need to be resolved in order for the individual to progress to the next stage of maturation. These stages reflected the Darwinian idea of evolution but cast the battle for survival in the struggle between a search for identity and the demands of social roles. I have always been fascinated by the sanity of Erikson's vision and believe that his characterization of the life story as a series of encounters may have a direct contribution to make towards the understanding of criminal behavior. So this is a perspective to which we will return.

The now classic profile used by popular novelist P.D. James depicts the extreme aggression shown towards women by the killer as a displaced attempt to gain independence from his smothering mother. The roots of this are seen as an inability to resolve the conflict, that all children are supposed to experience in their early years, between loving their father and being jealous of his relationship with their mother. By over-indulgence of the mother, or the absence of the father, the young boy is unable to metamorphose his jealousy into a socially acceptable conscience and so comes to have a hatred for his mother that he can express only in attacks on other women. This rather exotic theory, which has spawned many Hollywood thrillers (perhaps most notably Rod Steiger's *No Way to Treat a Lady*) is replete with the weaknesses I mentioned earlier, but by looking at the developmental roots it is also clear that the theory has a hard time explaining why most criminals are men. Why do we get no women serial killers living with their overindulgent, elderly fathers?

Some psychoanalysts see this early childhood conflict re-emerging in adolescence. Then it is the characteristic rebellion of teenagers against their parents. They suggest that the rebellion will be particularly violent if it is not dealt with effectively before the person's hormonal activity creates such extremes of emotional response.

While there are many flaws in psychoanalytic theorizing, stripped of its dramatic language the Freudian perspective does have value in drawing attention to the power of family relationships in shaping a person's ways of dealing with others. Our attention is drawn to the fact that the impact of biological processes, at different stages in a child's development, will be modified by the way he or she is dealt with by people who have significance for him or her.

The extremes of destructive relationships in childhood are those in which parents or others abuse children. Freudian theory has, therefore, possibly been of even more value in alerting us to the impact of the abuse and exploitation of children on their later psychological development. The recognition of the profound effect of child abuse is rather ironically linked to Freudian theory. Sigmund Freud argued that his patients' recollections of sexual abuse by their parents were wish-fulfilling fantasies. Yet the American psychiatrist Jeffrey Masson has demonstrated in his challenging book *The Assault on Truth* (1984), that there is every likelihood that then, as now, there was considerably more incest of many kinds than was generally recognized. Freud's patients may have been describing real events, not fantasies.

Certainly, most of the violent criminals to whom I have spoken, as well as those whose biographies I have read, do show early failures of relationships within their families. Whether this is a cause or a consequence of their criminal propensities is often difficult to disentangle. There is also the problem of explaining all those cases where people do survive disruptive, destructive family life without becoming serial rapists or murderers.

From the investigative point of view, the Freudian approach to criminal development alerts us to the significance of the family history of offenders. It also draws attention to the possibility that the criminal actions in a violent assault are likely to have precursors in the earlier life of the man for whom the police are looking. But exactly where to look and what to look for are not really indicated unless we stay close to the loner who lives with an elderly female relative.

The greatest contrast with the Freudian perspective on personal development lies in the work of leading learning theorists such as Burrhus Frederic Skinner, an American psychologist born in 1904. He applied the Darwinian idea of evolving species directly to the evolution of actions and habits. He set about explaining how a person's behavior is shaped directly by the particular experiences of the consequences of that behavior.

Skinner's concern was to build a science that dealt only with observable behavior, not the unconscious, inaccessible assumptions of psychoanalysis. Although more policemen will have heard of Freud than have ever heard of Skinner, his approach is more obviously relevant to police investigators. After all, all they have to go on are the actions of the criminal. They have less direct access to his thoughts and fantasies and certainly less opportunity to explore his unconscious than does the therapist.

Many of Skinner's studies focused on the simple habits of animals, especially pigeons, trained to respond in particular ways to particular stimuli. He proposed that people also could be considered as active organisms, like pigeons whose activity is shaped as a result of the consequences of prior activities. Activities that prove painful do not recur and those that prove satisfying are likely to increase in frequency, according to the Skinnerian theory of reinforcement. Few psychologists doubt the general validity of Skinner's models of learning but many question their relevance to daily experiences. Certainly in recent years psychology has become more cognitive in its orientation. Concern about studying the internal processes of thought and feeling, which help to give structure to human actions and experiences, has grown.

The basic challenge here is to answer questions about

how an individual recognizes situations as being similar, so that the satisfactions associated with those situations are linked to a common experience.

If a person is simply seeking to repeat experiences found as satisfying, then that person could move between a great variety of different experiences, any one of which might produce the same levels of satisfaction. In order that behavior should be shaped by the experience of satisfaction, those experiences have to be linked to similar or common types of situation. This is not a problem for the scientist studying a pigeon in a box. If the pigeon is given only one type of stimulus with or without a particular type of reinforcement, then this pigeon does not need to make complex discriminations. Even as the range of stimuli are increased and the pigeon has to exhibit more subtle discriminations, the bird still is discriminating in relation to one particular reinforcement. The life of a human being outside of a cage is far more complex than sat. The rewards and punishments take place within an unfolding human context.

Like the Freudians before them, then, learning theorists discovered that each individual moves through a sequence of stages that shape and structure subsequent patterns of behavior. For the Freudian these sequences are battles, conflicts that must be won, in which the individuals' inner desires have to be tempered by the external demands of civilized society. For the learning theorists, the sequences are more fluid and flexible and it is only really the consequences of the experiences for the individual that determine the eventual effect of those experiences. The manifold possibilities for arbitrariness, in terms of what a person experiences, that are implicit within the learning theory framework are tempered by the structure of society, which tends to expose people to particular experiences in a particular order.

Indeed, our search for an evolution in the actions of offenders during the course of their crime series was itself stimulated by notions from learning theory.

A more direct application of the learning theory approach to crime is the simple, but often ignored, point that most criminals can be expected to learn from their mistakes. "Richard", a serial rapist, told me that after the struggles he had had with his early victims he subsequently took with him a knife and material to bind them. In disentangling the offenses of Martin and George, Rupert and I had to work out what the likely changes had been in their actions as a result of the reactions of their victims. We needed to see what "mistakes" they might have made, such as leaving semen at a crime scene, and how they had learned from that mistake to take more care not to leave such evidence in the future. The effect of any involvement they may have had with the police investigation was another aspect of their "learning". George had become aware of police interest in blood-testing him; Martin had not had the same learning experience and consequently was less careful.

The weakness of this approach for investigations is its lack of specificity. Which actions change through the experiences of the criminal and which remain constant? What particular experiences are likely to be salient to him? Are the same things salient for all criminals? There may be ways of answering these questions, but they will probably take us beyond the traditional learning theory focus on limited aspects of behavior.

Although Freudian theory and Skinnerian theory are fundamentally opposed in their approach to science and to psychology, there are many strands that they have in common. Like evolutionary theory on which they are built, the most notable commonality to these two schools of psychology is that they see human life unfolding through a series of episodes. The outcome of each episode carries implications for what will happen in the next stage of growth. Distortions in these learning processes, or in the resolution of conflict situations, leave their mark on the individual, in disturbed ways of behaving, in neurosis and psychosis, in styles of interacting with others and modes of expression. Both approaches leave conscious thought processes out of the picture. For Freud and his followers, unconscious motivation is of central interest. For Skinner and the learning theorists, the focus is on behavior.

A Fourth Perspective

To understand how a person's way of thinking may develop we have to turn to a third giant of modern psychology: Jean Piaget, the Swiss psychologist born in 1896.

For Piaget, unlike for Freud and Skinner, experience was secondary to the unfolding of the natural processes of maturation within the individual. Provided the growing infant was able to have access to the appropriate mixture of environmental possibilities, he would develop through a series of stages from specific, concrete operations on the world through to more abstract formal dealings with representations of the world.

Piaget revealed two especially relevant points. One is the notion that there is almost a mathematical inevitability to the sequence of stages in human maturation. The second point is that these developments move from the more concrete to the more abstract. The importance of these two points stems as much from the general framework they provide for considering human cognitive development, as from their particular application to the ways in which young children evolve into intellectually mature adults. It is proposed that adults may go through parallel processes of increasing cognitive sophistication whenever they move into new realms of thought, whether it is architecture or fraud.

In other words, Piaget draws attention to the process, and that can help us solve crimes. This is an especially subtle point that requires a little more detail.

Piaget's studies focused on the ways in which children develop an understanding from infancy to young adulthood of basic concepts such as size, shape and number. He showed these basic concepts were fundamental to other more intricate issues, notably, for us, morality. Thus, one suggestion from these ideas is that criminals will have reached only a low level of moral development. In other words, criminals are depicted as operating at a concrete stage of moral thought in which they evaluate crimes only in terms of the likelihood of being caught or the pleasures of the crime itself. More morally mature adults are expected to think in terms of what is socially acceptable, or, at the most mature levels, in terms of general ethical principles. Unfortunately, the research evidence does not support these elegantly simple views of criminal ethical understanding. People appear to be able to operate at different ethical levels, depending on the circumstances, and known offenders are no less able to see morality in terms of general principles than are those who have not committed crimes.

This stage of moral development should not be mistaken for a sort of static personality characteristic, rather than as a phase in an unfolding process. Piaget gives us a way of understanding what unfolding criminal sophistication might mean. The young offender operating out of immediate Opportunity has little cognitive sophistication. The possibilities of the moment are paramount, just as the much younger child can act only as if objects are what they appear to be. As the offender becomes more experienced it would be hypothesized that he will see his criminal actions more abstractly, and be able to form a view on their implications and consequences. I know of no systematic research testing these ideas but the biographies of violent criminals provide a great many illustrations of the process in action. Duffy's career in crime offers a graphic example of a man whose initial actions are casual and unsophisticated, but who was later able to take an overview of what he was doing and plan his crimes in some detail.

Jeffrey Dahmer's series of murders also were appallingly clear. His first murder was a sudden, unplanned outburst, but he eventually developed a procedure for finding and drugging his victims. Eventually, this procedure became a criminal calculus for providing him with relics of his victims.

The ideas of cognitive development go beyond the learning theorists'. Not only are criminals' actions expected to show an increased effectiveness, greater "success", "learning from mistakes", but cognitive development would lead to plans evolving for crimes; principles and procedures being developed by the offender to make his objectives more achievable.

Another way of viewing cognitive sophistication refers to our earlier discussion of what it meant to regard FBI agents as "experts". In contrast to the novice, the expert had increased sensitivity to salient aspects of the situation and could draw upon implicit knowledge of known patterns of action. The criminal who becomes an expert develops analogous cognitive skills.

Putting the psychoanalytic, learning and cognitive perspectives together indeed provides a dynamic quality to our understanding of human actions and experiences. Combined, they provide a mixture of themes for growth and change within the individual. The natural unfolding of human maturation processes is modified by the particular satisfactions and pains a person experiences. Both internal and external developmental processes reflect a natural sequence of interpersonal conflicts that each person must resolve. But these formulations are still too academic, in the sense of being too removed from the details of daily life, to provide a thorough basis for translating a rapist's or murderer's actions into directions for criminal investigations.

Responsibility For Actions

The biological, psychological and social explanations of criminal behavior get close, but not very close, to the problems detectives face. The developmental processes tend to focus on the early years of childhood or to be couched in abstract terms across the life-span. The detective needs a framework that is more immediate in its relationship to particular crimes. There is a further weakness in many of the different psychological explanations of violent crime: para-doxically, they all place the actual perpetrator at some distance from the cause of his actions. His genetic make-up, or his inner conflicts, or his social group and upbringing are seen as the cause of the crime, never the person himself.

This is strangely at variance with our everyday under-standing and with fundamental legal assumptions. In only the most extreme cases does the law accept that a person is not responsible for his actions. These are cases where it is clear that a person is acting in ways far beyond his conscious control, or that he is unable to comprehend the moral impli-cations of what he has done. In all other circumstances the courts follow the common-sense view that the individual standing in front of them is accountable for his deeds. Can academic explanations of crime ever be compatible with this common-sense approach? Could explanations that give the criminal a dominant role ever be of use to police investi-gators?

The common-sense approach sees the criminal as an active agent. He is not pushed by his hormones or uncon-scious drives, dragged by the fates or shaped willy-nilly by those around him. Neither is the criminal on a helter-skelter ride of destruction, produced by mathematically inevitable consequences of his ways of thinking. All those processes may indeed have an influence but the main role is played by a person seeing, thinking and acting. Through his actions the criminal tells us about how he has chosen to live his life. The challenge is to reveal his destructive life story, to uncover the plot in which crime appears to play such a significant part. Furthermore, in violent crimes, as I have mentioned, we need to understand how a secret pattern of criminal actions evolves together with the more overt, less threatening, daily dealings of the perpetrators.

The assignment of a dominant role to the person in his dealings with the world relates to a distinct tradition within psychology. This is the approach to understanding people that is much more self-conscious than those I have already, briefly, reviewed; a tradition that focuses on the person's own understanding of his experiences.

However, clinical psychologists clearly demonstrated that a person's interpretation of his life's events could be very distorted. Clinicians try to help patients whose ways of experiencing the world are clearly unsatisfactory; that is why the patients seek help. So the introspections of their patients may be regarded as biased accounts that do not accurately or productively reflect what the patient knows, wants or feels.

George Kelly, an American psychologist, who published his major work in 1955, showed how each person's unique biases can be understood. He argued that the set of constructs that a person puts together to give sense to his life has to be the key to our understanding of that person. Does he think of people in terms of power and glory, or in terms of support and friendship? Where does any individual place himself in this matrix of concepts? In many conversations with violent men, I have been struck by the power of Kelly's insights. These criminals often cast the world into winners and losers, men who are real men and those who are wimps. In the language of Kelly their construct systems are limited and maladaptive. For Kelly the role of therapy is to help to rebuild construct systems that will enable the person to operate more effectively.

Inner Narratives

In a nutshell, a person is the consequence of both states and processes. We have also seen that each person becomes an expert on their own particular history of experiences, although their expertise will always be biased and will not always be helpful. A person's experiences will have moderately stable components, derived from the person's capabilities and social milieu, but there will also be changing qualities as their skills and conceptualizations develop and evolve in contact with the world around them. How can each of us make sense of this dynamic stability? How do we form a view of ourselves as distinct people, aware of our biological propensities, our state of being, but also aware of the way our actions and experiences are shaped and change? How do we resolve the paradox of being one person yet of constantly changing?

Over the past few years, a number of writers from many different disciplines have answered this central paradox of existence by proposing that we construct life stories for ourselves. We invent autobiographical narratives in which the central character has some semblance of continuity. The leaders of this movement are happy to find origins in the work of Freud and especially Erikson, or of George Kelly. They emphasize the stages in human narratives and the significance of particular episodes in moving a person's personal narrative on. Narrative psychologists also see important connections with explorations in history and studies of literature. This is revealed most clearly in how seriously they take the modes of expression by which personal stories are recounted.

The narratives with which we are concerned are expressed in violent actions and the traces left in the aftermath of those crimes. They are like shadow puppets telling us a life story in a stilted, alien language.

When considering personal narratives it is tempting to regard everyone as a polished autobiographer who has written out the plot against which he will live his life. There is also often an assumption that if a person is telling a story about themselves, then that story will be a fiction. Narratives may be confused and distorted but they can still be fruitful ways of understanding a person's life. The stories we tell ourselves and each other about ourselves do have great power in giving shape and meaning to our lives. It is the narrative form of these accounts, not their elegance or veracity, that it is crucial to understand. Arthur Danto, an analytic philosopher, wrote in 1965: "Narration exemplifies one of the basic ways in which we represent the world. The language of beginnings and endings, of turning points and climaxes, is [such] that our image of our own lives must be deeply narrational."

Talking to violent criminals about their lives reveals that they often understand their actions as episodes with "turning points and climaxes". One burly offender, in his early thirties, convicted of many violent assaults including rape, told me about his life entirely in terms of events when he had had contact with the police. He indicated that he had spent some time getting a trade qualification, but that was not a significant episode in the life story he presented to me. He saw himself as a child rejected by his mother on the death of his father and misunderstood thereafter in incident after incident.

A deeper understanding of how narratives inform our lives comes from attempts in the 1970's to develop computer programs that could communicate effectively with their users. Two very different psychologists, Roger Schank, concerned with computer intelligence, and Robert Abelson, a social psychologist, set about—trying to outline "how concepts are structured in the human mind", with the intention of discovering how to program computers so that they "can understand and interact with the outside world". They found that computers could not interact effectively unless they knew the "script" on which the interaction was based. Many psychologists quickly recognized that it was not only computers that needed scripts to be able to know how to act. We all do.

People learn ways of acting through taking on, or being assigned, particular roles. These integrated groupings of learned habits become dominant scripts that shape people's lives until they require modification because they are no longer found to be effective. What the cognitively oriented computer programmers discovered was that in order for their computers to have any semblance of understanding they needed to contain a set of rules of how a person would react under particular circumstances. These computer programmers even found they needed to put certain limits on what was possible in a particular situation, otherwise the program would cover too wide a range of options to be feasible.

What a person considers possible in any given situation is the script the person has for that situation. A script is a way of achieving a particular goal, but once the script is in action the original goal may be forgotten. The person may not even realize that he is living out a script that he has developed for himself. Narratives, then, are patterns of expected actions, organized, often loosely, around personal objectives. A person may decide that he must relieve his sexual frustration and that he deserves such relief, but thinks that the only way this can be achieved is by coercing a vulnerable woman. From previous knowledge, gained perhaps in domestic encounters, he may utilize a particular form of coercion. If this is successful from his point of view, the "rape script" will be born and the original objectives may be forgotten. His personal narrative has changed and he now sees himself playing the role of "rapist". In Duffy's case, as with a number of other serial rapists, the script became so dominant that, as the prosecution emphasized in court, he carried with him the props for his role in the form of a "rape kit" consisting of tissues and matches to destroy evidence of his assault.

A narrative links the actors to their actions. It provides a coherent framework in which to see the meaning of the shadows that criminals cast. As Donald Polkinghorne put it in 1988: "Narrative is the fundamental scheme for linking individual human actions and events into interrelated aspects of an understandable composite." For Polkinghorne, the crucial contribution of a narrative approach is that it shows the ways in which events have significance for one another. It is out of the recognition of the connectedness of the events that lives take on meaning. Thus narrative encapsulates both the dynamic and the episodic nature of human existence at the same time as it provides meaning.

By indicating direction the narrative framework also "Configures a sequence of events into a unified happening". The storyline gives shape and meaning to the whole flux of human affairs. The dynamic linking of episodes into a meaningful whole out of which the individual's own agency emerges as a dominant strand, therefore brings together both the episodic significance of the Freudian framework, without necessarily accepting the particular episodes to which Freud draws attention, and the unfolding maturational perspective that is the great contribution of Piagetian theory. The fact that the events and episodes have consequences for individuals (and provide a natural basis for expecting people to change the direction of their storyline) also accords comfortably with Skinnerian doctrine.

Identity

The plots we live by make another crucial contribution to each person's experience of the world. Our notions of our unique identity come from the parts played by our role in our autobiography. One man convicted of violent assault told me that he could not tolerate being insulted. He had waited two years to beat up a man who cheated him out of money, nursing his grievance as a matter of personal esteem, building up a plot that he would eventually act out in what he saw as an heroic climax.

We give shape to our contacts with others and our personal experiences by an implicit acceptance that the sequence of our lives has a central protagonist, our self, who lives through various episodes, reacting to the consequences by drawing upon a repertoire of possible actions. Although this all sounds desperately self-conscious, most of it happens below the levels of personal awareness. By adulthood, our views about ourselves and our capabilities are firmly fashioned and usually accepted unthinkingly.

From time to time, as in all stories, there are crucial episodes that challenge our views. The tendency is to act to maintain the established character, but sometimes these critical episodes lead to a reassessment of the central plot and a reconsideration of how it is likely to unfold. The story-lines are therefore usually shaped by our experience of our capacities and abilities in relation to the possibilities we perceive in the world around us. Although we invent ourselves, for most people these are not fictitious inventions. They have direct roots in our encounters with reality.

Richard, convicted of a number of violent rapes, told me that his first assault was an attempt to force a girl he knew to have his baby. He said he grabbed her by the throat so that she allowed him to rape her with little fight, although she was profoundly distressed by the assault, shouting at him that if she was pregnant she would just flush it down the toilet. But his story was already unfolding. He remembers the feeling of power afterwards, the sense of control. Not long after that episode he went armed with a kitchen knife looking for potential victims. He cast himself in the role of rapist.

The first violent assault Richard committed was an episode from which he learned that another exciting, secret narrative could be lived. The hidden story did not burst out fully formed. He went through a period of great confusion. He attempted suicide and unsuccessfully sought psychiatric help. He was searching for another way to live that would give him the feeling of significance and control that the first attack gave him. After he attacked the same girl a second time he knew the secret life for which he was reaching. When further attempts to get others to help him find another track failed, he started following women he did not know and viciously raping them.

Richard shows us that the evolving life story of which a person is aware is in effect their identity. The American psychologist Dan McAdams put this view very clearly:

"Identity... is a dynamic narrative configuration, taking initial shape in adolescence and
continuing to evolve there-after, that binds together
past, present, and future, bestowing upon the individual that sense of inner sameness and continuity."

Dan McAdams, Power, Intimacy
and the Life Story: Personological
Enquiries into Identity,
1988, p. 29.

In McAdams's fascinating book he argues that life stories take on their shape in late adolescence. Such a view is certainly consistent with the fact that most offenders commit themselves to a life of crime or avoid such a career in their late teens. If this is the time at which dominant life stories are established we would expect a frequent harking back to that era in the accounts people give of themselves. Certainly, novelists frequently turn to their adolescence to explain the roots of their inspiration.

McAdams also draws attention to another important point. Life stories may be confused or clear, or as he calls them well-formed or ill-formed. There is likely to be more tension and confusion in the ill-formed life story, of course. Ill-formed stories may break up into very separate, possibly conflicting, narratives. They may also be changed dramatically by episodes in which the central character experiences relatively minor mishaps. Perhaps here is the clue to the hidden nature of the narratives that violent offenders live: their dominant narratives are confused and sensitive to episodes that most people would ignore; their plots can be set off course by experiences that their friends and relatives might never notice. This may give violent criminals the experience of living a number of separate lives. Their narrative does not have any coherence, so it is experienced as many stories not just one.

The multiplicity of life stories is the starting point for therapy for Miller Mair, a British clinical psychologist. He emphasizes the fact that a person may live a number of different storylines at any point in time, different narratives emerging for different purposes in different situations. As a psychotherapist, Mair regards this as an important issue, using the therapeutic setting as a way of bringing to the surface many different plots that a person may be living.

Mair and other clinical psychologists see their role as the repairing of damaged stories, or as enabling people to examine different plots that might be relevant to the same events. In the most extreme circumstances they encourage people to recognize quite different events as salient in order to build different histories for themselves, and as a consequence more comfortable and psychologically acceptable futures. But such reconstruction would probably be extremely difficult for most violent offenders. The different tectonic plates of their lives are often so distinct that it would take a major life-threatening upheaval to bring them back together.

For many of us the narratives we live are openly, often proudly, expressed. In our work the career path we follow is likely to be a public story of successes and failures with key episodes and central roles as well as many walk-on parts. In the family the roles of father and mother, son and daughter will have unfolding themes that also have a recognized progression to them. But besides these, and the other stories we live by, are the hidden narratives; the people we see ourselves as being. They will draw upon the experiences and developments in all the other, usually more public, storylines but they will also have their own covert dynamic. For most people these inner narratives are either consistent with the other stories they live or they are well hidden, drawn upon perhaps for reverie. For the violent men who rape and kill, the inner narratives erupt into action.

Many violent men are aware of the different lives they live, recognizing in themselves the extreme fictional expression of this state in the story of *Dr Jekyll and Mr Hyde*. In one recent case on which I advised, the police arrested a man who lived an apparently happy family life with his wife and two children. After careful, almost gentle, questioning the man said: "Look I want to tell you the whole story. I really got two lives." He then went on eventually to admit raping eleven women. Cohn Pitchfork provides a different, but equally graphic example. As he was being driven to the police station, having admitted his murders to his wife, he said to the police officers escorting him: "There's two parts to me, a good and a bad side." Then, referring to family and friends who knew only the "good side" of this ex-scout leader, he said: "I must let some people know what's happened before they read it all in the papers."

More recently Andrei Chikatilo, a schoolteacher in Rostov, convicted of killing fifty-three children and young women over a period of twelve years, said: "I gave myself to my work, my studies, my family, my children, my grandchildren, and there was nothing else in my life, but when I found myself in a different setting, I became a different person, uncontrollable, as if some evil force controlled me against my will and I could not resist." Yet the Soviet psychiatrist who interviewed Chikatilo said: "He feels no remorse for his victims, only pity for himself."

Culture

Where do these life stories come from? Stories and their associated scripts are all around us. Oedipus, Hamlet, Frankenstein, Jekyll and Hyde, James Bond, Clint Eastwood's man with no name, Rambo, the characters in *Reservoir Dogs* and many other well-recognized fictional protagonists all encapsulate strong personal histories on which we draw. In other words, the stories that we use in constructing our inner narratives are drawn from the culture and society in which we live. The exploits that one person extols to another, the achievements that family, friends and work colleagues admire or deride, the escapades that newspapers choose to report and follow to their conclusions, fictional stories from nursery tales to Hollywood movies with soap operas in between, all prov ide a rich repertoire of possible roles and ways to act them out.

Each person has access to different subsets of this repertoire and pays note to different parts of it. The salient characteristics of the actors in our scripts are also identified by the issues that are of concern around us. One consequence of this differentiation is that different plots are dominant for different groups. For example, the typical representation of women as victims rather than protagonists is reflected in the fact that it is relatively rare for women to write themselves into actively violent scenarios (except as victims).

At a larger scale it would appear that cultures, and sub-cultures, have dominant themes in their common narrative. Indeed, variations between cultures are variations in the stories that they prefer. The world-view held by a culture is a view of what happens to their heroes and their victims. There can be no coincidence that Japan has a high incidence of suicide and also enshrines within its classic dramas of *Kabuki* and *Bunraku* the resolution of the hero's central conflict by him committing *seppuku*. The differences in the way violence is handled on the screen, its causes and conse-quences, between the few films made in Britain and those made in the USA appear to reflect the differences in the degree and nature of violence in those countries. In many films from Hollywood the violent killing of another person is an achievement, an indication of strength of character. For British films it is more likely to be an awkward necessity or a sign of incompetence.

For violent offenders there must therefore be some significance in the stories they consider. It is a chilling fact that Duffy spent many hours watching videos before he first killed. Dahmer watched *Exorcist II* over and over again during his last period of systematic killing. In recent court cases of vicious crimes committed by children not yet in their teens, these children have spent large proportions of their waking hours watching violent films. There is no suggestion that the films caused these horrific crimes, but it is plausible that a person, confused about his own life story, could watch simple tales of violent heroism to seek out scripts that would give his life more sense.

The stories told in a culture both reflect that culture and facilitate the continued production of personal narratives, so that a cycle of mutual support is maintained. In societies where dominant non-destructive narratives break down, as is currently happening in the former Yugoslavia, then inhuman violence is legitimized and emerges as the theme of the stories many people think they should live. There is nothing new to this. Throughout history people have denied the recognition of full humanity to others with whom they come into contact. Centuries of religious wars against "unbelievers" and "infidels", the enslavement of other races and Hitler's "final solution" are all examples of how other groups are seen as less than human and therefore objects to be used, exploited or killed. The role of the vanquished is well defined in the plots which we teach our children. No amount of abstract political debate in former Yugoslavia can produce new scripts for the plots that the various ethnic groups have written for themselves. Just as no therapies have ever changed the inner narratives of violent criminals.

Twisted Stories

To decipher a criminal's actions we need to know what narrative he is drawing upon. It would help to know if there is a very large range of such narratives available, or if there are just a few key plots which each person modifies for his own purposes. Narrative psychologists are divided on this matter. Some believe that there is a limit to the variety of possible structures for all life stories. Polkinghorne, in particular, emphasizes that there are relatively few convincing ways of telling a story. Kevin Murray has even gone so far as to suggest that all life stories can be seen as one of four classic types—comedy, romance, tragedy and satire—equating them respectively with *M.A.S.H.*, *Star Wars, The Elephant Man* and Monty Python's *Life of Brian.* These benign examples may have some relevance to Murray and his students, but it seems unlikely that any of them captures the experiences relevant to violent rapists and murderers.

The proposal that people take their life stories off the video shelf does, of course, contradict the active, autobiographical quality that is so attractive in the narrative approach. The cafeteria view of life stories pulls the framework back into the realms of static characteristics. Instead of having distinguishing ear-lobes, criminals can be recognized by the particular heroes they endorse. Life is not that simple. Narratives are moving targets that change their shape in response to changing circumstances.

The questions still remain. Are there different types of plots? Is there a finite limit to the plots available? How are the plots constructed? It is clear that the storylines that unfold for violent criminals are a limited subset of all possible life stories. Comedy and satire are certainly not for them and it seems unlikely that the optimistic objectives of romance fall within their realms of thought. Killers and rapists live broken, destructive lives. We must understand how these distorted, disjointed, debilitating life stories are written.

It helps to remember that most violent men write their own tragedies against the backdrop of acceptable civilized behavior in which they are able to participate. In this regard they are akin to people who are required to live secretly destructive lives in the service of the state; spies, saboteurs and torturers. These officially sanctioned criminals have to build up new narratives through a learning process that moves in acceptable steps from the old storyline to the new.

Violent crime is not a broadening of experience but a narrowing of it. The offender's shadow belies the bleakness of his life, the two-dimensional existence in which the abuse of others becomes paramount. We will understand what causes these somber shadows by recognizing the limited narratives of these offenders.

Chapter Nine
LIMITED NARRATIVES

Consistent Patterns

The limits on the lives of criminals are implicit in the order of their behavior. Crime is not haphazardly distributed through time and space. Criminals are not a random sample of the population at large. Even the darkest human evil has a pattern. Whatever the attack, it contains themes, recurring elements, dominant characteristics, and identifiable structures.

A violent criminal's shadows flicker and change, but they are identifiably his. Like a predator that has only a few ways of catching its prey, a criminal has a repertoire of actions. The serial rapists and murderers we studied have shown us that this portfolio of behaviors can often be surprisingly restricted. The area in which the crimes are committed, the type of victim targeted, the approach taken to overpower the victim, and many other aspects of an assault are typically quite consistent for any one offender.

The range of crimes a criminal commits may be considerable. Certainly, young offenders are usually not specialists in the types of crimes they commit. Most rapists do have previous convictions for theft or dishonesty, but when they carry out their violent assaults they do it in a distinctive way. We have found, for example, that a rapist who commits a number of assaults indoors is unlikely to carry out an assault outdoors. Fewer than ten per cent of those that we studied have attacked both indoors and outdoors.

We have seen many examples of the criminal's

limitations. Babb assaulted only elderly women in a limited area. Nilsen, Dahmer, Sutcliffe, and even Jack the Ripper, were constrained by the types of victims they picked. All Dahmer's victims, except the first, were black men of a similar age. Duffy bound and mutilated his victims in very similar ways. The similarities helped police link his murders, and to link the murders to the rapes. Even the growing area of his offenses was characteristic of Duffy, just as both Sutcliffe and Jack the Ripper's avoided an area in which they had recently attacked.

Often a criminal's recurring motif will appear arbitrary and idiosyncratic. One rapist whose attacks were spread over a number of years always asked his victims if they were clean. Another made his victims solemnly swear that they would not report him. Yet another often told his victims that he had already served a prison sentence for rape (which was not true).

Consistent, recognizable patterns go beyond the usual notion of *modus operandi*. MO probably plays a less important role in actual investigations than it does in many detective stories. Attempts to produce computerized "M.O. indexes" at great expense (such as the system used by the British police, or the FBI VICAP system) have failed. Computers list particular actions or descriptions, but have no capacity for that most human of capabilities, the recognition of patterns. It is not the simple addition of elements such as the color of a car, the wearing of a mask and the selection of a blonde victim that form a pattern. A pattern has shape and meaning, it adds up to something more than the sum of its parts. It tells a story, one with an underlying theme.

The process of identifying significant themes, or facets of crimes, differs from the interpretation of a unique clue. Any action may have multiple implications, and various combinations of actions can change those implications. For example, the targeting of elderly victims in a city where many other potential sexual targets exist would carry very different implications from similar attacks in a retirement community. The meaning of a particular action in a crime lies in the thematic pattern of which it is a part.

The themes typifying individual offenders emerge from a backdrop of characteristics common to subsets of crimes. For example, the ages of offenders is not evenly spread. People in their mid teens commit the majority of crimes, but these offenses tend to be opportunistic. If teens continue their criminal lives, the nature of their crimes will evolve as they develop a more sophisticated understanding of the possibilities.

The average ages at which different types of crime are committed help us understand the unfolding life patterns of each offender as he weaves his distinctive web. Unfortunately, few such statistics are available. Most statistics are collected in order to reveal general trends and to predict future prison populations. From my own research and the few published studies, however, some trends may be seen.

People who commit a number of rapes on strangers tend to be in their late teens or early twenties. The average age of men who murder strangers is a little higher than that of serial rapists, twenty-three or twenty-four, although their age ranges overlap. The average age is also different for various styles of murder: a man who carries out a gangland slaying will probably be in his late twenties, whereas the person who kills an elderly woman during a burglary is likely to be five or ten years younger.

When other types of crime are considered, broad differences are also apparent. The average age of writers of threat letters and those involved in more complex blackmail and extortion is typically at least ten years higher than the average age of murderers. People who assault children are likely to be either older or younger than is typical for those who kill.

The typical young teenage crime is, therefore, a sudden violent outburst or unpremeditated theft. By the late teens a vicious attack, or prepared burglary, on selected targets is more prevalent. An older man, determined to kill, or to abduct young children, is likely to think more about how he can get away with the crime with minimum risk to himself. Children molested by strangers are likely to be violently assaulted only by younger offenders. Men in their thirties and forties who sexually molest young children usually act cautiously to avoid suspicion, such as offering to help fix a bicycle, or to provide some imported chewing gum, as Chikatilo did.

Some individuals may go through stages indicated by the changes in average age. But, even if they come to their crimes by some other route, their own stage in life will be reflected in how they commit their crimes. This suggests that the themes on which a criminal draws vary. They change as he grows older. These general trends demonstrate the need to identify themes across all violent crimes and not to focus solely on variations within one type of crime.

A further dominant characteristic of criminals may also clarify the limited themes that underlie their narratives. Men commit most crimes. Virtually all violent crime is committed by men. Criminal narratives must therefore be drawn from those that our society provides for men. Stories of nurturance and sharing are therefore unlikely to be the basis of an offender's life-story.

Central Themes

Themes about personal relationships are central to the criminal's story. Loneliness and the distorted search for intimacy, may ignite feelings of impotence and isolation, embedded in anger towards those seen as crucial in defining the criminal's identity, typically women. In their different ways, violent men attempt to use their victims to achieve their own particular ends.

Intimacy and Power

This search for control is reflected in the ultimate actions of rape and murder. The static, recurring components of their narratives therefore portray particular facets of the power they wish to have over their victims. Other facets will reflect distortions in the forms of intimacy for which they are searching.

It was Dan McAdams who emphasized that power and intimacy were the dominant facets of all life stories, but he focused on effective, productive life stories. The lives we are considering are the very opposite. The breakdown in the fruitful search for acceptable power and appropriate intimacy characterizes the inner narratives of violent men. These men are the antithesis of the processes that keep society stable; supportive relationships between people and the empathetic use of influence and control. Perhaps this is another part of the general fascination with violent crime. It reveals how readily the processes that keep society in balance can be turned inside out to produce mayhem and destruction.

Experiences

The impact of experiences upon criminal storylines— apart from age factors—must be carefully examined. There are also dynamic components to unfolding criminal storylines. As we shall see, the experience of the crimes themselves can change the criminal narrative.

The themes of intimacy, power and criminal development can be extracted from the whole pattern of activities in a crime. These themes point to different features of the criminal and can help in his capture.

Here, we are no longer merely identifying types of offense and offender. Overlapping criminal storylines generate a much richer matrix of possibilities than the limited typologies, as will become clear.

The criminal's personal narratives assign everyone but the narrator a subsidiary role in his attack. His personal vision is so distorted that he never gets beyond the childish view that others are objects to be used to satisfy his own appetites.

A Breakdown in Empathy

I suggest that violent criminals are incapable of creating private dramas (narratives) in which others share center-stage. Giving an equal role to other people is the major aspect of empathy because it accepts that others have life stories too. Without empathy, one can easily rape and murder. Violent crime, then, is the result of breakdowns in empathy and distortions in feelings for others.

For the detective an important question is the relationship between the roles an offender assigns to his victims and the roles he assigns to other people in his life.

To build on these ideas for detective work it is necessary to break the idea that criminals are alien monsters. Their crimes are a product of the inner, secret narratives they are living, not the public face they present to their wives and workmates. By watching someone walk down the street, we cannot decide whether they have a superb talent for mathematics or a special disregard for other people. Most human beings present themselves in socially accepted patterns, making variations difficult to discern during normal contact. Perhaps our fascination with violent criminals lies precisely in the desire to uncover the mystery of their hidden depths.

Yet these inner experiences are created from contact with others. They are the internalization of external events. They reflect the consequences of previous actions. There is there-fore likely to be some sign of what those earlier experiences have been.

Hidden Stories

What sorts of hidden stories do criminals live? One theme consistently occurs, that other people are treated as less than human. They become objects of anger or desire, vehicles to satisfy the perpetrator, jealously guarded possessions, targets for his vicious acts. The criminal cannot empathize, cannot assign an active role to anyone else in his life story. From this view there is little fundamental difference between murder, rape, violent non-sexual assaults or child molesting—all are onslaughts on other people. They may differ in the target or consequences of their actions, but the central theme is the same.

Many subtle variations play on this theme, each variation as characteristic of the person who produces it. The range of variations is immense: from the edges of an abyss of grotesque crimes—like those studied daily by the FBI at Quantico—to the fringes of normal, often accepted conduct, such as "date rape". All reflect man's inhumanity to woman (or man). For the detective, the particular shape of the criminal's story is key to crime solving.

The question becomes: what role does the victim play in the life of the offender? This will be revealed, at least in part, through consistent themes running through the criminal's actions, themes such as the vulnerability of his chosen victim, the risks in his method of approaching her, and the security of the location he selects for the assault.

The Search for Identity

None of us is born human. Our humanity is shaped

throughout our lives from contact with other human beings. As we grow we learn who we are and what are. Our physical capabilities unfold from our experiences, all shaping, urging or constraining our behavior. The person we become is neither God-given at birth, nor inevitable from our upbringing.

First dimly, then with increasing clarity, the young child develops an idea of the sort of person he is and his place in the world. This is an imaginative creation shaped by direct experience. It is an evolving personal history that acts as a script to guide future actions. We are each the central character of our own drama. Whether we see ourselves as heroes, victims, villains, losers or superstars depends on how we see our personal story unfolding. Our early years give us a view of our own worth and whether our personal narratives are romances or tragedies comedies or melodramas. Not only do we learn to be human, we learn what sort of human being we are.

The parts in our life dramas are not assigned to us at birth, although there may be a limit to those that we can most readily fill. In the first few months of life babies experience themselves as objects, requiring other objects to satisfy their desires. Slowly the child's acceptance of himself as a person grows through episodes of support or frustration, leading to the realization that other people exist whose experiences may be like his. But this process is never complete. There is always a search to understand the unique experiences of other people.

In our early years the inner narratives guiding our actions are constant modified. Initially, other people more rigid than us mold our clay. In leaving an impression of themselves they also leave an imprint of what it means to be human and of the significance of other people to our sense of ourselves, and the stories we live by.

Like the people in Plato's cave, we can only see the

shadows of ourselves and other people cast on the wall. We all develop an understanding of what the shadows mean by inventing stories to describe the actions we think the shadows illustrate. Our experience is central to these narratives, but the meaning and significance of that experience derives from how we are treated by other people; the parts we are told that we play in their dramas.

In part, our views of ourselves, and the views that others have of us, are defined in terms of what we possess and what we have achieved. In cultures that enshrine material well-being as the paramount attainment of the society, the role of possessions is dominant. This is crucial to understanding violent assault because in the early stages of human development no distinction is made between people and objects. The child has to invent the idea that others have minds; and experience time, space, delight and anger in ways analogous to his own experience.

Aristotle favorably quotes Plato as saying that it is important to be brought up to find pleasure and pain in the right things, arguing that it is from this appropriate search for reward that moral virtue grows. Where a person finds pleasure or pain will be influenced to some extent by the capabilities and sensitivities with which a person is born. How much it is influenced is a matter of intense debate among psychologists.

Some sex offenders, without doubt, have an abnormal sexual appetite, yet others do not. But whether a man with intense sex drive ends up as an isolated person who turns to serial rape or as a football star, regarded as having admirable sexual prowess, is a complex product of how he sees himself, the group he is part of and the mixture of personal propensities he has. All of these combine in the story he writes for himself.

It seems very likely that violent offenders' narratives are distorted from their earliest years in a number of ways. They may simply not have models of empathy from which to learn because the people around them never illustrate the relevant processes. Or they may be told conflicting things about themselves; a mother who dotes on them and for whom they can do no wrong and a father who demeans them, treating them as failures, are not uncommon in the background of violent men. But there are many other ways in which the growing boy can be unsure about his identity and unclear as to which of the available life stories is appropriate for him. He will turn to the possibilities offered by the narratives around him that often include violence, aggression and the exploitation of others.

A number of men who ended up as violent criminals experienced a period where their lives made sense. Richard had a skilled trade as a plumber. Colin Pitchfork was a baker. Adrian Babb worked as an attendant in a swimming bath. John Duffy was employed as a carpenter. All these men appeared to have lived "normal", non-criminal lives before changes occurred that awakened their dormant stories and led them toward rape and murder. At present we know very little about the backgrounds of those rare criminals who seem to come from caring, supportive families and become involved in violent crime for the first time after their mid-teens. I believe that distinct aspects of their family experience sowed the seeds for later violence, followed by critical episodes that allowed those seeds to thrive.

Many acts of violence seem to erupt at a time when the perpetrator is searching for identity and personal meaning. This may be why so many crimes are committed by teenagers. Adolescence is often the time when people explore the most appropriate life story for themselves and the boundaries of social acceptability are tested. In terms of future crime, these years are therefore crucial in determining which inner narrative will become dominant.

By the mid-teens most people will have formed a view of

their own identity that includes a description of their intellect, power and ability to cope with various demands. It will also include self-perceptions of characteristic ways of relating to other people and the significance of others in their lives. Part of this self-identity will undoubtedly include notions of what is socially acceptable and the extent to which the person will attempt to operate within those bounds.

If the view a person holds of himself is shaped before he is free of his family, it is no surprise to find that later violent acts mirror his actions within the family.

Sadistic criminals often were cruel as children and, for example, tortured animals. Just as the infant prodigy in music or mathematics usually grows up in a family where music and mathematics are encouraged and enjoyed, later to reflect this in the behavior the adult reveals to the world, in the same way there is a consistency in the earlier activities of criminals who attack people, clearly demonstrating through the viciousness of their actions the lack of any real awareness of or feeling for the consequences of their actions. Such men have usually grown up in a household where people were treated as objects, where feelings for others were less important than acting for oneself. Certain groups or classes in any society may be more prone to create families that have these weaknesses, but it is not the class membership that creates the propensity to crime. The conditions can be found in all social groups.

The criminological and psychiatric literature is replete with accounts of the distressed and deprived childhoods of criminals. Various forms of abuse and lack of support are commonplace.

But what is it that they have missed in their upbringing that can help us locate them when they turn to crime?

The opportunity of learning empathy has been absent from their early lives. The technical term used by some social scientists is learning "to take the role of the other"; to step inside somebody else's shoes and experience a particular situation as they would. In the language of story-telling, this is an inability to script dramas in which all the players have similar relevance. As Richard told me of one of his more violent attacks, "She was crying as I penetrated her, but none of it was registering." He explained that he got home through back alleys very quickly, but "when I got in it was just like it never happened".

In the home life of all children who develop as rapists or murderers I suggest there will be a social discourse that lacks real empathy. Often, of course, this is because there is no home life. The child brought up in an institution, where those who care for the children do it as a job, almost inevitably learns that he is a commodity to be dealt with. Half of the children brought up in institutions find their way into homelessness and crime. But many families create an institutional mood all their own. This may be through overt physical or sexual abuse or by more subtle indications to the child that it is appropriate for one individual to treat another as an object.

The cycle of destruction and abuse may stretch back for generations. People appear to be almost as able to inherit a predisposition to sudden anger as they are to inherit blue eyes, but this inheritance may not need to be transmitted through the genetic make-up. It can just as readily be communicated through the way parents and children treat each other.

For reasons not fully understood, such a background appears to be more likely to give rise to violent crime when it is the boy who suffers, rather than the girl. Perhaps girls learn to survive in these circumstances by writing stories that cast them as exploited victims, whereas boys draw upon the popular stereotypes of men as the users of other people. If you are shown from an early age that you are less than fully human, this not only leads you to think of other people as instruments, but also to think of yourself in a similar way. The two roles as vengeful monster, and as the instrument who suffers from other people may be adopted by those whose upbringing lacks empathy. In our culture it appears that women are more likely to accept that they will be used and men are more likely to seek reprisals.

The process of learning to be human is one of building a world in which contact with other people is satisfying and productive. The human isolation and separation that a generation of novelists wrote about ignored the fact that most people do not feel alienated. Close personal contacts provide a feeling of self-worth and connection to others. The term "love" has become trite and overused because it captures the search for personal significance, to become fully human through contact with others. Because we feel what others feel, most of us also feel part of a social group. For the violent criminal, various weaknesses, which everyone experiences (such as upsurges of anger, awareness of. Injustice, desire for revenge and lustful urges), are not tempered by any sympathy for the suffering caused by his actions. These weaknesses take many forms, their differences reflected in different types of crime and criminal.

This does not dismiss the variations between people that are present at birth. Just as there are variations in physical characteristics and the potential for some illnesses, there are variations in general, abstract intelligence, in the broad levels of stimulation people find most pleasant, and probably in such matters as extremes of emotional response, which may or may not be related to expressed sexual drive. But the distribution of these variations in the population is a continuous one. Subtle gradations distinguish people from each other. It is through transactions with others that the clay is molded.

The immediate family is only one part of the contact that shapes human experience and behavior. Studies of abuse show that it is often friends and close relatives who are typically the perpetrators, rather than the immediate family. We make as much impression by exposing our children to particular possibilities outside the home as in those we provide directly for them within it.

The extent to which an "ordinary" family can generate a mood that leads to violent crime is a vexed and open question. One brother may become a policeman and another a villain with little in their circumstances to choose between them.

Physical make-up and the particularities of individual situations cannot be ignored. Studies do report higher than average histories of head injury in some samples of violent criminals, but then there is a more intensive searching for such injuries in that population. One child may already be independent when a family crisis occurs that scars his brother for life, although there are only a few years between them. Another may be too young to be aware of the trauma. These are the complexities that will always keep alive the debate about the causes of violent crime. Many overlapping currents in a shifting sea of forces give shape to our actions. Dominant trends may be identifiable but the wave never washes on the beach at exactly the same spot.

Sexual Narratives

For violent criminals, sexual appetites seem to have acquired a particular significance in defining the person they believe they are. These appetites are a dominant characteristic of the protagonist in his personal narrative. They are not unique in this; our culture appears to give great significance to aspects of gender and sexuality as ways of defining people. For many of us the roles that we ascribe to other people are overlaid with sexual significance.

How is it that the acts of sex are so important in defining

who people are and their social worth? Why is it that a violent physical attack on a wife by her husband may not even lead to a criminal charge, while forced sexual intercourse by a stranger that was not especially vicious can lead to many years of imprisonment? How have the sexual act and the potential for the sexual act come to dominate so much of our imagery, literature, conversation and consciousness? Why is private sexuality so important that people who in all other ways are seen as capable human beings, are redefined because their choice of willing sexual partners is seen as abnormal?

One rapist asked by the police if he had any special sexual problems replied that he masturbated a lot more than was appropriate for a man of his age. "Wanker" is still an insult. Most people regard stimulation of the erogenous zones as a fundamentally interpersonal activity. It is this social nature of the sexual act that gives it significance and power. It is telling us a story of how we exist in the world, about what our roles are. Once divorced from a personal relationship, sex takes on a separate, tantalizing existence.

Newspaper and magazine editors have found that sex sells products, to women as well as to men. Stories of the love lives of celebrities excite enormous interest. Politicians and others in public life increase in significance when their activities as sexual partners are openly discussed.

Pornography takes this one step further. It treats other people as objects of desire to be used to satisfy personal lusts. It turns women and men into willing playmates in make-believe stories. For those men and women who have been able to develop some empathy for others this may stimulate the enjoyment of their partner, but if that ability to take the role of the other is weak or absent then pornography will feed the deformed imagination. Unfortunately, the debates around this topic are distorted with old religious and ideological confusions. Clearly, pornographic materials are arousing; and, by revealing possibilities, to some extent can reduce inhibitions. That is why they are purchased. Most societies have found that any agent that lessens inhibitions, whether alcohol or other substances, is open to abuse by people who are especially vulnerable to its effects. Controls are therefore usually placed on the availability of these drugs. If the effects of these substances become too threatening for society, they are banned.

The people who live stories that take them to the extreme reaches of violent assault and murder are limited people. Consequently they draw from a limited set of narratives around which to live their lives. These narratives will often be confused. The offender will sometimes think of himself as hero and sometimes as victim, but the repetition of his crimes shows that the themes shaping his life have not changed. In order to find these men we have to understand the different, interweaving stories they enact. We need to be able to identify each different drama that brings the "shadow play" to life.

The Structure of Rape

If we are to read the character of a criminal from his violent actions we must disentangle the various themes that distinguish one rapist or murderer from another. Any act can have many layers of meaning. The human horror of violent actions may confuse us, but as I learned from the cold precision of the FBI Behavioral Science Unit and my own studies of behavior in major disasters, it is essential to peel away the different layers of significance that encrust even the most extreme inhumanities.

For any violent attack there will be hundreds of aspects of the offense to be considered. Each of those can carry implications about many different features of the offender. The scientific quest is to identify the structure underlying all these possibilities so that a manageable framework can be created. What story does the killer's actions tell?

A theme is a coherent set of actions. For example, there will be some actions, such as violent coercion of the victim, that are common to all sexual assaults. But the sub-themes will be revealed in the actions that are not common to all rapes, for instance exactly how the victim is approached, or the nature of the conversation that takes place during the assault. In order to distinguish these themes, then, we need to establish which actions fit together across rapes. The co-occurrence of actions could help us disentangle the themes that distinguish one set of assaults from another.

There are many problems in building theories of criminal actions solely on the cases brought to me by the police when they are looking for help. These cases are typically ones that present particular investigative problems. Moreover, many details will be ambiguous or missing until the cases are solved. Therefore, once it became clear that psychology could contribute directly to criminal investigations, Rupert and I started to amass details of solved crimes that would be open to systematic analysis. Because of our early interest in sexual assaults our studies started with the examination of rapes of strangers. Since that time other colleagues have joined us in studying a much wider range of crimes, includeing arson, murder, sexual abuse of children, fraud and extortion as well as the more common crimes of robbery and burglary. The studies of rape have made most progress. The results of those studies indicate some intriguing distinctions that may well be relevant to other crimes. Thus, let us look at some of the results.

The aim of the studies was to find out which actions tend to happen in the same assaults. The actions that form a coherent pattern will reveal the dominant themes of assaults, the objectives of the assailant and, consequently, the story he is living when he carries out the attack.

There are potentially hundreds of actions that can happen in a sexual assault. The first stage in the research, therefore, was to define very carefully every possible action. So, for example, somebody who talks his way into a flat by indicating that he needs help or has lost his way and then assaults his victim was defined as using a "confidence trick" approach. The confidence trick then became a datum point for comparison with all the other actions in the crimes. A large number of assaults were then examined. In the following illustration there were 105 separate attacks drawn from throughout England.

For each assault a decision was made as to whether or not a particular action had occurred. This produced a table of assaults against actions, similar to the much smaller table produced to help discriminate between the ten rapes of students in the Midlands. To help that inquiry we needed to carry out an analysis that would focus on the differences between those crimes. Here our objectives were more general, some would say more fundamental. We wanted to identify the themes that distinguished all the sexual assaults from which our sample was drawn, to find the underlying narratives of rape.

A powerful computing procedure allowed us to represent each action—for example, whether a weapon was used, or whether binding or gags were used, the type of sexual activity and so on—as if it were a point on some abstract map of criminal behavior. Those actions that frequently happen in the same crime, taking all 105 cases into account, are close to each other on this map. Those that seldom co-occur will be far apart. What we found was that somebody who wears a mask to hide his identity during the committal of an assault is very unlikely, as would be expected, to make the confidence trick approach. Therefore, the point on the map indicating the wearing of a disguise is well away from the point representing a confidence trick approach.

In the present example we have thirty-one actions, so there are thirty-one points on the map. If actions in sexual assault were opportunistic and random, with no apparent themes to them, then there would be no discernible structure to this map and we would not be able to interpret it. Yet what we have discovered in a number of studies of sexual assaults, as for other crimes, is that these maps do reveal underlying themes. Actions with narrative significance are found together on the map.

At the center of the map we find the actions that are characteristic of rape in general: a surprise attack, the removal of the victims' clothing and vaginal penetration. Moving out from this central area are actions with lowering frequencies so that on the very edge are those behaviors that occur in only a small percentage of rapes.

The exciting discovery is that major themes distinguish actions that occur in about a third of all cases.

One region of the map relates to how prepared and organized the offender is, whether he brought material with him, such as bindings and a weapon to be able to control the victim readily at the crime scene. A second region has within it actions that are overtly aggressive, including attempts to demean and insult the victim. This sits next to the region covering all the different sexual activities that can take place, showing that a variety of sexual acts is a distinct theme for rape, although it is close to aggression.

A third region of the map covers bizarre attempts to develop a relationship with the victim, a sort of pseudo-"intimacy". In this assault the offender implies that he knows the victim and may even compliment her and ask her about herself and for comment on his actions.

These three groupings of variables seem to me to reflect three different themes, or indeed underlying narratives, in the activities of the offender. One is the man who sees himself very much as the organized criminal. He might be classified

**The Computer Analysis of 31 Actions in a Rape
showing their similarity of co-occurence and the
central themes characteristic of each set of behaviours
(Based on 105 cases)**

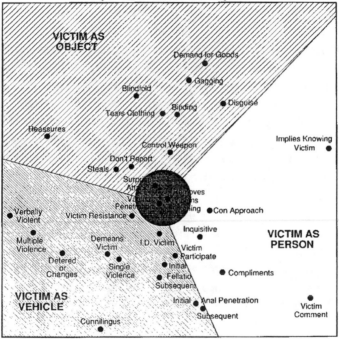

as a person whose storyline is one of effective control to get what he wants. The second is the aggressive offender who is reflecting his anger and his determination to exert his will on the victim by violent means.

The third is the offender who tells himself that he is developing some type of relationship with the victim and mistakenly sees an unfolding level of intimacy being produced by the sexual assault. Thus, the grouping of different activities carries implications for their central themes in the personal narratives of the offenders.

The advanced statistical procedure therefore gives us a way of bringing to the surface the themes that exist in a variety of sexual assaults and of relating these back to the general discussion on personal narratives that I have summarized above. The themes are not entirely unexpected. They group around the role of the victim for the offender and how he controls her to achieve his objectives. Of particular note is that the varieties of sexual activity are not distributed around the map; they appear to constitute a narrative in their own right. For some offenders the opportunity to indulge in a number of sexual acts with a coerced female is their distinguishing feature, although it comes close to violent demeaning of the victim in many cases. In other words, rape is not always about perverted sexual indulgence, although sometimes it is. It is about controlling a victim to achieve a variety of different objectives. Besides the distorted sexual relationship there may be the curious attempt to break through the offender's profound isolation by implying some sort of relationship with the victim. In the life stories of these men, women play very different roles from the object of sexual gratification in the former group.

Yet another role for the victim emerges from those actions typified by binding and gagging a woman before raping her. She is a dangerous object that must be trussed and coerced, whom the offender will neither attempt to demean nor cajole.

The inner narratives violent men write for themselves cast their victims in less than human roles. The horror of the actions lies in their lack of empathy and sympathetic human contact. We must identify the distinguishing features of these evil narratives to recognize the men who write them.

Chapter Ten
NARRATIVES OF EVIL

In building a psychology for criminal investigations, we realized that different forms of brutality and degradation, violence and coercion, could tell us about differences in the life experiences of the men who commit these crimes. The drama each criminal writes for himself features crucial distinctions that can be seen in the roles he gives to his victims.

Two Facets of All Rapes & Murders

First Facet: Whether a rapist or murderer treats his victim as, for example, a purely sexual object, or as someone to be insulted and demeaned, depends on his distorted search for intimacy. The particular forms of these distortions are key to understanding the rest of his violent behavior. What the criminal emphasizes in the vicious interpersonal contact is therefore the first major theme to consider when interpreting any violent crime. This theme shows the objective of the assailant's attack.

Second Facet: A second set of themes is revealed in how the offender acts to control his victims. The degree of power or aggression that he shows reflects his deformed approach to the control of other people. Variations on this theme run the gamut from Dahmer's acts of murder and mutilation to the verbal coercion and fraudulent coaxing of many child molesters.

The destructive mixture of a callous search for intimacy and an unsympathetic desire for control lies at the heart of the hidden narratives that shape violent assaults. The tangled variations provide a general framework for considering crimes as different as Ryan's spree killings in Hungerford and Martin's series of rapes in the Midlands. The offender may manipulate the broadly different roles he assigns to his victims, to exhibit different levels of power. The facets of intimacy and control combine to produce the unique brew that characterizes any particular attack.

Facet 1: Type of Contact with Victim

Even if we consider only three levels of lack of intimacy and three levels of violent domination, the multiplication gives us nine different potential mixes. This complexity is magnified when we consider the criminal's stage of development, too. Intimacy and power are two major components that describe the criminal's life story at a particular point in time. Earlier, we saw these as a "static" component, revealed through examination of any one of his crimes. But comparison between these crimes will indicate a "dynamic" aspect to his actions, the moving target that characterizes every life.

Therefore, as we have seen, to the first facet of the levels of *power* exerted by the offender, and the second facet of the levels of *intimacy* must be added a third facet of the *stage* in the unfolding evolution of an offender's use of power and intimacy. Together these three facets provide the dangerous compound that produces the particular offence. If we can recognize which special mix is revealed in a crime we can interpret a criminal's shadows.

To make this potentially complicated framework—of intimacy, power and development—comprehensible, we can organize these elements around one central premise: that the depths of distorted intimacy are fundamental ingredients of violent criminality. For simplicity, we will restrict the role of the victim to one of three levels: object, vehicle or person.

Victim as Object: The first and most callous level —victim as object—was clearly illustrated by Babb when he said that he liked women's bodies. The statement tells us that he saw his victims this way, as little more than animate objects. He knew there were certain things necessary to keep them reasonably comfortable, but he had no empathy for their reactions to him. In the assaults victims were not expected to play any active part at all. In these narratives the offender made no attempt to see the world from the point of view of the person who suffers his actions.

Victim as Vehicle: The second level—victim as vehicle —recognizes that the victim has some human significance. These rapists and murderers assign their victim a more active and sometimes even more brutal role in the violent drama. When Martin aggressively insisted on his rape victim "putting it in", or John Cannan, who was convicted of rape and the murder of Shirley Banks in 1989, beat all his victims beyond the need to subjugate them, they were both forcing their victims to carry meanings the men had derived from their contact with other women. The victims were not just objects but vehicles that had to bear a load.

Victim As Person: A third recognizable level of the role —victim as person—is closest to normal relationships in which the woman is a person with thoughts and feelings. The actual person is important in the formulation of meaning to the criminal. The brutal beating, and dismemberment of Lynette White illustrates the chilling attempt to obliterate a person.

Facet 2: Degree of Power and Aggression

The victim as object, vehicle or person implies certain reactions of the offender, but should not be confused with the nature of the violence itself. The violence is a product of the type of control the offender exerts—another distinct facet of the crime. This facet shows us how similar narratives, in terms of the relationship to the victim, can be seen in crimes as different as serial murder or "date rape". In both crimes, the victim may play a similar role, as object, vehicle or person, but the forms of control will be very different.

Total Subjugation. At the extremes of control the victim is possessed and reduced to total subjugation, but the significance of the victim to the offender varies considerably from one offense to the other. Mutilation of the body or extensive acts of savage brutality will take place when an assailant is transfixed by the need to exert his dominance to the point of obliterating his prey.

Murder Without Frenzy: In the chilling calculus of violence, murder without frenzy and mutilation is not the most extreme form of assault. It provides a second level for our facet of power and control. Murder can take many different forms and be committed for many different reasons. The framework here proposes that the difference will reflect the varying functions the victim has for the killer.

As we have noted, attacks on women rarely lack some sexual connotation. Murder of a woman unknown to the killer often includes overt sexual acts. Furthermore, a number of criminals we interviewed who admitted to serial rapes often also admitted they would have killed future victims if they had not been caught. Rape has the same roots as murder. The difference between the two lies in the form and degree of control the offender exerts over his victim.

Source of Satisfaction: The third level of control can therefore be identified when the assailant uses the woman who falls into his hands as a source of satisfaction for his lust. The desire for power over a woman is reflected in the rapist's demonstration of his own sexuality. By forcing his manliness upon her he feels that he is in control.

With a few central concepts a rich range of possible offenses and offenders can be drawn. Our research and similar studies, while still in the early stages, clearly supports the idea that consistent profiles can be drawn on the basis of intimacy and power. The following detailed examples help enrich the skeleton I have outlined.

Victims as Objects

The vicious serial murderer is often portrayed as a brilliantly evil man with superhuman powers of evasion, coldly prepared to wreak havoc and destruction. Robot-like, he feels nothing for his victims and is therefore able to torture, kill and mutilate without a shred of remorse—the kind of robot killers portrayed in Hollywood films and television programs. They all can trace their descent to Mary Shelley's monster created by Dr Viktor Frankenstein.

A close reading of that original monster story shows that what separates the nameless fiend from other people, and contrasts so totally with the reactions of his creator, is the absence of any remorse. Only at the end of the novel, with the death of his creator, does the monster show any sincere feelings for what he has perpetrated, but even then it is because this has finally sealed the loneliness of the monster's existence. Only Viktor Frankenstein had the skill to build him a female partner, so even this final loss is felt in entirely egocentric terms.

When considering real-life murderers and rapists who assault a series of strangers, *Frankenstein* offers a kernel of truth: the lack of any feeling for the victims, or the treatment of victims as *objects*. The cunning and unremitting desire to inflict pain and fear are not present in these men, at least not when they start their destructive adventures.

This lack of personal feeling is often reflected in the type of contact with their victims—in nondescript public places, on the streets, in supermarkets and parks, unless an accident brings a victim to the killer's door. Perhaps the criminal's sense of a victim as a person is less apparent when they are removed from significant places, products and people.

Bizarre sexuality often also dominates the personal narratives of these men. Their victims are little more than objects to be explored and played with. In extreme cases these acts have the strange innocence that will lead a child to take a toy apart, not realizing the destructive nature of the action. Because the real lives of their women victims are so irrelevant to these men, the women tend to be vulnerable victims of opportunity. Such men do not stalk and target a specific person. Any woman who is available and fits into the broad range of interest to the assailant may become a victim if the situation allows.

In cases where the criminal exhibits extreme control, where the desire to have power over the victim is especially intense, we find excessive mutilations of the victims both alive and dead; the keeping of body parts as mementos; cannibalism and other practices that treat other human beings as inanimate. A startling example of this type of violent offender was Ed Gein, a farmer from Wisconsin, convicted for murder in 1957. He kept relics from at least fifteen bodies as gruesome "ornaments" around his house. He started his ghoulish activities by digging up bodies to examine them, wearing their skins about him, going on to kill in order to obtain other body parts.

Albert Fish, convicted of murder in New York State in 1934, mutilated and ate his victims, most of them young children. He illustrates also how such men often regard their own bodies as little more than objects to be controlled. He frequently flagellated himself, burned himself and inserted needles and other metal objects into his pubic regions.

Gein and Fish are at the very extremes of sanity. The stories they and other similar criminals live would probably not be open to any coherent account. The offender has a virtual lack of contact with most of normal human reality, and an inability to distinguish thoughts from secret voices, or fantasy from reality. Such a state will color all the criminal's actions and make normal existence extremely difficult for him. He lives a grotesque, magical existence that keeps him in a twilight world of rules far different than those of ordinary people.

The term *psychotic* is often used to describe this group, dragging in with it such psychiatric classifications as schizophrenia and paranoia. But these terms of mental illness are not our focus here. Indeed, the courts in many countries have often found such extreme criminals fit to plead and sane enough to be convicted, and in some cases executed. It is also important to recognize that people who are mentally ill are only rarely violent. The axe-wielding madman is rare indeed. Most mental patients are far more dangerous to themselves than to anybody else.

These offenders are one example of a group that has no real understanding that other people do indeed feel as they do. The racist or fascist who defines people of other colors or creeds as less than human also exposes the difficulty he has in feeling the experience of others, but these very disturbed criminals take that process one stage further, not really aware of the existence of others, except perhaps in lucid moments.

Such an all-embracing inability by a criminal to feel the victim's reactions must put him on the outer edges even of criminal society. Personal relationships of any normal kind will be difficult for him. Other people are devices whose inner workings mean little. But he does not have to be obviously out of touch with reality in the sense that he is *psychotic*. He may be of very low intellectual ability. One man who had murdered a number of old men and women, evading police detection for some time, sat in the court during his trial masturbating, apparently oblivious to his surroundings.

Such rare offenders are unlikely to write their auto-biographies or volunteer to be interviewed by the FBI. Indeed, FBI agents who have tried to interview such men gleaned little from them, other than the extraordinary nature of their thought processes. The ones who do offer an account of their deeds are more intelligent and have some hold on reality, and some desire to keep manipulating their image of themselves through their actions.

In the FBI framework, these men exhibit the classical picture of disorganization in both their crimes and lifestyles, possibly moving in and out of institutions or living solitary, disheveled existences punctuated by the excesses of their crimes. In terms of detection, these men often will be known in the local community as relatively harmless eccentrics. From time to time, their erratic behavior may annoy people with whom they have contact. Their bizarre ways usually develop so secretly and slowly that their deeds come to notice quite accidentally.

As might be expected, their background and upbringing are typically disturbed and unhappy, spent in institutions with frequent changes of parental figures, in poverty and degradation. This does not mean that they cannot find periods of stability and sanity. Albert Fish was known in his earlier years as a shy married man who doted on his six children. Like all personal narratives, significant episodes can have great importance. Fish's killings started after his wife had left him. In fact, it is unusual for these men to still be living with a partner at the time of their offenses.

The driven, distorted focus of their narratives is so limiting that these men likely will travel far to commit their crimes. They may not even try to evade capture, escaping more by luck and the incompetence of local police than by careful planning. They are still often aware, though, of the criminality of their actions and may spread their net wide to reduce the risk of being stopped.

Once captured, they are frequently prepared to give a full account of their deeds. They happily speak of the voices and mission that spurred them on, keen to reveal the hidden narrative they have been living for so long; their need for human blood to fight the poisons around them; their instructions from God to rid the earth of evil. But these storylines have only an internal logic. They omit the more realistic facts that enabled them to continue killing: the reasons for hiding the bodies, the care to make contact with their victims without any overt threat, their change of venue once people had been alerted. The overt logic of the crimes, not the inner narratives, leads courts to find these murderers fit to plead—sane and guilty.

When possession and control are less extreme, yet where the victim remains an object, the style of murder will be different. Here the victims are more likely to be selected for very special qualities. Sexual contact will be more dominant than in mutilation and dismemberment. Murder will follow as a consequence of the violent actions, not necessarily as an objective of the assault.

These men have not yet found their way to more distorted perceptions. Thus, there may be little evidence of bizarre mental thoughts or psychosis in their actions. They are obsessed with victims and how they can obtain them. Dennis Nilsen, keeping bodies under his floor, and Jeffrey Dahmer with a fridge full of body parts are typical of this group of serial killers.

These men are obsessed with special types of bodies, such as young men or girls, and the desire to control them for their own special purposes. Their distortions typically are centered on the objects of their obsession, so they plan and think about their crimes carefully. They will try to create some lair in which to keep their prey without disturbance.

Although they may present themselves to the world as inoffensive, their hidden pre-occupations will tend to keep them separate from others. "A quiet young man," the neighbors will say, "we didn't see very much of him." He probably will hold down a non-demanding job that allows him the freedom to develop his hidden narrative, and does not require him to have much contact with people in general. He is probably not even aware of his own loneliness, so dominated is he by his secret pursuits.

When a rapist kills his victims in order to reduce the risk of detection, he is indicating an even more callous and egocentric view of his crimes than those offenders who allow their victims to live. Killing the victim treats her as an object the offender now considers a mere risk. Such a viewpoint is likely to come later in criminal experience, when the assailant has already learned to treat his victims as less than human. It is far along the road of evil. Later in the chapter we will consider this journey.

Babb can be regarded on the low end of control over the victim, while still treating his victims as objects. Unlike the "vampires" and "cannibals," violence had no dominant role in his crimes other than to keep the victim under control. But related psychological processes can still be perceived in his actions. The milder nature of his crimes was reflected in the less peculiar lifestyle that he, like other offenders in this sub-group, lived. These are men who are likely to be more in touch with those around them, although essentially they are still alone. Their obsessions have not yet totally dominated their lives.

These men will prowl areas they know will yield likely prey. Typically they will commute to these areas until the pressure of public concern, or police presence, force them to move further afield. They will say little to their victims, but may come to the scene with weapons and binding, prepared to overpower them with minimal struggle.

These offenders often puzzle those who arrest them, answering questions about their crimes in neutral, almost disinterested terms as if they do not really understand what all the fuss is about. At a psychological level they do not understand. The victims have no more significance to these rapists than does the quarry to a hunter.

I have argued that, in some ways, all violent men treat their victims as objects. In this sense they are all evil. But in order to develop our science, subtle discriminations are necessary. Men whose actions reveal no concern at all for the reactions or feelings of their victims, who at the extreme of control treat the actual physical body of the people they have killed as a thing to be used, have been placed in this first group for whom their prey are nothing more than animate objects. In the following groups the inhumanity of the depravity is less extreme. This makes the offenses no less abhorrent, but possibly more understandable.

Victims as Vehicles

When the murderer is concerned with what sort of people his victims are, and what they represent to him in his personal life, the processes of violence are very different. Here the victim must carry the load of the offender's desires. She is a vehicle for him to use.

Anger with himself and the fates that have led him to his desolate situation is the central theme of such men's stories. They cast themselves in the role of tragic hero, living out in their assaults the sense of power and freedom they feel is absent in the other stories they live. If our first set of themes reflects the offender's view of himself as a sort of nameless monster, this group would see themselves as more akin to dramatic heroes such as Oedipus. The fates have combined against them to deny them their rightful place, and so by seizing the moment they briefly steal back the initiative, recognizing the inevitable doom that lies ahead.

The most extreme examples are the spree killers who drive into fast-food restaurants and kill all, or who sit on a rooftop and shoot passers-by. It is difficult to see suicide as an expressive act, as a desire to tell a particular story and make an impact on the world around you, but when Michael Ryan went out with his assault rifle to perform the Hungerford massacre he was declaring his inner turmoil. He was a formidable example of a man who had to destroy the people around him to exert his identity, and in so doing, kill himself. There is a biblical parallel in the story of Samson who could destroy the Philistines only by killing himself. I have also noticed this "Samson Syndrome" in people who find that they cannot survive in an organization. They feel that if they cannot cope within the organization then it should not continue to exist either. They therefore try to destroy the organization before they leave it.

At a less extreme level of control, when the path to self-destruction is not so all-embracing, and the man is possibly more aware of a destructive mission, his crimes will take on a more controlled, serial form. Some of these men may even believe that they are grasping a mission that they will eventually want to describe. Many will wish to see their biographies written. They are the serial killers who will sit and talk at length to FBI agents. Because they are so willing to give an account of themselves they are often thought of as typical of serial killers, but this very willingness to express their views is what distinguishes them from other violent criminals.

Their ability to express themselves and to make contact with women is at the heart of their crimes and typifies the ways in which their crimes are committed. These are offenders whose native intelligence and life opportunities have enabled them to learn how to present a sociable face to the world. They may be labeled *psychopath* or *sociopath.* Both are curious terms that imply a medical, pathogenic origin yet in fact describe someone for whom no obvious organic or psychotic diagnosis can be made. The seemingly informed technical term is therefore more an admission of ignorance than an effective description. It is also confusing that the smooth manipulator of others is as likely to be called a psychopath as the man who carries out forced abductions and violent assaults with no attempt to "con" his victims.

The technical terminology is an attempt to characterize those people whose actions are clearly and consistently criminal, often violently so, but who seem able to reveal an inner world of thoughts and feelings that are not as bizarre as their actions. These are the criminals who come nearest to exhibiting pure evil. They know what the story of human relationships ought to be, but this always appears to be a part they play, not a role with which they are one. They can recognize what empathy may mean but they never feel it.

The play at empathy cannot be stage-managed without at least some glimmering of how others see the world. Therefore, such people are one stage removed from the sadistic and psychotic alienation of our first group. These sane but remorseless criminals have never fully developed the capacity to see the world as others do. This leads them to feel no blame or guilt for the consequences of their actions. Their lives are littered with people who thought that it was possible to share their feelings, only to find themselves used and abused. As rapists these criminals may use subterfuge to gain access to their victims, asking for help, then take advantage of their quarry's vulnerability to carry out their assault.

Their ability to make contact with others will often mean that their initial approach will seem open and non-threatening. But because their victims signify something for them they will select or target women of a particular appearance. These victims may therefore be conventionally attractive, or be seen by the killer as typical of women of a particular class or style. He will have much more apparently social contact with his victims than our first group, but this will be an interaction in which the victim has to be harnessed to the offender's will. It is not sufficient for them just to be used; they must be exploited.

Key episodes in the criminal's life story are crucial. The break-up of a relationship or the death of a loved one will fuel the inner despair that drives these men. In one recent case, following my work with the police, they arrested a man, who I will call Allan, for a series of violent rapes. They thought that a murder in the same area could also have been Allan's work, but they were not completely confident that he had done it and had little forensic evidence. Allan admitted the rapes but denied the murder.

When police officers asked me about the possibilities I requested details of the life crises Allan had undergone around the time of his crimes, a chronology they had not considered. It emerged that the rapes had started around the time of the break-up of his marriage, but that a month or so before the murder, the woman who had brought him up and who had always supported him had died, unexpectedly and quite young. I told the police that the coincidence was too great to ignore and they should keep a careful watch on Allan and keep in contact with his associates. Not long after, an acquaintance of the suspect reported to the police that Allan had confessed to the murder when in a very morose state. The reported confession contained many details that had never become public and would be known only to the killer and to investigators who had found the body.

These killers may apparently have much in common with those who treat their victims as objects, but there are a number of important differences. They will tend to have backgrounds that are more stable and conventional. There will be obvious episodes in their lives that trigger the emergence of their violent inner narratives. The locations they choose as central to their drama will be far from arbitrary and will go beyond opportunism. These locations will carry a special significance for the offender.

These men are extremely dangerous in any assault because there is no basic compassion on which they can draw to limit the horror of their crimes. The mildest reaction from their victims can lead to murder. Even those whose manipulation of others implies some degree of access, some possibility of sharing their victims' feelings, may still be so distant from any genuine empathy that they avoid detection by killing their victims.

John Cannan had been a moderately successful car salesman. He was a "lady's man" who had an affable, easy way of talking to people he met for the first time, polished by his education in an expensive private school. His family background, unlike those of most serial murderers, was unremarkable. Certainly his mother and father, brother and sister had no history of criminality or abuse. Yet he is now serving life imprisonment for the murder of Shirley Banks, a newlywed with whom he had had no previous contact. She disappeared from Bristol in October 1987. Her body was found 50 miles away in Somerset a year later. He also admitted to a number of violent assaults and rapes and was suspected of a number of other murders.

Close examination of Cannan's unfolding life story shows exploitative use of women. They were possessions or creatures to comfort him, never partners. He built up a private world, near alcoholic at times, developing an account of his activities that, increasingly, lacked any reality. From time to time he faced his own failures and this was followed by violent outbursts against those near to him. By his late twenties the pattern of superficially normal behavior had become the minor theme in his life. The major theme was using his charm to make contact with women, then raping and sometimes killing them.

Cannan is thus a clear example of the offender for whom his victims are vehicles to carry his own emotions; they have no personal significance. As one of the women friends whom he attacked said: "He only ever really loved himself." His anger with himself burst out in his sexual assaults, which he may even have believed started as viable relationships. There is still the search for control over others, but it is constrained by the desire to demonstrate some sort of personal contact with his unwilling victim.

In the FBI's definition of such men, they will tend to be organized in their offenses, traveling far and wide to make contact with suitable victims. The victims themselves are, for the offender, a reflection of significant women in their lives. Attempts to rebuild their broken relationships are central to their missions.

The confusion in labeling these men "psychopaths" is illustrated by the fact that they are just as likely to earn the label as the very different killers in our first category, who treat their victims as objects. They are seen as "psychopathic" because they appear to break all bounds of human morality. People like Cannan are put in the same category for a very different reason. They seem able to operate as normal human beings, may even be regarded as socially skilled, but they use and exploit their victims without any apparent remorse.

These offenders have taken longer to move along their personal path to reach this state of violence, with many broken relationships along the way. It is therefore not uncommon to find that they are rather older than many that we have been considering. Also, their previous relationships often have produced children.

Richard was not quite as far along the line of determined control as Cannan. For him the excitement came from the power and freedom he felt in the adventure of stalking and raping women. He had never had a long-standing relationship that he was trying to rediscover; his path of violence had opened earlier. His search for victims was therefore clearly one of marauding, moving ever further out into territories where he would be less at risk from alert citizens or policemen. The targets of his assaults were selected, though. He was a black man brought up in the streets of Liverpool. Almost accidentally he attended a school where most children were white, an environment where whites tended to be just a bit better off. When he grew older his family and friends forbade him any contact with the white women he considered superior. As his life story collapsed, he found a special excitement in overpowering attractive white women and raping them. He admitted that he had long thought of himself as "white with black skin". Somehow in his assaults he could live out this very different identity.

When the focus of his attack represents some particular sort of opportunity for the assailant, rather than just a body to use, there is an exploitative quality to the relationship between victim and offender which many women who survive find especially distressing. This is reflected in studies we have carried out of the traumatic effects of rape. Where there is some pre-existing relationship between the man and woman the victim is likely to exhibit more obvious psychological trauma. Indeed, the ferocity of the assault will tend to be greater for pre-existing relationships. I would suggest that if the rapist believes there is some form of existing relationship, whether valid or not, then the victim is forced to carry some of the attacker's anger, to be a vehicle for his desire to impose his will.

Victims as Persons

Those violent offenders who do recognize the existence of their victims as particular people get close to what many people would regard as normal behavior. Like the great majority of criminals, they see in others distorted representations of their own experiences. They try to understand the experience of their victims and often believe they have done so, although this is inevitably a parody of real empathy. The inner narrative of these men puts them as heroes in dramatic adventures. Here you find the rapist who has shattered a woman's life in a violent assault telling her to be more careful next time because somebody nasty could have attacked her. This is also typical of the rapist who so misunderstood the reactions of his victim that he agreed to meet her the next day, not appreciating that she would have the police waiting for him.

Violent criminals who come close to normal social interactions are those who expect to use others. For them the control of others is a natural part of daily transactions between people. Here you have George pushing his hand fiercely into his victim's mouth to control her. Men who carry out such assaults are drawn from a subculture in which sex can be stolen like any other possession. Some may be driven by anger, jealousy, desire for revenge over wrongs they think women have inflicted on them or a confused combination of these, but all are impervious to fear, shame, anger and guilt.

Bar room brawls and other forms of violence that police officers refer to as "public order" crimes fit into this category, as do the "domestic" killings that are the majority of murders. Often in these cases, it is an accident of circumstance which person ends up as the victim, and which one the murderer. A relationship between two people that has been tense for some time boils over into violence. Where guns or other weapons are readily available and are regarded as legitimate means for exerting influence over others, these outbreaks can end in death.

We have all felt annoyance or even anger with someone close to us; anger that would not be felt if they were anybody else. Who they are is pivotal to our reactions. This everyday reaction can erupt into violence if the criminal is part of a social group in which vicious actions are commonplace and possibly even accepted. Paradoxically, when it is important to the assailant that the victim is a particular person, not just a body or a representative of a type of person, there is a reasonable chance the attacker has a long and checkered criminal history behind him. Such men often attack indoors, near where they live, spilling over into this violence from other criminal activity, such as theft or burglary. Their actions though can run the full gamut from brutal murder to confused sexual assault.

Another of type of murderer, where the particular victim is important to the killer, attacks elderly people living alone, often frail women. These murders are often part of burglary or fraud, rarely with any sexual connotations. This type of murderer is typically an adolescent boy who lives less than a few hundred yards from the crime scene. Usually the boy knows the victim and may even be a distant relative. He has decided that the person can easily provide them with some gain. A particular person has been forced to provide for the killer. It is therefore less likely that the assailant will kill in this way again.

Rapists who seek out victims they can talk to, in the confused belief that there is some personal relationship in the assault, are only one step removed from the exploitative, murdering adolescents. The victim may be followed for some considerable time, her house broken into before the assault. During the assault the rapist may ask personal details of the victim such as her name and information about her boyfriend. These offenders tell them-selves stories about their attractiveness to women, sometimes even having the confused belief that once they have sexually penetrated them their relationship is assured. Rape can become a way of life for these men, their preferred form of sex.

They start their assaults close to home in almost a recreational fashion, quite often with friends. The rapes may even start as attacks on women they know, the partner of a friend, a girl met at a party. Such men will be known by their associates as two-faced, given to grabbing what they want without much concern for others. They may even have wives or regular girlfriends. The women who marry these men, though, are likely to be younger than their husband, subservient to him, and probably collude in the life of petty crime they know their partners live.

It is tempting to broaden this group to cover a great range of crimes founded in such destructive human emotions as jealousy, greed and indignation. But that would take us far beyond the crimes for which psychological theories and methods can help in police investigations. Where there is a known relationship between the criminal and his victim it is much more likely that established, competent police procedures will lead to the apprehension of the assailant. For cases in which there is no obvious link between offender and victim the characteristics of the attacks are important in two key ways.

One is in drawing attention to the possibility that the offender feels the victim has particular significance. The second is that many violent offenders who are known for their attacks on strangers (as vehicles or objects) have started their criminal careers with crimes against people they know. Understanding "the victim as person" may therefore be very helpful in understanding the genesis of most personal narratives of violence.

Criminal Careers

How do criminal narratives develop? How does a person continue to treat other people in so callous a way and move on from minor crimes to major ones? After all, criminals are human beings. Although it is tempting to dismiss the perpetrators of violent crime as "monsters" or "perverts", as people who are not within the normal realms of human experience, the simple fact is that, one way or another, criminals survive in our towns and cities, making some friends, holding down jobs, at least for a while, drinking in bars, speaking the local language. Even the most depraved serial murderer is not an alien being driven by processes totally beyond normal experience, if he were it is highly probable that the police and others would have become aware of him long before his crimes became a series. In 1888, a London newspaper commenting on the character of Jack the Ripper pointed out: "we may infer that the assassin must appeal to his victims in some way that disarms suspicion. In other words, he cannot suggest by his appearance that he is the bloodthirsty miscreant."

Such a comment raises the curious question of what a "bloodthirsty miscreant" should look like. Certainly in the last hundred years the photographs of serial-murderers that have covered the front pages of newspapers have usually shown young men of surprisingly benign appearance. Most people would pass John Duffy in the street unaware. The fictional characters who insanely devastate towns with chain-saws, who become transformed overnight, or at phases of the moon, into freakish fiends, the Dr. Jekylls and Mr .Hydes, are representations of how we feel about violent, unprovoked assaults. These invented stories may even relate to how some violent men try to excuse their own actions, but real-life perpetrators draw upon narratives that we all share. They have much more about them that is normal, everyday, than is not.

We cannot assume that the actions we see carried out by a man in his mid-twenties were potentially apparent in his actions when a young boy. Some of the seeds may be recognizable, but just as training and experience can turn one child into a brilliant gymnast it can turn another into a hardened criminal. Experience and training are involved. Learning to cope with your own fears, seeing the power you can have over others, getting accustomed to thinking of yourself as a man who uses other people's bodies, all these prepare and shape a person so that he eventually does go far beyond the realms of ordinary human actions. Focusing on the end result of these processes of personal development emphasizes how different these criminals are from other human beings.

Although criminals are limited people they fall within the range of human experience. They may be extreme examples of the human condition but they are not outside it. The themes to their lives are ones with which all of us have had contact. But for the men who rape and kill these themes develop and evolve far beyond the normal range. These personal evolutions of behavior have much in common with the normal processes of human development. The distortions of maturing processes, recognized in a milder form within ourselves, are at the heart of all criminal activity.

The men I have studied all have committed more than one crime, typically numerous crimes before they are caught. These earlier crimes will influence subsequent behavior.

The most extreme example of criminal development can be seen in Albert DeSalvo, eventually given a life sentence in 1967, after killing at least thirteen women. His criminal career had started by the time he was twelve years old, when he had been arrested for larceny and breaking and entering. By his early teens, which he spent in a school for delinquent boys, it was clear that he had an enormous sex drive and by the age of twenty-three he was charged with his first sexual assault.

In his mid-twenties DeSalvo was well established as an unusual confidence trickster. He talked his way into apartments on the pretext of representing a modeling agency searching for models. He was nicknamed "the measuring man" for touching women, whom he claimed willingly allowed him to record their physical details. After subsequent imprisonment for burglary his measuring activities became more violent, tying up his victims and raping them. The green trousers he wore during these attacks earned him the nickname, "green man".

The initial stages in which he had related to women as people, well enough for some to believe he represented a modeling agency, had given way to treating them as vehicles for his sexual proclivities. In the final stages of his violent career he started killing his victims and desecrating their corpses. This was when he became known as the "Boston Strangler". The women were now objects to him.

John Duffy also illustrates a parallel process of criminal development. In the earliest rapes attributed to Duffy, he was the reluctant partner to a more determined and aggressive attacker. He showed real concern for his victim and anxiety at being caught. He treated his victim as a person, although less than fully aware of the impact his assault had on her. By the time he was attacking on his own he had already raped his estranged wife. His victims were becoming more distant vehicles for him. Yet all these early offenses took place near where he lived in Kilburn. As I would now predict from his lack of extensive criminal background, he always attacked unknown women outdoors. Unfortunately we do not have full physical descriptions of his victims, but some that I saw did look similar to his estranged wife.

When Duffy started to attack on his own he still showed the attempts at intimacy and concern for his victims, characterized as typical of the third category of rapist. For example, with one of his earliest victims Duffy said: "If you do everything I say I won't hurt you." The victim also reported: "He fondled my breasts and said, 'put your arms around me and kiss me'". With one victim, whom he had blindfolded and left, he later returned to give her directions home. But as the location of his offences moved further and further away from his home, his need for control combined with his growing perception of his victims as objects to be manipulated, resulting in the carefully created ligature that strangled a young girl in a bluebell wood.

At last we can get closer to answering the question that Lesley Cross kept asking me during the Duffy inquiry. "Why had a man who had escaped with rape so often gone on to murder?" I now believe that the experience of rape without capture prepared him for even more violent crimes. His inner narrative led him along a path requiring more than sexual possession of his victims.

Chapter Eleven
DECIPHERING CRIMINAL SHADOWS

When Vince McFadden asked me to help his inquiry, virtually no one outside the police force and only a few inside, knew what "profiling" was. Today, a professional framework for police work is being built from scientific psychology, as well as many other sources. When firm principles for detective work have been established within the behavioral sciences, investigators will become more competent at helping courts both convict evil criminals, and free those who are innocent.

The suspect's "intention" to commit a crime is central to the legal case. Someone who goes into a house determined to kill is seen as more culpable than someone who kills accidentally during the course of a burglary.

The law recognizes gradations of intention: going to a scene with a murderous weapon indicates more preparedness to kill than hitting out in self-defense. But the story the court tries to establish assumes some single, central purpose, or motive, and attempts to see how that unfolds in the commission of the crime. The court is trying to establish whether or not a criminal is a badly-programmed Frankenstein's monster with uncivilized desires. If the offender appears driven to satisfy unacceptable desires then he must be locked away where he can do no harm.

The story of the crime takes shape according to how it is presented to the court, and investigators play a significant role in the presentation of facts. As we have seen, detectives have little formal training beyond what occupational psychologists call "sitting next to Nelly"; that is, learning through a form of apprenticeship from experienced practitioners.

But, with a firm understanding of the natural and social sciences, they can stop being tradesmen and start becoming professionals.

The decision about which person to present in court as a criminal should not be reached any differently than the decision to diagnose and treat a disease. A doctor is not expected to operate on hunch and intuition, to learn his trade merely from hearing about how others have treated patients in the past. Physicians have firmly established principles to operate upon, and procedures to follow. They are not expected to turn their hands to solve complex problems in very different areas of discipline without any specialist support. Nor can we expect a detective to do all these. After all, life and death often depend upon a single detective's decision.

Still today national trawls are conducted for potential suspects of many crimes. A man known to live hundreds of miles away is treated with similar suspicion as a local man. Yet we now have principles that could help detectives narrow the list, making wider searches unnecessary. These are principles, not procedures or routines to be carried out unthinkingly—as in the classic film, *Casablanca*: "Round up the usual suspects...."

Many police officers, knowing how a crime will be perceived in court, seek to identify a central motive that might guide the criminal's actions. If the criminal is out for financial gain, but kills to avoid capture, then that dominant motive will be used by the detective to look for someone with a history of theft. A man who rapes is seen as motivated by enormous sexual appetite and therefore is suspected of having committed previous sexual crimes. The focus on motive can lead officers to almost obsess about "Why did he do it?"

Legal accounts of crimes have a simple shape. A defendant had an objective and sought to achieve it by unacceptable means. This viewpoint may be helpful in court, but not in police investigations. The criminal may be easier to apprehend if his actions in one particular offense are recognized as the outcome of that offender's own, evolving story. Instead of looking for a man who has shown his uncontrolled sexual desire by assaulting a woman, detectives can search for a man who has found excitement in burglaries and now is building upon the feeling of superiority those crimes gave him to stalk and rape women

Our examination of criminal actions challenges legal notions of direct cause and effect, motive and mission. A rapist brings to his crime habits and attitudes that he has nurtured over many years. A murder may have been committed in the offender's mind many times before the victim was struck. The legal distinction between premeditation and impulse will usually be difficult to defend in the light of the life history of the offender. Motives, encapsulated in legal definitions of crimes, such as burglary, rape or murder, are obscured by the feelings of adventure, revenge, anger or justification within a person's own narrative.

The contribution of psychology to criminal investigations, then, can help replace the legal perspective on the narrative of crimes with the inner narrative that shapes the criminal's own actions. Criminals write their own stories; psychology may help us read them.

How can detectives read a criminal's inner narrative? If we look directly at his story we can get to the heart of his criminal actions. The narrative perspective, or search for a storyline, provides detectives with a practical, convenient framework for investigations. Let us review the basic principles.

Characters, Setting & Roles

A story is always unfolding. The actions in any particular crime are the culmination of many other activities and the interplay between many lives. The investigator therefore needs to try and understand what has led to the particular event.

The role of the main characters, especially the offender himself and the part the victim is assigned, will be the foundation of the story. The setting and meaning the attacker assigns to the characters will also help clarify his objective. The actions themselves will reveal the relationships that the rapist or murderer has established. At the heart of these relationships are indications of the particular types of possession and control characteristic of the offender's ways of dealing with people. All these aspects will show developments within and across crimes.

Separating Offender from Citizen

The psychological detective must attempt to fathom the criminal's hidden narrative, separating it from the normal, acceptable life the killer shows on the surface. These two counterpoints as offender and citizen are reflected in how his crimes are committed, telling us about different aspects of his existence.

Control: The criminal story unfolds skillfully, but it is always linked to a confidence that comes from being in control

Experience: The feelings associated with intrusion reflect stages in the hardening of a criminal's sensibilities. They are the internal counter-part to growing criminal experience. The way a criminal commits a crime portrays his experience as a criminal, loosely connected to his degree of criminal sophistication.

Personal World: The way in which the criminal's story unfolds will also tell us about the personal world he inhabits. Violent control over others will be central to his inner narrative. He will seek criminal opportunities to live out that story and may well have committed earlier crimes as precursors, or had relationships with other people that would reveal similar themes.

Fear of Capture

Another way the criminal's story evolves is through the degree of care he takes to avoid capture. The person who sees himself as a professional prides himself on not taking what he regards as unacceptable risks.

Degree of Experience: The extent of the criminal's history is revealed by the degree of experience he shows in his crime. This can be used to indicate how likely it is that the perpetrator is already somewhere in the police record system. The amount and kind of risk that the offender takes can be added to this formula to clarify his criminal antecedents and to indicate the types of crime for which he may have been responsible in the past.

Even if the police can locate suspects from their records, they must still select from many possibilities. This is where personal characteristics and the types of crimes for which they may have been convinced become highly important. In sexual assaults, for example, police in the past have often assumed that the offender is most likely to have a history relating to sexual crimes, indecent exposure, voyeurism or more violent sex-related crimes. This may be the case for the deviant individual who attack impulsively in settings offering a potentially high risk of detection. However, many rapists, possibly the majority, do not have any obvious history of sex crimes.

Structure of the Attack

If criminal history or behavior patterns suggest the offender has no prior, this fact in itself tells the detective something about his distinguishing characteristics. The nature of the relationships within the attacks—their shape or structure—is the key.

More erratic and eventually more violent actions can show different characteristics from the start. Duffy's skilled job could be gleaned from the planning and intelligence revealed in some of his assaults, but their varied and erratic nature suggested that he would not be a reliable worker. For Duffy, the vicious ligatures he used to strangle his victims revealed more about him than his signature at the end of a letter. They showed controlled anger, controlled to the point that even day-to-day casual contact with him would reveal.

Unusual aspects of a crime can indicate the type of alien individual others may recognize. By contrast, the preparedness of the assailant to talk to his victims reveals how comfortable he is holding a casual conversation and therefore whether he is likely to do that in normal circumstances. Broadly, being able to place the offender along the range from the bizarre psychotic to the misanthropic criminal enables investigators to locate them within their likely social context, with all its concomitants.

Role of the Victim

When not committing crimes, offenders develop life stories similar to those around them. These contain habits of thinking that carry over into how and where they carry out their crimes; their familiarity and knowledge of the areas where they live, their day-to-day relationships with other people. But, most importantly, they carry into their crimes ways of dealing with other people. The search for intimacy with a victim perhaps will be revealed through a paradoxical attempt to take care of her, in contrast to the encounter where sexual activity is the overriding objective. Women play a very different role in each case. Does he cast her as victim or culprit, as object for venting his feelings or subject of his personal drama? That is what he reveals in every aspect of his criminal actions.

Locating the Criminal

The possibility that we can locate where the criminal lives based on his "profile" strongly signifies how fundamentally limited they are. A large number of criminals live within a few minutes' walk of their crimes. We may eventually find those who do not live so close by studying the availability of targets for them and their access to transport. Their unfolding story may also indicate how far they have travelled to commit a crime. Those for whom the victim is a relatively arbitrary object are less likely to travel far than those who are looking for a special vessel for their desires. Both groups will broaden their area of search as they become more engrossed in their life of violence. Our studies also hint at differences between black and white assailants and those who attack indoors and outdoors. Distinctive subgroups appear to have characteristic uses of the city as venues for crime.

Changes in the law have increased demands on police. To make effective use of the limited time available during an interview, police officers must be much more prepared than in the past. Anything that might be relevant about the suspect could benefit this planning. In the future police may rely far more heavily on behavioral science.

If detectives do develop psychological understanding and associated procedures this will reshape how they organize their material for the courts. Replacing current types of criminal stories with the psychologically rich narratives that result from profiling may provide more convincing briefings for prosecutors, and thus have a far-reaching impact upon our legal processes.

A New Investigative Psychology

All of this adds up to a new area of applied psychology. It covers different facets of criminal behavior, developments of police interviewing to examine this behavior, changes in the group dynamics of police inquiry teams, and changes in the psychological theories and computing procedures associated with all these aspects of investigations. Taken together, they offer a coherence and focus appropriate to a sub-discipline that has earned its own identifiable existence. *Investigative Psychology* seems an apposite name for this field.

A person's shadow can be read because people have a coherent, interpretable form. Try as hard as we will none of us can act in a random way. No one can maintain an enigmatic persona for very long. My earlier studies of the experience of places and of how people coped when faced with a life-threatening emergency clearly show that people impose meaning on even the most fleeting or ambiguous of experiences. We all create significance in our lives through the actions we perform. For others to discover that significance they need to understand our acts and the meanings they have for us.

Violent assaults on other people reveal the personal narratives that both reflect and structure a criminal's life, the signatures from which their personality and way of living can be interpreted. As I have shown, some of these signatures are graphic, others subtle. If properly understood they give us access to many other aspects of the person to whom they are linked.

The storylines of violent criminals are different from those of other people in society because of distortions in their themes of intimacy and appropriate use of power. The distorted relationships they have with other people may consequently be of value in contrasting the criminal against normal society. The ability to relate with empathy to other people, and to maintain personal esteem without the need to exert coercive control over others distinguish us from rapists and murderers. The extent to which we cast ourselves in roles that recognize the valid existence of others is an index of the distance we each keep from becoming violent criminals. The ways in which we deal with other people indicate something of the inner narratives we are living, just as what a victim suffers reveals the inner narrative of the assailant.

By carefully following the actions of criminals, we uncover the stories they tell themselves. By staying close to the details of what they do, we are attempting to get into their shoes, not their minds. The same is true of the people we live and work with; the way they walk or laugh is not random, accidental or arbitrary. It can tell us something about them, provided we have the science and the patience to decipher it.

A shadow can be disguised, but it can never be shaken off.

AFTERWORD

Since the publication of the hardback edition of *Criminal Shadows*, many senior police officers mentioned in earlier pages, including Vince McFadden, John Hurst, Thelma Wagstaff, have now retired. The generation replacing them no longer sees offender profiling as some exotic idea. Journalists still get excited about the notion that psychologists are helping police investigations, but even they now tend to use psychological profiles as a standard way of filling out a story on a major case. In one recent investigation, that enthralled the national newspapers for weeks, it was routinely reported that "police and psychologists" were looking for the offender, as if everyone would accept psychologists' natural role within a team of detectives.

In all the cases that have grabbed the headlines since *Criminal Shadows* was first published, such as Cohn Ireland's killing of gay men, the murder of Jamie Bulger or the bodies found buried in Cromwell Road, Gloucester, the contributions of psychologists, using procedures that derive from those I have described, have been widely acclaimed as highly valued by police. All this is a far cry from the situation when I started writing this book.

Despite my satisfaction with the progress we've made in this field, many dangers lie in too rapidly assimilating investigative psychology into police work.

Few people in the police force are qualified to evaluate profiling or discern the quality of the information they are given. The mystical image exists of the quasi-magical "profiler", whose opinions are derived from his (rarely her) personal experience, rather than any systematic, scientific study. For some police officers, "profilers" have merely replaced psychics who were occasionally consulted before.

Many people who now produce profiles for police, indeed, fall into the same categories as psychics and are used by investigating officers for similar reasons. Some profilers may be able to help on some occasions, but, without any understanding of how they produce their reports, the results always will be wildly unpredictable.

An even more important long-term consideration exists. In order to have a basis for improving accuracy, we have to know how a profile was produced.

Profiles based on the intuitive creation of an individual with little scientific backing are just flotsam on a sea of crime. The scientific psychologist's role is to build sturdy ships that will help detectives sail through what almost literally amounts to an ocean of information. But there is no point expecting profilers to operate like "hit-and-run" robbers, quickly turning up at an inquiry and giving an unsupported opinion without time to closely study all the facts. We need to develop the science of Investigative Psychology.

Fortunately many police officers and psychologists are prepared to put forth the effort to study and develop this branch of science. They have already taken many ideas from the present volume and tested them exhaustively, developing powerful new theories and procedures of this model. Many conference presentations and academic publications have flowed from their work over past months. The narrative theory I outlined has proved especially fruitful and already appears effective in several areas of crime not mentioned in this book, such as robbery and arson.

Using the approach to offender profiling outlined in this book, an international network of specialized police officers and research psychologists has emerged. Their successes have been quietly acknowledged among police officers, but have not attracted the same public interest as the "hit-and-run experts". Curiously, the media seems less impressed that an employee of the police, whether officer or civilian, should use new scientific procedures to help solve crimes than that a lone individual, acting outside the police can give "extra-ordinary" help. Conan Doyle clearly has a lot to answer for.

Fictional accounts, such as the successful television series *Cracker* therefore continue misleading the public into believing that "profiling" depends on the special gifts (probably disturbed) individual. I strongly reiterate that the process of making inferences about a person from the way he commits a crime is a natural development that can be seen in scientific psychology, thus it is a teachable, learnable skill.

Using psychology to improve the effectiveness of detective work is only one side of the story. The answers a suspect gives to a trained detective, illuminate some dark corners of criminal psychology. The value exceeds that of simply helping apprehend the perpetrator. This new psycho-logical perspective will have implications for the judicial procedure as well as for treatment. Indeed, one police officer who had studied with me was asked in a courtroom cross-examination to prove his qualifications for saying the accused had committed all the rapes for which he was charged. I would like to have been there to see the attorney's face when the police officer replied with a detailed account of his own academic study of rapists' behavior.

Clinicians are already researching treatment programs that respond to the variations between offenders, drawing from the close examination of their behavior profile. For example, an offender who recognizes the human, personal qualities of his victim really needs a different sort of treatment from an offender who uses victims totally as objects.

Crime prevention procedures can also doubtless be

improved by drawing upon the psychological theories of profiling.

Again, though, a little knowledge can, potentially, be very dangerous. Juries, when presented with profiles whether for the defense or prosecution, will find it difficult to evaluate them. Opinions masquerading as scientific fact could be given too much credence by an ill-informed judicial system. The courts might be better off relying on traditional forms of evidence.

Similarly, clinicians might drift towards an investigative role, focusing on details of the crime rather than the nature of the person who carried out the offense. The only way to reduce the danger of the profiler's work being misinterpreted or misappropriated is to emphasize long-term scientific studies. These longer-term studies must address the central question: "How do criminals differ from each other?"

The criminology literature is remarkably quiet about variations between criminals, usually preferring to treat them all as one particular kind of person. Typically the variations mentioned relate to stages in their development as criminals. Yet the whole process of profiling is based upon the assumption that there will be some features that distinguish one criminal from another across his criminal career. What does it do for the theories of crime to propose that there will be many different styles of criminality? Are the causes of crime different for different types of offender? Are they likely to respond to punishment in different ways?

One of the meanings of "shadow" in the title of this book is that hidden, secret part of all of us we keep under control in order to act in a civilized way. Our shadows have criminal features. For a variety of reasons some people reveal their criminal shadows more overtly by committing offenses.

By understanding more fully the shadows revealed by criminals we will gain deeper insights into our own being.

ACKNOWLEDGEMENTS

Rupert Heritage is present on most of the pages of this book, which would never have existed without his full co-operation. I hope it is a suitable tribute to his wit and friendship. More recently two other police officers, Rick Holden and Stuart Kirby, have taken up studies with me. Many of the things they have taught me have found their way into the present volume. I am very grateful to them for their insights and goodwill.

A number of senior police officers have supported and helped the work covered in this book and contributed to its subsequent development. Out of many, I owe very special gratitude to John Grieve, Vince McFadden and Thelma Wagstaff. They all openly welcomed me into the world of criminal investigations. I also greatly appreciate the support which John Hurst and John Stevens have continued to give me and my colleagues.

With some temerity I approached police officers who had been involved in the various cases that I describe in the book, asking them to look over the chapters I had written. Without exception they responded quickly and with courtesy, giving me detailed comments on the veracity of what I had written as they saw it. So, although they cannot be held responsible for my account of the investigations, I am grateful for their careful assistance. My contacts with the police have, however, taught me a certain discretion. I therefore think that it is probably best not to mention their names. However, there is no secret that the following forces have been of tremendous help both while I was writing this book and also in helping my colleagues me in the study of criminal behavior: Greater Manchester, Metropolitan, South Wales, Surrey and West Midlands. Other police forces and police officers also continue to contribute to the Investigative Psychology research and teaching at the University of Surrey. I hope they will see this book as at least a small, constructive repayment of the debt I owe them.

My secretary at the University of Surrey has specifically asked not to be named in this book. I am happy to acknowledge her help which is never anonymous.

Over a number of years Rupert and I have been privileged to keep in contact with the Behavioral Science Unit at Quantico. Robert (Roy) Hazelwood, Bob Ressler, Jannet Warren have been especially kind, and generous, John Douglas, Roland Reboussin and Ann Burgess also shared with us their thoughts, experiences and reports. The friendly guidance and warm encouragement them and their colleagues have been a continual source of inspiration. Their pioneering work and productive insights are the foundation of this book.

At the University of Surrey I have been particularly fortunate in the backing I have received from my colleagues. The Vice Chancellor, Anthony Kelly, has gone out of his way to facilitate my research and the writing of this book. Indeed it was from him that I appreciated the significance of Plato's shadows to the theme of my book. He gave me the greatest gift of all when he allowed me to take a sabbatical in which to write. Glynis Breakwell readily shouldered my administrative responsibilities to become Head of the Psychology Department, in which he has continued to assist my writing and thinking, ling many valuable comments on the manuscript unfurled. The sub-librarian for psychology, Mark Ashworth, has given me assistance far beyond the call of duty.

A number of undergraduates at the University of Surrey have worked with me during the writing of this book, giving help and advice in many ways. They include Adam Gregory (who helped prepare the illustrations for this book), Helen Hughes, Paul Larkin, Ellen Tzang and Graeme Vaughan. Many postgraduates have also contributed to my thinking, and added to the excitement of working in this area. They include Anne Davies, Jennifer Kilcoyne, Chris Missen and Jenny Ward. David Jordan deserves a special mention for making available to me his invaluable undergraduate dissertation on Michael Ryan.

Other friends have also eased the birth-pangs of this book. Elliott Leyton has been unstinting with his guidance and reassurance, allowing me to benefit from his enormous experience of writing and of killers. Eric Clarke and Les Blair both took time to show me where it was productive to focus. Celia Kitzinger and Amita Sinha have each given me a unique perspective of great value. Lorraine Nanke got me into crime and has continued to give me the benefits of her advice. Patrick Fleming, the television documentary director who put me in a helicopter over Birmingham, very kindly made his production notes available to me. His encouragement throughout the writing of this book is much appreciated. Thanks are also due to Margaret Wilson and Lynne Martin for details of their work on detectives' decision making.

I don't know who A. P. Watt was or is, but the agency that takes his or her name has provided me with the most delightful support team that an author could ever want. Imogen Parker nursed the book into being and saw it through various crises, Derek Johns charmingly continued her work while Nick Marston dealt wonderfully with the media spin-off.

My children have all made the work on this book more bearable. Hana reminded me not to become insensitive to horror of the material with which I have had to deal.

She has also done an excellent job in helping me to put

together the source notes and bibliography and in preparing the index. Daniel, Lily and my wife Sandra helped to ensure that I did not lose touch with the delights of day-to-day reality as I got absorbed by this writing project.

Without Sandra's love and support, as well as the benefits of her profound understanding of human nature, I'd never have written this book. This book is dedicated to her with deep love and appreciation for everything she shared with me.

REFERENCES AND NOTES

Throughout this book "he" is used to describe criminals and the victims are usually assumed to be women. This is because all the offenders I have considered in this book have been men and the great majority of their victims have been female. I know that men are often victims of sex crimes as well as other crimes and that there are an increasing number of violent female offenders.

However, the important matters raised by the existence of male victims and female offenders are not dealt with in the present volume. In the following notes books listed in the Select Bibliography are indicated by author and date. However, because I drew upon the books in the Select Bibliography throughout the writing of *Criminal Shadows*, I have indicated only very direct citations in the following notes.

The opening quote from G. S. Howard is from *Culture Tales: a Narrative Approach to Thinking, Cross-Cultural Psychology and Psychotherapy*, American Psychologist, March 1991, Vol. 46 No. 3, pp. 187-97. On page 196 Howard says that it is a paraphrase of Shakespeare, but Professor Howard has informed me that he cannot remember which quote it paraphrases.

ONE: A BETTER NET

See Kind (1987) and Swanson et al. (1992) for details of the information available at crime scenes and from witnesses.

The idea that it is possible to identify criminals from

their looks is most vividly explored in the works of Lombroso, discussed in Chapter Nine. Giovanni Morelli, the Victorian art connoisseur, who used details such as ears to identify fake paintings, possibly laid the foundations for the search for anomalies of a more psychological kind. See James Hairs article in the *Guardian* 15 July 1992 "An ear for authenticity", p 36.

The term "serial murderer" can be traced to J. Brophy, *The Meaning of Murder* (London: Corgi, 1966), p. 172: "Jack the Ripper, still unidentified and still the most famous of all serial murderers", pre-dating the FBI use of the term "serial killer" in the mid-1970s (Ressler and Shachtman, 1992, p. 35).

The historical development of our understanding of the psychology of insanity and its relationship to the development of medicine is summarized in Hearnshaw (1989).

Police Review, 22 January 1993,pp. 16-18 captures the interest by police officers in the application of psychology to detective work.

An account of the emergence of "The M'Naghten Rules" is given in Wilson and Herrnstein (1985), pp. 502-6.

The significance of forgetting a name was explored by Sigmund Freud in one of his earliest books, *The Psychopathology of Everyday Life*, first published in 1904.

An obituary of Dr Thomas Bond is given in the *Westminster Hospital Reports* for 1901, available in Cambridge University Library.

Haward, L. R. C. (1981), *Forensic Psychology*. London: Batsford. Gives a number of accounts of psychological contributions to military and police investigations.

Langer, W. (1972), *The Mind of Adolph Hitler*. New York: New American Library.

Watson, P. (1980), *War on the Mind.* London: Penguin. Describes a number of psychological contributions to military/political strategy.

Rendell, R. (1991), *Devices and Desires*. London: Penguin.

Tullet, T. (1986), *Clues to Murder: Famous Forensic Murder Cases of Professor J. M. Cameron*. London: Grafton Books

The development of the FBI profiling activities is best gleaned from Ressler (1992) and Hazelwood and Burgess (1987). Colin Wilson and Donald Seaman also provide accounts of a number of cases in their 1990 book *The Serial Killers: A Study of the Psychology of Violence* (London: W. H. Allen). The role of Brussel is also discussed in Leyton 1986).

Rumbelow, D. (1988), *The Complete Jack the Ripper*. London: Penguin.

Cross, K. (1981), *The Yorkshire Ripper*. London: Granada.

Wambaugh (1989) gives a very full account of the investigation leading to the arrest of Colin Pitchfork.

Canter, D. (ed.) (1990), *Fires and Human Behavior*. London: David Fulton.

Police and Criminal Evidence Act (1984) London HMSO
Shepard, M. (1985),*Sherlock Holmes and the Case of Dr Freud*. London: Tavistock Publications.

TWO: FIRST PRINCIPLES

Although the "hand-to-mouth" funding of research is still typically as indicated in this chapter, I am happy to acknowledge the support given by the Home Office, the US Army Basic Research Institute, DEC plc and the University of Surrey, for studies conducted subsequent to those reported in this book.

Accounts of the investigations leading to the arrest and conviction of John Duffy were given in most national newspapers on 15 and 16 January 1988, including; the Daily

Telegraph, Daily Mail and the Guardian. The Surrey Advertiser gave a particularly full account.

The computer-based statistical analysis mentioned in this chapter is the same as that described in Chapters Seven and Ten, technical details of which are given in Canter (1985). A brief summary of how the statistical analysis works is given in the notes to Chapter Seven.

The various psychological approaches to human development are briefly reviewed in Chapter Nine.

Psychological considerations of eyewitness testimony are given in Raskin (1989) and Stephenson (1992).

One study to illustrate the wide-ranging criminal experience of rapists is Scully (1990).

The learning of sexual behavior is discussed in Masters, W. H. and Johnson, V. B. (1966), *Human Sexual Response*. Boston: Little Brown.

The tourniquet quotation is taken from *Encyclopaedia Britannica* (1964), article on First Aid, Vol 9, p. 313.

Locard, B. (1931-39), *Traité de criminalistique* (7 vols). Lyon: Joannes Desvigne et ses Fils. d

THREE: ENRICHING INTUITION

Maltz, M. D., Gordon, A. C. and Friedman, W. (1991), *Mapping Crime in its Community Setting: Event Geography Analysis*, New York: Springer-Verlag.

Ratledge, B. C. and Jacoby, J. E. (1989), *Handbook on Artificial Intelligence and Expert Systems in Law Enforcement*. New York: Greenwood.

Groth, A. N., Burgess, A. W. and Holmstrom, L. L (1977), *Rape: Power, Anger and Sexuality*, American Journal of Psychiatry, Vol. 134, No. 11, pp. 1239-43.

See the following for further details on the work at Quantico: Házelwood and Burgess (1987); Kessler and Shachtman (1992); Ressler et al. (1988).

Perkins (1981) has a full exploration of the nature of intuition.

Holmes, K. N. *(1989), Profiling Violent Crimes: an Investigative Tool.* London: Sage. Provides a general overview of profiling as an art.

FOUR: CRIMINAL MAPS

Canter, D. and Larkin, P. (1993), "The Environmental Range of Serial Rapists", *Journal of Environmental Psychology*, Vol. 13, No. 1, pp. 63-9.

Brantingham, P. J. and P. L. (eds) (1981), *Environmental Criminology. Beverly Hills: Sage.* Covers most of the early studies on the geography of crime.

Evans, D. J. and Herbert, D. T. (eds) (1989), *The Geography of Crime.* London: Routledge. Reviews further issues in environmental criminology.

Begg, P. (1988), *Jack the Ripper: the Uncensored Facts.* London: Robson Books.

Scully (1990).

Morris, T. (1957) *The Criminal Area: a Study in Social Ecology.* London: Routledge and Kegan Paul.

Barker, M. (1989), *Criminal Activity and Home Range: a Study of the Spatial Offence Patterns of Burglars.* MSc Thesis, University of Surrey (unpublished).

Canter, D. (1977), *The Psychology of Place.* London: Architectural Press.

Hickey (1991); Kind (1987).

The Notting Hill rapes are considered in e.g. The Times, 7 April 1989.

FIVE: CONSISTENT CLUES

The Tower Block rapes are covered in the *Birmingham Post* and *Evening Mail*, 21 December 1989.

SIX: DISTINGUISHING ACTIONS

Groth, A. N. and Burgess, A. W. (1977), "Sexual Dysfunction During Rape", New England Jrnl of Medicine, vol. 297, no. 4, pp. 764-6.

Additional References and Notes

The statistical procedures described in this and subsequent chapters are a subset of the family of multivariate analysis procedures known as non-metric multi-dimensional scaling (Canter, 1985). The following description gives an indication of how these procedures work.

The computer deals with each crime as a row and all the types of behaviors that occur as columns. The first crime is the first row, below it is a row for the second crime and so on. Forcing their way down through these rows is a tuned platoon of actions, each action a column on its own. For the Midlands rapes, the first column indicated (a) whether the criminal in each offence row had gained entry to the house by a window. The second was (b) whether he had brought a weapon to the scene with him, and so on. The other eight behaviors were: whether or not (c) the victim was blindfolded, (d) the offender was masked, (e) the offender attempted to reassure the victim she would not be hurt, (f) the offender was viciously violent, (g) gagging was with a hand or cloth, (h) cunnilingus occurred, (i) fellatio occurred, (j) fondling occurred. These ten actions, (a) to (j), were found to be effective in pinning down the actions for the range of crimes in the Midlands. The rows and columns are known as a "data matrix".

Armed with this matrix of rows and columns it was possible to indicate at the intersection of these two phalanxes whether the particular action had occurred in the particular offence. The computers we used prefer a 1 if the action did not occur and a 2 if it did. Filling in the numbers from a close reading of the statements by the victims is a quite precise creation of a "profile", in a technical mathematical sense, of the offender as revealed through his actions. Each row of 1s and 2s looks much like any other string of numbers that might be used to feed the inexhaustible appetite of a modern computer.

Each row of 1s and 2s provides a very precise profile of the actions that happened in one offence. It is a real profile in the direct sense of specifying the outline of the offender's actions.

The computer can bring this flat fabric into a lurching semblance of life, forcing the numbers to reveal some of their secrets. Or, like raw recruits who have been through basic training, the platoon of 1s and 2s can be paraded through various maneuvers until their underlying similarities and differences can be seen.

The task was to establish, first, if there were subsets of crimes that shared characteristics to the extent that we could reasonably assume that the same person was responsible. We could then build a better understanding of the perpetrators from the common characteristics of each subsets examining changes within them over time, and groupings in particular parts of the city, as well as particular reactions to certain victims. These patterns can also be compared with the patterns of known criminals. It seems reasonable to assume that the personal profile of known criminals would be parallel to those of the unknown assailants who had a similar behavioral profile. A simple example would be that if two attackers both snapped instructions at their victims in what might be thought of as a military style and we knew one had had a military training, then a reasonable starting point would be to assume that the unknown attacker had a military background as well. Of course, the more examples of behavior we could compare the more confidence we would have in our assumptions. But how are we to compare these patterns of behavior?

Like rows of soldiers, we had a platoon of numbers standing in lines one behind the other. The comparison of one row with another is the computer's way of comparing one crime pattern with another. Similarities between each row had to be assigned a value. We had to measure the correlation between the crimes. This is done by mathematical comparison of the string of 1s and 2s. The highest correlation between two crimes would be produced if the profile of 1s and 2s were the same for each row; the lowest if they were opposite (1,2,1,1, for example, being challenged by 2,1,2,2). All the values between indicate the other degrees of similarity. The calculations are unbiased and objective in not giving special weight to any particular action that might apparently seem especially awful.

Such calculations are meat and drink for the modern electronic computer. Reducing it to its simplest, it is straightforward to work out the total number of times the figures in each row are the same as each other. This total is an index of just how close, in broad, direct terms, is the similarity between the pattern of behaviors for each crime. Statistically we have done something quite bold here. Two strings of qualities have been compared and an overall quantity has been derived to indicate their similarity.

This enables us to move from the world of descriptions, where like can only be compared with like, to the much more manageable world of arithmetic in which measures of similarity, correlations, can be manipulated to reveal underlying trends.

In order to make sense of the similarities and differences of the ten crimes we were concerned with in the Midlands, it was necessary to consider all the possible correlations between the crimes. There are ten crimes of interest. Elementary mathematics reveals that if every crime is compared with every other one we would end up with forty five comparisons. This would seem to add to the complexity of what we are studying rather than simplifying it

Fortunately, statistically-minded-psychologists have developed many procedures for reducing the complexity inherent in multiple comparisons and revealing the central trends behind all the correlations. The approach used in the present book (described in detail in Canter, 1985) is based on having each row of numbers, each crime, represented as a point in space. This is one of those abstract spaces in which mathematicians like to live. It floats, unfixed, defined entirely by what is going on within it. But the easiest way to think of it is as a blank, empty square. Inside this square there are points. Each of these points represents a crime; in the Midlands case ten points for ten crimes.

The statistical cunning comes from the process of assigning points to locations in this space. This process can be thought of as fastening each point to every other one with a piece of string. The length of the string represents how unlike the two crimes are. The shorter the string the higher the correlation between crimes. The computer attempts to pull all these strings tight so that the closer together any two points representing two crimes, the more similar are the actions in those two crimes. The points in the square will therefore be spread out in clusters, not unlike constellations of stars in the night sky. These groupings help us to see, in one summary picture, what is going on across a number of crimes at once, but they did not tell us definitively which crimes were distinct from which others. They gave us a basis on which to build the case for such distinctions.

There is one important technical problem in all this drawing of maps from correlations. Only in circumstances where the mathematics were exceptional would all the strings become taut on a flat sheet of paper. On a limiting two-dimensional surface it would be only under very special conditions that the relationships could be mapped within those constraints. They would always end up with an approximation. Some of the pieces of string would be slack and some would be stretched, possibly beyond breaking point. The computer gives the best approximation to a map that it can.

In the Midlands investigation we already had information available on a known London rapist We therefore took the details of three of his offences (simply adding a further three rows o the data matrix and repeated the analysis for all thirteen crimes. We found that the "marker" crimes from London did help to clarify some of the ambiguities that were present when the Midlands cases were the only ones that the computer analyzed, by spreading out the Midlands rapes into more distinct groups.

SEVEN: OBJECTS OF MURDER

Toolis, K. (1991), "The Game of Love and Death", *Weekend Guardian*, 11-12 May, pp. 4-6.

The feminist view of rape is discussed in Scully (1990).

Jordan D. (1988), *A Psychology of Mass Murder, BSc Thesis, Portsmouth -Polytechnic* (unpublished), provided me with considerable detail on the life and death of Michael Ryan.

The high prevalence of existing relationships between murderer and victim is clear from *Home Office reports, e.g. Criminal Statistics: England and Wales* 1990. London: HMSO (Cmnd 1935), p. 81.

EIGHT: STORIES WE LIVE BY

The terms "plot", "story", "narrative"; "theme", "plan", "goal" and a number of others, can be distinguished in important ways for further elaboration of the issues in this chapter, but that would take the discussion into academic niceties that are inappropriate for the present book.

Wilson and Herrnstein (1985) Bartol, C. R. (1991), *Criminal Behavior: a Psychosocial Approach.* Englewood Cliffs: Prentice

References and Notes

Malone, Dr. Gary L, medical director and chief of psychiatry at All Saints Episcopal Hospital in Fort Worth, Texas. He is an assistant clinical professor of psychiatry at Southern Medical School, and a teaching analyst in the Dallas Psychoanalytic Institute.

Hollin, C. R. (1989), *Psychology and Crime: an Intro-duction to Criminological Psychology.* London: Routledge.

Sutherland (1978) is the general reference, but the quotations are taken from the third edition published in 1939.

Lombroso, C. (1911/1968), *Crime: Its Causes and Remedies.*

Montclair: Patterson Smith.

Norris, J. (1988), *Serial Killers: the Growing Menace.* London: Arrow.

Goring, C. (1913) *The English Convict: a Statistical Study.* London: Darling and Son.

Readers wishing to get a more detailed introduction to current psychology, as well as overviews of the works of Freud, Piaget and Skinner, should consult Atkinson, R. L., Atkinson, R. C., Smith, E. E. and Bem, D. L. (1993), *Introduction to Psychology.*

London: Harcourt Brace Jovanovich. A review of Darwin's influence on the development of psychology is given in Hearnshaw (1989) and particularly on studies of individual differences by Wiggins, J. S., Renner, R. K., Clove, G. L. and Rose, R. J. (1971), *The Psychology of Personality.* London: Addison Wesley.

Stephenson (1992) reviews the studies of criminality, self-esteem and moral reasoning. Wilson and Herrnstein (1985) review the ages of criminals.

Masters, B. (1993) *The Shrine of Jeffrey Dahmer.* London: Hodder and Stoughton.

Erikson, E. H. (1963), *Childhood and Society.* New York: W. W. Norton.

Masson, J. (1984), *The Assault on Truth: Freud's Suppression of the Seduction Theory.* London: Faber. West (1987).

Kelly, G. A. (1955), *The Psychology of Personal Constructs.* New York; W. W. Norton.

Polkinghorne, D. E. (1988), *Narrative Knowing and the Human Sciences.* Albany: State University of New York Press. McAdams (1988).

Danto, A. (1965), *Analytic Philosophy of History.* Cambridge: Cambridge University Press.

Schank, R. and Abelson, R. (1977), *Scripts, Plans, Goals and Understanding: an Inquiry into Human Knowledge Structures.* Hillsdale; Lawrence Erlbaum.

Mair, M. (1988), Psychology as Storytelling, *Intl Journal of Personal Construct Psychology,* Vol 1 pp 125-37

Murray, K. (1985), "Life as Fiction" *Journal for the Theory of Social Behavior,* Vol. 15, No.2, pp. 173-88.

The studies of child sexual abuse are being carried out by Stuart Kirby and are, as yet, unpublished.

The consideration in this chapter of the backgrounds and motivations of violent men, especially sex offenders, draws on the general psychological and psychiatric literature, see e.g. Groth (1979), West (1987).

NINE: LIMITED NARRATIVES

One of the earliest comments on offenders' inner narratives was Bolitho, W. (1926), *Murder for Profit. New*

York: Garden City, who wrote "They very commonly construct for themselves a life romance, a personal myth in which they are the maltreated hero, which secret is the key of their battle against despair."

Reviews of the early experiences of violent criminals and the significance of the "role of the other" are given by Athens, L. H. (1980), *Violent Criminal Acts and Actors: a Symbolic Interactionist Study*. London: Routledge and Kegan Paul; and Athens, L. H. (1989), *The Creation of Dangerous and Violent Criminals*. London: Routledge.

The list of behaviors drawn up for the analyses presented in this chapter do owe a lot to the detailed discussions of crimes provided by Hazelwood and Burgess (1987), Ressler et al. (1988) and Leyton (1986).

The analysis of actions in rape is taken from the data collected and content analyzed by Rupert Heritage, the first tranche of which was published in Canter, D. and Heritage, R. (1990), "A Multi-Variate Model of Sexual Offence Behavior", *Journal of Forensic Psychiatry*, Vol 1, No. 2., pp 185-212. The full account of this research is given in Heritage, R. (1992), *Facets of Sexual Assault: First Steps in Investigave Classifications, Mphil thesis*, University of Surrey (unpublished).

The statistical procedure illustrated in this chapter has many similarities to that described in Chapter Seven. Except that this analysis (known as Smallest Space Analysis I, or SSAI) represents the behaviors, derived from the columns of the data matrix, as points in the spatial plot, whereas the procedure described in Chapter Seven (known as Multi-Dimensional Scalogram Analysis I, or MSAI) represents the rows of the data matrix as points in the spatial plot.

Studies of varieties of murderer, drawn on in this and other chapters, are being carried out by Rick Holden and are, as yet unpublished.

TEN: NARRATIVES OF EVIL

A special issue of *Criminal Behavior and Mental Health*, 1992, Vol. 2., No. 2., is devoted to "Psychopathic Disorder". Helen Hughes' (unpublished) 1992. undergraduate dissertation at the University of Surrey explored the correlations between the amount of violence in rape and the pre-existing relationship between offender and victim.

Laurie, R. (1993), *Hunting the Devil: the Search for the Russian Ripper*. London: Grafton.

Hickey (1991) provides details of the criminal life of DeSalvo, the self-confessed "Boston Strangler".

SELECT BIBLIOGRAPHY

Canter, D. (ed.) (1985), *Facet Theory: Approaches to Social Research*. New York: Springer-Verlag.

Groth, A. N. (1979) *Men Who Rape: the Psychology of the Offender*. New York: Plenum.

Harris, T. (1989), *The Silence of the Lambs*. London: Heinemann.

Hazelwood, R. R. and Burgess, A. (eds) (1987), *Practical Aspects of Rape Investigation: a Multidisciplinary Approach*. Amsterdam:Elsevier.

Hearnshaw, L. S. (1989), *The Shaping of Modern Psychology*. London:Routledge.

Hickey, E. W. (1991), *Serial Murderers and Their Victims*. California:Brooks/Cole.

Katz, J. (1988), *The Seductions of Crime: Moral and Sensual Attractions in Doing Evil*. New York: Basic Books.

Kind, S. S. (1987), *The Scientific Investigation of Crime*. London: Forensic Science Services Ltd.

Leyton, E. (1986), *Hunting Humans: The Rise of the Modern Multiple Murderer*. Toronto: Seal Books.

McAdams, D. P. (1988), *Power, Intimacy, and the Life Story: Personological Inquiries into Identity*. New York: Guilford Press.

Perkins, D. N. (1981), *The Mind's Best Work*. London: Harvard University Press,

Raskin, D. C. (ed.) (1989), *Psychological Methods in Criminal Investigation and Evidence*. New York: Springer Publishing.

Ressler, R. K., and Shachtman, T. (1992.). *Whoever Fights Monsters*, London: Simon and Schuster.

Ressler, R. K., Burgess, A. W. and Douglas, J. E. (1988), *Sexual Homicide:Patterns and Motives*. Massachusetts: Lexington Books.

Scully, D. (1990), *Understanding Sexual Violence: a*

Study of Convicted Rapists. Boston: Unwin Hyman.

Stephenson, G. M. (1992), *The Psychology of Criminal Justice*. Oxford:Blackwell.

Sutherland, E. H. (1978), *Principles of Criminology* (10th edn). New York: Harper and Row.

Swanson, C. R., Chamelin, N. C. and Territo, L. (1992.), *Criminal Investigation* (5th edn). New York: McGraw-Hill.

Wambaugh, J. (1989), *The Blooding*. London: Bantam.

West, D. J. (1987), *Sexual Crimes and Confrontations: a Study of Victims and Offenders*. Aldershot: Gower.

Wilson, J. Q. and Herrnstein, R. J. (1985), *Crime and Human Nature*. New York: Simon and Schuster.

INDEX OF KEY WORDS AND PHRASES

Printed in the United States
56360LVS00002B/211-213